The Superna
in Short L

The Supernatural and Fantastic in Short Detective Fiction

A Survey, 1841–2000

LAIRD R. BLACKWELL

McFarland & Company, Inc., Publishers
Jefferson, North Carolina

LIBRARY OF CONGRESS CATALOGUING-IN-PUBLICATION DATA

Names: Blackwell, Laird R. (Laird Richard), 1945– author.
Title: The supernatural and fantastic in short detective fiction : a
survey, 1841–2000 / Laird R. Blackwell.
Description: Jefferson, North Carolina : McFarland & Company, Inc.,
Publishers, 2020 | Includes bibliographical references and index.
Identifiers: LCCN 2020044350 | ISBN 9781476681283 (paperback : acid free paper) ∞
ISBN 9781476639451 (ebook)
Subjects: LCSH: Detective and mystery stories, English—History and
criticism. | English fiction—19th century—History and criticism. |
English fiction—20th century—History and criticism. | Detective and
mystery stories, American—History and criticism. | American
fiction—19th century—History and criticism. | American fiction—20th
century—History and criticism. | Supernatural in literature. | Fantasy
in literature. | Short story.
Classification: LCC PR868.D4 B57 2020 | DDC 823/.08720937—dc23
LC record available at https://lccn.loc.gov/2020044350

BRITISH LIBRARY CATALOGUING DATA ARE AVAILABLE

ISBN (print) 978-1-4766-8128-3
ISBN (ebook) 978-1-4766-3945-1

Surrealistic front cover image of the invisible man
© 2020 Alexander Sviridov/Shutterstock

Printed in the United States of America

*McFarland & Company, Inc., Publishers
Box 611, Jefferson, North Carolina 28640
www.mcfarlandpub.com*

Table of Contents

Preface

It seems that my early "book" life was a bit schizophrenic or perhaps just eclectic, for from as early as I can remember, I had a profound love of all sorts of fantastic literature—from *Dragons of Blue Land* (Ruth Gannett), *The Wizard of Oz* (L. Frank Baum), *Mary Poppins* (Mary Travers), and *Wind in the Willows* (Kenneth Grahame) to *Journey to the Center of the Earth* (Jules Verne) and *At the Back of the North Wind* (George MacDonald)—and an equal passion for detective fiction, from Sherlock Holmes and Uncle Abner to Hercule Poirot and Ellery Queen. These two types of fiction seemed so different in so many ways, yet I recognized that they both appealed to my love of adventure, of the marvelous, and of all that took me out of my daily existence. Even though most of the detective stories appealed to my "crossword puzzle" fascination with discovering clues and solving problems, while the fantastic tales aroused my romantic enchantment with fairy-tale worlds of make-believe, talking animals, and unseen wonders, I felt the same excitement with both types of books—something bigger than life, something marvelous lurking just beneath the surface of my daily reality.

And then I found *Freddy the Detective* by Walter Brooks (a talking pig as sleuth), and a little later I discovered the metaphysical puzzles and bizarre landscapes of Chesterton's Father Brown, and then the whole fantastic world of the "locked-room" mystery and other impossible crimes where the crime (at least at first) seemed to transcend any rational or natural explanation. The gap between my two literary loves was now at least partly bridged, for here was fantastic literature that had a detective, and detective fiction that had elements of the fantastic, although the Father Brown stories (and most impossible crime tales), in the end, explained away the fantastic with rational solutions. Even so, the sense of the marvelous and the fanciful lingered with me far beyond the rationalization. But as I grew older and more sophisticated in my reading in both domains, including the fantastic in the form of the supernatural—vampires and werewolves and ghosts and possession—I found that this bridge, other than the presentation of the *apparently* fantastic in the "impossible crime" subgenre, seemed to be rarely travelled in any serious way, that most detective fiction (including the impossible crime stories) was firmly entrenched in the rational, the realistic, and the "clue-puzzle," while most fantastic literature seemed to be far removed from these "real-world" realities.

But still later, I discovered, much to my surprise, that the supernatural (or "occult") detective was a literary phenomenon of long standing; however, not surprisingly, the supernatural detective was often dismissed by fans and critics of detective fiction as a somewhat unrespectable "half-breed," while the lover of supernatural fiction often denigrated detective fiction as "much ado about nothing" and overly intellectual and convoluted. At this point I still wasn't sure if it was possible to effectively use the fantastic, especially the supernatural, in a detective tale in any way other than as a red herring or as a straw man to be discredited by reason.

As I discovered more stories that crossed the fantasy and detective genres, especially those of detectives of the occult, I found many tales that were not especially satisfying either as detective or as fantastic—whose fantastic elements "cheapened" the detection, turning it into mere encounters with "ghosts in the night," and where the attempts at detection deadened the emotional impact and larger meaning of the fantastic. I began to think that this "bridge" was too flawed to endure, too contrived to bear any weight. The early "rules" of the detective genre certainly discouraged the bridge, and early fantasists thought of their genre as light years away from the magnifying glass and deerstalker hat.

However, as I continued to read in both genres, I found what I felt to be some effective integrations by authors who managed to unite the power of the strange, the fanciful, the fantastic, and, in some cases, the supernatural with the fascination of the more-or-less familiar and completely rational. And as I delved deeper, I found more successful integrations, and I was encouraged to believe that perhaps the bridge was possible after all and could bring the two worlds together to the benefit of both.

This monograph is an attempt to use my long experience venturing back-and-forth on the detective-fantastic bridge to address the question of how and how effectively the fantastic and the supernatural can be incorporated into the usually highly rational world of the detective story. Our study ranges from stories that use the fantastic as intriguing and colorful "red herrings" to be debunked by a rational solution to stories that use touches of the non-rational to entice and engage readers to tales that use the fantastic and the supernatural as a "genuine" part of the mystery and its solution. Is a detective-fantastic "hybrid" of this last sort always an uneasy failure "without a country," as some suggest, or can it sometimes be a "bilingual" showpiece of strength in diversity? With the recent increasing popularity of fantasy literature and the supernatural detective, including the publication of numerous anthologies of 19th and 20th century supernatural detective stories, it is now much easier to study the genre and to reach some informed conclusions.

Introduction:
Bringing the Fantastic and
the Detective Together

"All supernatural or preternatural agencies are ruled out
as a matter of course."
                                                    —Knox, 194

One view of the detective story—a very traditional view—is that it is a kind of intellectual game, a battle of wits between the criminal and the detective, between the reader and the detective, and ultimately between the reader and the author. In this view, there is no place for fantastic or supernatural agencies or occurrences, for "a reader has a chance when matching wits with a rationalistic detective, but if he must compete with the world of spirits and go chasing about the 4th dimension of metaphysics, he is defeated *ab initio*" (Van Dine, 190). Todorov, in *The Fantastic: A Structural Approach to a Literary Genre*, argues that the detective story, despite having similarities with the fantastic structurally, "is also the contrary of the fantastic: in fantastic texts we tend to prefer the supernatural explanation; the detective story, once it is over, leaves no doubt as to the absence of supernatural events" (50). According to Todorov, the reader of detective fiction is interested only in the finding of the final solution, which is a logical, analytical, rational process. This view—that detective stories are primarily, if not exclusively, clue-puzzle intellectual exercises—has a long history, but it is only part of the story—of the detective story, that is.

The tale of fantasy—whether folk tale, fairy tale, myth, the supernatural, or the weird—has a long history, for "Those who did not want to read about the dreariness they saw everyday around them could find other realities in certain books of strange and beautiful myths, of quests and journeys, of sanctuaries and secrets, of touchstones and

5

Introduction

talismans.... Above all, there was the sense of the numinous, of the wonder and awe to be found in the world" (Valentine, 2015, vii). What Shelley says of poetry can equally apply to fantasy—"[it] strips the veil of familiarity from the world, and lays bare the naked and sleeping beauty, which is the spirit of its forms" (Swinfen, 9). It is important to recognize, then, that fantasy is not divorced from our material reality, but, at its best, can reveal and celebrate the true nature of that reality in all its wonder and mystery—"All serious fantasy is deeply rooted in human experience and is relevant to human living" (231). And not only is it relevant to human living, but it has the potential to reveal the true nature of that living:

> ...to remind us that the world is no mere dust-heap, pullulating with worms, as some old-fashioned scientists tried to make us believe; but that, on the contrary, it is a rendezvous of radiant forces forever engaged in turning its dust into dreams ... a world, too, so mysterious that anything can happen, or any dream can come true ... the mystery and wonder of being alive, the marvelous happiness, the wondrous sorrow, and the divine expectations [La Gallienne in Higgins, 4].

Perhaps this is too "divine" to expect or even to hope for from detective fiction, but it probably is not too much to hope that at least some of that fiction will go beyond the intellectual and material, beyond the presentation of a problem in logic to solve with completely rational solutions, to in some way explore the wonder and magic of life and even its as yet undreamed of possibilities. So perhaps at least some readers of detective fiction are not just seeking an intellectual solution to a problem, but also want to be awakened to the possibilities of life beyond the material, beyond the intellectual and rational.

In some ways all detective fiction is fantastic, for it takes us out of our daily routines to events, characters, and mysteries larger than life—or at least larger than *our* lives. Ironically, however, it is also fantastic in its creation of a world that is "smaller" (or at least simpler) than the world we experience, for the daunting existential problems of life are transformed into puzzles that can be solved (by the detective)—"detective fiction can provide us with ... the escape into the world of justice, the world in which the *problem* of evil becomes only the *puzzle* of evil, and the sufficiently skilled detective can always bring the world to 'a sort of moral attention'" (Rabkin, 66). So, although all detective fiction may, then, be "fantastic" in these two senses, this monograph explores the more problematic and debated question of whether detective fiction and the "fantastic" in the sense of the *non-rational* can comfortably coexist. Can detective fiction that goes beyond the rational, that "in a world governed by materialism and scientific rationalism ... sets out to explore the immaterial and irrational" (Swinfen, 2), be viewed by readers and critics alike as "legitimate" and appealing?

There has been much debate over how to define "fantasy" or "fantastic" when it comes to literature, but most versions come down, in the end, to "what seems to have slight relation to the real world because of its strangeness or extravagance" (*The American College Dictionary*) or, much more stringently, "works in which non-rational phenomena play a significant part ... works in which events occur, or places and creatures exist, that could not occur or exist according to rational standards or scientific explanations. The non-rational phenomena of fantasy simply do not fall within human experience or accord with natural laws as we know them" (Tymn, Zahorski, and Boyer, 3). Todorov, in his critical study, *The Fantastic*, adopts an even more stringent and specific definition—"The fantastic lasts only as long as a certain hesitation: a hesitation common to reader and character, who must decide whether or not what they perceive derives from 'reality' as it exists in the common opinion" (42). For Todorov a reader experiences the fantastic only when he is unsure of whether something is "natural" or not—it is this period of uncertainty, this hesitation that entails the fantastic. In this monograph we categorize works that illustrate the second definition (things that could not occur according to rational standards) as "supernatural" (involving such "imaginary" beings as vampires, werewolves, and ghosts). These stories are discussed in Part 3. Works that only "seem to have slight relation to the real world" are said to have a "touch of the fantastic" and are discussed in Part 2. Works that evoke uncertainty about whether something is natural or not are discussed in Part 4. Part 1 deals with the much less problematic works that seem, at first, to be fantastic or supernatural, but in the end turn out to belong to the "real world," having completely rational explanations.

The Detection Club's biting critique of those detective stories which suddenly, gratuitously, introduce non-rational "Divine Revelation, Feminine Intuition, Mumbo-Jumbo, Jiggery-Piggery, Coincidence, or the Act of God" (The Detection Club, 198) to solve a mystery that has been up until then presented in a rational context has validity, for this sudden switching of "ground rules" is not only unfair to a reader approaching the story with a strictly rational mindset, but usually is also a plot copout on the author's part (a "magical" way to escape a self-created dead end) and a severe let-down to the reader. Supernatural mysteries have long been popular, but the reader of these is prepared for a different set of rules and expectations, not trying to apply logical solutions to non-rational situations—"Mysteries involving the supernatural seek to disarm the reader's power of logical thought [and the detective's] by arousing fear" (Murch, 13). So, is it true that detective fiction and fantastic/supernatural fiction live in two different worlds, creating two different and antagonistic mind-sets and expectations in readers? It would seem that both deal with mysteries but mysteries of vastly different types: in the former, a highly contained mystery of how, who, and why a crime has been committed with a logical solution, while in the latter, an all-pervading mystery of the very nature of life, whose "solution" leads far beyond logic and the intellect. As Ellery Queen (a staunch advocate of the traditional, rational clue-puzzle detective story) puts it, "The real and the unreal are seldom compatible in a single short story: straight detection is usually earthbound, grounded by the realistic demands of cold logic and credibility; fantasy, on the other hand, has wings—it may soar into the stratosphere of the weird and even the supernatural" (Queen Introduction, *EQMM*, September 1945, 98).

However, before we conclude that detective fiction and fantastic fiction are incompatible, it should be observed that Queen's statement of their incompatibility includes the word "seldom" *and* is found in the introduction to one of those "rare crime stories which combines pure detection with pure fantasy" (98)—"The Adventure of Mr. Montalba, Obsequist" by H.F. Heard (see Chapter Six)—so even Queen does recognize the possibility, however rare, of the two genres "living in harmony." Detection and fantasy may be two different worlds, but this doesn't mean that these worlds can't coexist or even co-habit. Murch (quoted above) echoes Queen's caveat when he says that "paradoxically a few detective story writers have found a use for supernatural themes. Very occasionally an author has gone so far as to show his detective grappling with other-worldly mysteries" (13). He does go on to say that using the *appearance* of the supernatural as a straw man for logical detection is much more frequent—"far more often the writer excites the reader's apprehensions by hinting at supernatural causes for some terrifying mystery which is eventually proved by the detective to have a perfectly rational explanation" (13). He cites Algernon Blackwood (and his occult detective John Silence) as one of the rare examples of the "very occasionally" and Doyle's famous *Hound of the Baskervilles* as a classic example of the "far more often."

This monograph argues, then, that although the relationship between the fantastic (including the supernatural) and the detective story is, because of often contrary assumptions, purposes, and expectations, frequently an uneasy one, an author's inclusion of fantastic and even supernatural elements in his detective fiction, if done honestly and skillfully, can deepen the scope and appeal of the detective story— "Todorov may not be right when he insists that the reader of the detective story is only interested in the finding of the final solution, as well as his conviction that the detective story always tries to extinguish all supernatural elements.... [In some of the best stories] the reader is enticed and excited by the possibility of the supernatural element and hungrily reads on because of it" (van der Beek, 25).

Not surprisingly, given the problematic relationship between detective fiction and the fantastic and supernatural, we will see that there is indeed a large body of detective fiction where the fantastic elements are used as dressing, but not as the salad, where the fantastic is a sort of red herring to "excite the reader's apprehension by hinting at supernatural causes" (Murch, 13), but not the solution, as that turns out to be completely rational. This is the easiest and least problematic way to bring the fantastic into the detective genre, for the story benefits by the mood and mystery of the fantastic while the conventions of the detective story can still be followed—the "hocus-pocus" is only an illusion created by the criminal, a clever diversion, but the puzzle still needs to be solved by logic and deduction, and the solution is still "reason-able." This type of story, at its best, can be an engaging and memorable blending of the rational and the non-rational—"so that fact and fancy, half-way meeting, interpenetrate, and form one seamless whole" (Melville, 535). Most "locked-room" and other impossible crime stories use the fantastic in this way, for the solution to the mystery that at first seems "naturally" impossible turns out to have a rational (though often convoluted or improbable) explanation that the detective, using reason and logic, can discover and the reader can uncover. This type of story, demonstrating that the "impossible" isn't really impossible but conforms to natural law, can be deeply satisfying and comforting, for it is reassuring that a world that sometimes seems chaotic and unpredictable and threatening is ultimately logical, orderly, and knowable:

> The detective was the supreme rationalist, grappling with a crime that seemed to violate the very laws of nature. If he failed to find a logical explanation, if only the supernatural would account for a murderer's ability to appear and disappear, or

9

walk across snow without leaving footprints, then we would all be plunged back to a time of ghosts and witchcraft, a new Dark Age far more frightening than Russian spies and secret agents... [Levison and Link in Carr, 1981, vi].

In Part 1 ("The Apparently Fantastic Shown to Be Natural") we examine many of the best stories that use the fantastic in this "teasing" way before eventually discrediting it. In all four chapters in Part 1, several of the best stories are discussed first as "exemplars" with discussions of many other successful stories following. In Chapter One we explore some of the many "locked-room" and other impossible crime stories where the fantastic or supernatural seems to be the only possible explanation of the crime, but in the end the solution is revealed to be completely logical and natural—contrived by the criminal (and the author) to look supernatural or fantastic. In Chapter Two we examine other types of stories where the fantastic appears to be operating but is de-bunked in the end. In Chapter Three we explore stories where the fantastic takes the form of superstition, prophecies, or curses that eventually are revealed to be fabricated or used by the criminal to disguise or conceal his crime. To finish Part 1, Chapter Four examines stories of the "charlatan supernatural detective," where the detective purports to be using non-logical, supernatural investigative methods to solve the crime, but the reader knows or comes to know that these methods are actually completely rational and logical. Part 1 demonstrates that there are many popular and acclaimed stories where the fantastic is used in this way—as a "red herring" to make the final rational solution all the more dramatic and satisfying. Few critics, even the most traditional, object to the fantastic being used in this way, as the conventions of the traditional detective story remain intact and respected.

In Part 2 ("A Touch of the Fantastic") we explore stories which offer a bit more challenge to detective story conventions. Chapter Five examines detective stories where the crime or mystery is shown to have a rational explanation, but it is solved by detectives with non-rational abilities—intuition, a special sense for evil, or supernatural sensitivity. Chapter Six explores detective stories in which the non-rational plays a central role (it is the salad itself), but the non-rational is not supernatural. In most cases, the explanation turns out to be psychological or mythological (which could have been viewed as supernatural in earlier times). In a few of these stories, there is a science fiction element (beyond natural laws as we currently know them) and in others, the explanation turns out to be rational, but the crime is embellished with fanciful, fabulous, or near-absurd trappings. Although bringing a "touch of the fantastic" to detective stories can be precarious, we will see that, as in Part 1, there are numerous stories where this "touch" enhances the detective elements, and the two work well together. As in Part 1, we first discuss the very best stories of this type as "exemplars" with discussion of several other successful stories following.

Part 3 ("The Supernatural") examines still more problematic territory—the detective stories where the supernatural is in full effect, where there is no rational explanation for the mystery, and the story is populated with werewolves, vampires, ghosts, possession, thought-transference, or other psychic beings or phenomena. In some of these cases, the detective uses traditional, rational methods, but in many, he/she calls upon supernatural methods to solve the case and combat the danger. This is where Knox, Van Dine, and other traditionalists might scoff at the detection (and the mysteries) as "hocus-pocus, and higgledy-piggledy," but others find that in some stories the detection fits the crime and the supernatural elements can add interest, intrigue, and mystery. In Chapter Seven we explore stories where the detective experiences and investigates the supernatural (the supernatural is not always ominous or threatening), while in Chapter Eight we look at stories where the supernatural is dangerous and is combatted usually at the detective's great peril. Not surprisingly, given the challenges in integrating "serious" detection with supernatural mysteries, we will see that in most of these stories the supernatural terror predominates, while the detection is less emphasized and often more formulaic and mundane. Those who argue that the fantastic and high quality detective stories are incompatible receive some support in this section, for although there is a large body of supernatural detective stories, many of them are more interesting and engaging for their supernatural horror than for astute detection—in many of these tales the detective does more surviving and combatting the horror than actually detecting its causes and motives. However, we will find that there are a few classic stories where the two genres intertwine smoothly and effectively, creating tales of great detective interest and supernatural fascination, so it would seem that successful "intertwining," though difficult and infrequent, is at least occasionally gloriously possible. To support both aspects of this claim, in Chapters Seven and Eight the "exemplars" are those few "gloriously possible," while the other discussed stories demonstrate the "difficult" or at least those stories where the supernatural and the detective elements are not equally successful.

Introduction

In Part 4 ("Supernatural or Natural?") Chapter Nine examines the very few supernatural detective stories which are "fantastic" in the limited sense advanced by Todorov—where at the end, the reader (and often the detective) is unsure of whether the solution to the mystery is supernatural or natural. We are left in doubt, in "hesitation" about the explanation, and so also about the nature of the mysteries of life. These stories are among the most intriguing and provocative of all the stories examined, for the questions are left hanging to haunt and intrigue us. As in Parts 1 and 2 of this monograph, exemplars are discussed first followed by other effective stories.

As we've said, there are far more successful examples of stories in Part 1, where the rational "triumphs" in the end, and Part 2, where there is only a touch of the fantastic, than there are in Part 3, where there is no rational or even psychological explanation or solution, or in Part 4, where it isn't certain whether the explanation is rational or not. Clearly, using the fantastic or supernatural as window dressing or as a foil has proved to be much easier and more acceptable than incorporating it wholeheartedly into the mystery and the detection. (It should be noted that some of the stories illustrate more than one of the categories, e.g., a "sensitive" detective who experiences the supernatural, so they have been placed in the chapter that they seem to most strongly represent.)

Finally, the Conclusion sums up our study of the intersection of the classic detective story with the world of the fantastic and supernatural. It is argued that although this intersection is fraught with risk, it is also rich with possibility as is evidenced by some resounding successes. (Fair warning: it was necessary to provide some detail about the stories for analysis purposes, and in some cases general statements are made that reveal some aspects of the solution or explanation, but every attempt is made to avoid giving away details or spoiling surprises.) It also should be noted that although an intensive and detailed search of "fantastic" detective stories has been undertaken for this monograph, no claim is made that all such stories have been included (though hopefully most or all of the best have been).

There is a long and continuing history of fantastic and supernatural detective *novels*, which is beyond the scope of this monograph; here we examine only the domain of the short story. The "supernatural" detective story (novel as well as short story) has become much more popular and prevalent in recent years—in print, film and television (some might say because modern life for many has become increasingly materialist and mundane)—and although these recent trends are intriguing, this mono-graph limits its scope to the 160 years between 1841 (the appearance of what is acknowledged by most literary historians to be the first detective short story, Edgar Allan Poe's "Murders in the Rue Morgue," which, though celebrating ratiocination, certainly had a fantastic element) and the first year of the 21st century. One recent development helps our analysis and will help the reader judge its conclusions—numerous anthologies have recently been published of classic 19th and 20th century supernatural detective stories, so many of the stories included in this study are now readily available.

PART 1

The Apparently Fantastic Shown to Be Natural

As has been stated in the Introduction, although detective stories and tales of the fantastic and supernatural both deal with the solving of mysteries, they often are quite different kinds of mysteries with different types of solutions. The detective story usually presents the crime or mystery as an intellectual puzzle to be solved by clues and logic (not infrequently with a bit of intuition or leaps of imagination mixed in), while the fantastic or supernatural excites or menaces our emotions and challenges the assumptions and "laws" of nature that underlie our understanding of reality. Some conclude that these differences are too fundamental for the detective story and the fantastic to co-exist. In Part 3, we examine this claim by assessing stories of supernatural detectives in which serious supernatural occurrences are investigated or combatted, but in Part 1 we will see that there are numerous examples of highly successful and acclaimed detective stories where traditional methods of detection are able to peel back apparently fantastic occurrences to reveal completely natural, human-contrived crimes and mysteries. We will see that some of the most popular and celebrated detective stories use the fantastic or the supernatural to color and embellish the classic detective tale with intrigue and mystique while enhancing, not diminishing, the appeal of detection by observation, reason, and deduction. So, these types of stories bring the appeal of the fantastic and the supernatural to the detective tale without creating a conflict between the differing intents, assumptions, and values of the two different genres, for the fantastic or supernatural is discredited in the end by the powers of reason and the skills of the detective.

15

One

Locked-Room Murders and Other Impossible Crimes

All "locked-room" or other impossible crime detective stories—where it appears that the crime could not possibly have happened—are by their nature fantastic, as the crime seems to violate reality as we know it. The main appeal of these stories is their cleverness as the seemingly impossible is shown to be not only possible but real. In some ways this transformation of the explanation from the fantastic into the natural and reasonable gives the rational even more credence and power, for the non-rational is vanquished in the end, and reason is victorious against all odds.

John Dickson Carr, acknowledged to be one of the great masters of the impossible crime story, especially the locked-room tale, is also known for his extensive delineation of the "possible impossible"—in Chapter Seventeen of *The Three Coffins*, the famous lecture by Carr's detective Dr. Gideon Fell lists the various types and subtypes of solutions with exemplar stories (mostly novels). Scores of authors of detective stories, including Carr, have worked over the decades to create the most fantastic, seemingly inexplicable crimes which still have "natural" solutions, but all (or almost all—see, for example, Boucher's "Elsewhen" in Chapter Six, Crispin's "The Name on the Window" below, and de la Torre's "Murder Lock'd In" below as exceptions) have fit somewhere in Carr's classification. So the logical solution to the seemingly illogical crime has itself a set of logical parameters and limitations. To go outside these may take the story into the "truly fantastic" or even supernatural.

Exemplars

Christianna Brand

Acclaimed by the critic and author Anthony Boucher as a writer "in the Christie-Carr-Queen manner, a brilliant juggler of clues and deductions" (*EQMM*, January 1958, 36), Brand wrote some ingenious impossible crime stories, especially "Murder Game" (1968), which is made all the more fantastic by the introduction of such bizarre features as the murder victim's last gasping of "Got me by the throat ... and something about the window and something about vanishing into thin air and something on a suddenly rising note of terror about the 'long arms'" (Brand, 101), and dark, foreboding life histories and heredities. In typical, masterly Brand fashion, a series of clever but plausible solutions are offered to this locked-room mystery, all of which are shown to be false, until the final just-as-plausible and actually true solution is revealed. Also typical of Brand is the secret disclosed in the last few sentences, a secret which divulges whole new depths to the story and to the crime. Brand certainly rivals, if not surpasses, Christie, Carr, and Queen, as an artist of the fantastic blending with traditional detection, the former giving color, vitality, and mystique to the latter, while the latter grounds the former with reason and veracity.

John Dickson Carr

Carr, that connoisseur and practitioner extraordinaire of the locked-room mysteries, always had an affinity for the fantastic mixed in with logical detection, but rarely was he as adept at intermingling the two, while respecting both, as he was in the exquisitely crafted "The House in Goblin Wood" (1947) in which a young woman disappears from a "sealed" cottage right in front of the detective, Henri Merrivale, leaving behind only her disembodied voice. What makes it all the more remarkable is that it is an almost exact re-enactment of her similar disappearance years earlier when she was a young girl. While others had explained that she was "a child of the fairies who'd been spirited away by pixies" (Carr, 1947, 8), she herself (after just as mysteriously re-appearing) attributed it to her power to dematerialize and rematerialize at will. Then, just as we are in that "fantastic" mood, Carr follows the usual pattern of traditional detective stories that play with the fantastic by debunking it with a logical explanation (the cottage had a trick window when the first disappearance occurred). We sigh with relief that the puzzle's solved but with some disappointment at such a cheap trick, but here is where Carr's genius shines, for in a clever double twist, the fantastic is re-invoked (we discover that the trick window had been nailed shut after the first disappearance so can't explain the second one). And finally, when we've settled in to the fantastic once again, Carr plays his last card—a devilishly clever, completely natural, murder plot. The ongoing give-and-take between the natural and the fantastic in this story gives to both more voice and more credence and keeps us gasping to keep up.

G.K. Chesterton

Many of Chesterton's Father Brown stories feature apparently fantastic crimes that turn out to have rational (and extremely clever) explanations. In the third collection of these stories, *The Incredulity of Father Brown* (1926), the crimes (usually murder) are thought by most to be the result of superstitions, prophecies or curses (see Chapter Three), but Father Brown (incredulous of these fantastic explanations) proves otherwise. A couple of the stories in this same collection involve locked-room mysteries, the best of which is undoubtedly "The Oracle of the Dog" (1923) in which a man is stabbed to death in plain sight in a summerhouse with only one entrance, which was under constant observation, and no weapon is found. Father Brown not only deduces the rational solution, but in the process also discredits the superstition about the dog's fantastic ability to know when and by whom his master was killed—"at the very moment when the beast [the dog] came back from the sea and bellowed, his master's soul was driven out of his body by the blow of some unseen power that no mortal man can trace or even imagine" (Chesterton, 1951, 324), and "The moment Nox [the dog] saw that man, the dog dashed forward and stood in the middle of the path barking at him madly, murderously, volleying out curses that were almost verbal in their dreadful distinctness of their hatred" (324–325). Father Brown, in a brilliant bit of "naturalizing" the non-natural, asserts that the dog's actions *do* point to the solution to the crime, but not by some fantastic "dog-sense" ("the dog had super-normal vision, and was a mysterious mouthpiece of doom," 331) but by the behavior completely natural to dogs—trying to retrieve sticks and barking at people they don't like.

Melville Davisson Post

Uncle Abner, that fire-and-brimstone champion of the weak and mistreated, always has a touch of the fanciful and mythological about him. Many of the stories in *Uncle Abner: Master of Mysteries* (1918) are rich and heavy with the atmosphere of a dark and stormy night, exotic crimes and clues, and the "hammer" of divine justice, but a few evoke the fantastic more overtly, none more than the famous "The Doomdorf Mystery" (1914) in which "he that killeth with the sword must be killed with the sword" (Post, 1977, 162), in this case the sword of an assassin who "not only climbed the face of that precipice and got in through the closed window, but shot Doomdorf to death and got out again through the closed window without disturbing a grain of dust or a thread of a cobweb" (168). The solution, though not supernatural or divine, is certainly guided by a marvelous justice and inviolable law beyond human intervention.

Clayton Rawson

Rawson's magician/detective Merlini solves many clever locked-room mysteries in the collection of short stories *The Great Merlini* (1979) all of which have, of course, a touch of magic, but a few of which go beyond magic and illusion to evoke the fantastic and the supernatural. In the best story (in response to a challenge by John Dickson Carr), "Off the Face of the Earth" (1949) describes the impossible disappearance from a watched phone booth involving the "Lords of the Outer Darkness." Although the supernatural is presented in such a way that neither Merlini nor the readers ever take it seriously as a possible explanation of the fantastic disappearance, it does provide color, amusement, and temporary distraction from the slow and inexorable unfolding of the natural explanations.

Joel Townsley Rogers

The author of one of the wildest, most fantastic mystery/detective novels ever, *The Red Right Hand* (1945), Rogers also wrote some taut, gripping short stories, one in particular a dark, ominous, locked-room, detective story—"The Hanging Rope" (1946). Weaving in with traditional clue-puzzle detection is not only the enigma of the locked-room murders, the second done with police at the door and a slew of suspects, but the foreboding atmosphere of gloom and horror—"There was something inexplicably dismal about that window. Like a great rectangular inhuman eye. Like the blank face of nothing. Like the shape of a grave that is filled with dark earth and dark water" (Rogers, 205)—and fantastic figures lurking in that dark—"It was a face, an apelike ghostly face, with a wide grinning mouth, with juglike ears, with a pair of great moist glistening eyes like the eyes of a lemur. The face swam toward the dirty window pane, staring back at him as he stared out" (207). Even the devil himself makes an appearance, for it was "nuttings human, but it vass det Old Vun out of hell dot had come to get his own" (185). Two detectives and their tools of the trade—fingerprints, witnesses, imagination and reason—finally pierce the madness and the fantastic to reveal the "classic of crime simplicity" (157) hiding in plain sight.

Other Stories

Margery Allingham

Albert Campion, Allingham's unostentatious, decidedly uneccentric detective, rarely encounters anything even verging on the fantastic, but in "The Border-Line Case" (1937) he is consulted on a murder that "seems to be a miracle, for the man who shot the fellow dead couldn't possibly have done so" (Allingham, 704). But in typical Campion, and Allingham, fashion the fantastic is shown to be quite natural, and even mundane, by the simple expedient of answering the question, "When is a policeman not a concrete wall?" (707).

William Arden

Ellery Queen comments in *EQMM*, June 1970, that "we are experiencing a renaissance of the Locked Room Mystery. More locked room detective stories have been submitted to *EQMM* in recent months than usually come our way in years; indeed there have been periods in the past when not a single new locked-room story turned up from one lustrum to the other. But, happily, the locked-room 'tec theme is now being revived" (102). In "The Bizarre Case Expert" (1970) in that edition of the magazine, Detective Marx, specialist in impossible crimes, what his department calls "circus cases," solves a murder where no one entered or left and no weapon was found. Before it joins other mysterious cases in the "unsolved" file, Marx reduces this fantastic crime to a rather commonplace human one—commonplace except for the peripatetic, purple phone and the quick thinking of the killer.

Robert Arthur

"The 51st Sealed Room" (1951) is a devilishly clever take-off on locked-room mysteries at the same time as it is an ingenious locked-room (or, more accurately, a sealed room) murder story in itself. But what makes this story such a dazzling illustration of the fantastic "in deadly embrace" with the realistic is the layer upon layer and twist upon twist of the real and the fictional—"The world's foremost writer of locked-room mysteries had been rather gaudily murdered in a locked-room" (Asimov, 1982, 193), and he was murdered for the "completely new way to escape from a locked room" (189) he had dreamed up for his latest locked-room novel, *and* the murderer had used his plot idea to accomplish the murder, *and* a competing writer trying to surreptitiously solve the murder so he himself can use the plot in his own book is, in turn, murdered by the same killer using the same method in the same locked room! That's a lot of "and's" and a lot of fantastic twists and turns! And, just to add a couple more fantastic elements to the mix, real writers of detective fiction (and members of the Mystery Writers of America) are characters in the story and are presented larger or at least as large as life, *and* the real author of this story is, himself, a renowned mystery writer who dreamed up a brand new method to commit a locked-room murder. We can only hope that he doesn't meet the same fate as did his fictional detective.

Stephen Barr

"The Locked Room to End Locked Rooms" (1965) is in a way just that, for as the story points out, "The locked-room problem isn't a mystery at all: it's a self-contradiction ... the murderer got out when he could not. That, by definition, is absurd" (Penzler, 585). However, absurd or not, the story illustrates that even when the contradiction is resolved, you can still have a mystery and a paradox—"You say he could not have got out of the house. That was your mistake—not realizing that you were absolutely right" (590). The "impossible" murder is shown to be quite possible, though certainly at least a touch fantastic.

Lawrence Block and Lynn Wood Block

Block's stories of Bernie Rhodenbarr (thief and detective) are especially entertaining with their light humor and frequent allusions to the detective genre and some of its classic books. "The Burglar Who Smelled Smoke" (1997) is a particularly engaging tale of locked-room murder, and quite an extraordinary locked room it is—"He slipped the irreproducible key into the impregnable lock and opened the unbreachable door" (Penzler, 525) to the massive library with its reinforced concrete walls and impeccably controlled climate. Amid cameos from the works of Stout, Chandler, Hammett, and Lovesey, a clever "impossible" murder is committed, the victim (Karl) surrounded by his beloved detective books and, in the end, murdered by his fascination with the locked-room crime—"It's classic, and it would have appealed to Karl, given his passion for crime fiction. If he had to die, he'd probably have wanted it to happen in a locked room" (532). Although the fantastic nature of the crime is refuted in the end, it still is uniquely clever, brilliantly imaginative, and deviously bibliographic.

M. McDonnell Bodkin

Author of several collections of short stories about the detective, Paul Beck, one of the deluge of immediate successors to Sherlock Holmes, Bodkin explored the fantastic murder in a locked-room motif in a few of these tales. Most are easily forgotten, but "Murder by Proxy" (1898) stands out, not for itself, but for the later classic tale it inspired— Melville Davisson Post's Uncle Abner story, "The Doomdorf Mystery." Although Beck is called "You devilish bloodhound" by the murderer (Greene and Adey, 169), the killer probably deserves the "devilish" more, as he ingeniously makes nature his unthinking accomplice.

Jon Breen

In his collection of parodies *Hair of the Sleuthhound* (1982) Breen has a field day with some of the best known detective story authors of his day including Carr, Christie, Biggers, Hoch, Ross Macdonald, Van Dine, and Queen. In "The House of the Shrill Whispers" (1972) he not only satirizes Carr's corpulent detectives Gideon Fell and Henri Merrivale, but also Carr's mania with locked-room mysteries and the fantastic. In this rollicking tale, a murder is committed in a sealed room surrounded by untracked snow, and the solution, though not what you expect, nonetheless debunks the fantastic, though not the absurd.

William Brittain

In Brittain's long series of stories about Leonard Strang, high school teacher and amateur detective, there are several impossible crime stories, including "Mr. Strang Accepts a Challenge" (1976) in which the "impossible" murder "seems immune to any logical approach" (Ashley, 2000, 359), but eventually succumbs to Strang's impeccable reasoning. As with many natural solutions to seemingly fantastic crimes, it takes the criminal (and the author) all sorts of complicated maneuvering and contriving to create the appearance of the impossible, although in this case the complexity lies carefully hidden behind the simple act of putting on the water. In "Mr. Strang Takes a Field Trip" (1980) in which a valuable Incan gold mask "impossibly" disappears, Strang "was considering that black magic was involved" (Brittain, 2018, 147), but eventually discovers that it's marsupial magic instead. In "Mr. Strang Finds an Angle" (1971) the locked room isn't locked and isn't even a room, but the vanishing of the murder weapon is nonetheless impossible, and the angle Strang finds isn't a point of view. In maybe the cleverest of the Strang impossible crime tales, "Mr. Strang, Armchair Detective" (1975), a corpse that didn't leave but isn't there turns out to be an ingenious final act of an aspiring opera singer.

"The Impossible Footprint" (1974) is a clever non–Strang impossible murder story. Although there is an official detective, the real sleuth in this story is strictly amateur (clearly a forte of Brittain's), an avid reader of detective stories in the penny dreadfuls. A man whose leg is caught in a bear trap in winter has apparently amputated his leg and dragged himself across the snow in a desperate but futile attempt to survive, but fantastically a footprint from the severed foot is discovered by the amateur detective near the body now some distance from the trap—"Is it yer contention that the severed leg, takin' on a life uv its own, somehow got out uv the trap an' then hipperty-hopped down here to the body like a pogo stick, an' then later returned and put itself back into the trap?" (Ashley, 2007, 147). Although it may be true that "the real police cases aren't like the shows on TV" (150) where everything's neatly wrapped up at the end, a "phantom" footprint turns out to be just a bit more than an annoying loose end, as the fantastic is disclosed to be instead the ingeniously fabricated.

Fredric Brown

Both in his science fiction and his detective stories, Brown demonstrates an "offbeat—'cockeyed' some critics have said—view of humanity" (Greene and Adey, 108) nowhere more evident than in "The Spherical Ghoul" (1943) in which it appears a "ghoul hath murdered sleep" (125), but the reality is at least as cockeyed and ghoulish, as a corpse's face is mutilated in a locked morgue. The entire story is drenched in the atmosphere of the fantastic—a dark night in a morgue, "ghosts, ghouls, vampires, werewolves" (111), a thesis on the superstitions and early customs of mankind, and a shadowy figure carrying a black sphere of oblivion—and the rational solution is only slightly less fantastic than the premise of ghouls.

John Dickson Carr

Though perhaps not quite at the level of genius as "The House in Goblin Wood," the early Carr stories of Henri Bencolin—"The Shadow of the Goat" (1926), "The Fourth Suspect" (1927), "The Ends of Justice" (1927), and "The Murder in Number Four" (1928)—provide a strong hint of the Carr taste for the fantastic and the "locked-room" brilliance to come. Especially "The Shadow of the Goat" and "The Murder in Number Four" weave a hint of the supernatural in with impossible crimes, the former tale featuring a devilish figure who apparently can enter and exit locked rooms at will, commit murder then evaporate; the latter involving the murder of a diamond smuggler on a "haunted" train ("Sometimes there rides in the cab a blind driver named Death," Carr, 1991a, 94). Both tales lead to logical reasoning and clever detection and, amazingly, a rational solution, although Bencolin protests that it wasn't all reason but a bit of the fanciful as well—"Nobody is more apt than a detective to say a lot of windy, fancy things about reasoning, deduction, and logic. He too frequently says 'reason' when he means imagination. I object to having a cheap, straight-laced pedantry like reason confused with a far greater thing" (110). Reason or imagination or both—natural law in these stories dissolves the spell of the fantastic, though a trace of that spell, and of Carr's burgeoning genius, linger long in the mind well after the tale is told.

And a few years later, Carr's locked-room genius takes another step forward as demonstrated in the long short story "The Third Bullet" (1937), where impossibilities compound impossibilities as there are two guns too many and two bullets too few—"What sort of witchcraft or hocus-pocus happened in the next two or three seconds?" (Carr, 1991b, 323). For a while (a long while) it does appear that "djinns and afreets were fooling around in a bewitched house" (324), but eventually Colonel Marquis sorts it all out, and the fantastic fades into natural treachery and deceit.

In Carr's collection *The Department of Queer Complaints* (1940) Colonel March specializes in fantastic crimes, not just "impossible" but downright "queer"—"If somebody comes in and reports (say) that the Borough of Stepney is being terrorized by a blue pig, I've got to decide whether it's a piece of lunacy or a mistake, or a hoax, or a serious crime" (59). Although all seven March stories in the collection (there are four non–Department stories as well) are about the last category (serious crimes), they do seem to be touched with at least a little of the first category (a piece of lunacy) as well—a footprint in the snow atop a hedge ("The Footprint in the Sky," 1940), a murder in a room that doesn't exist ("The Crime in Nobody's Room," 1938), a mentally invisible piece of furniture ("Hot Money," 1940), a shower of deadly rain ("The Silver Curtain," 1939). Colonel March restores order with sanity and reason, as the incredible transforms into the possible and even, in most cases, the plausible.

Leslie Charteris

Although Charteris' Simon Templar, the Saint, is known most for his criminal tendencies, not infrequently does he become detective in order to advance his nefarious enterprises, but the locked-room case, "The Man Who Liked Toys" (1933) is a bit of an exception as here the Saint detects just to detect. In the suicide that is "murder just the same" (Penzler, 739), there is a hint of the fantastic—"Mr. Teal's spine tingled with the involuntary chill that has its roots in man's immemorial fear of the supernatural" (739)—but it ends up more psychological manipulation than occult suggestion.

G.K. Chesterton

The first collection of Father Brown stories, *The Innocence of Father Brown* (1911), includes several impossible crimes that apparently have only fantastic solutions—a corpse with one head too many ("The Secret Garden," 1910), an invisible killer and an equally invisible corpse ("The Invisible Man," 1911), a fatal blow of the hammer only God could have wielded ("The Hammer of God," 1910)—but are shown by Father Brown to have "natural" explanations. However, part of Chesterton's genius and appeal is that even though the "fantastic" is shown to be illusion, the "natural" that replaces it is almost as fantastic—fanciful, incredible, eccentric, extravagant, yet somehow plausible and even reasonable (within the bounds of the story).

Charles B. Child

In his wonderful collection *The Sleuth of Baghdad* (2002) Child sets the scene and tone for his Indian detective, Chafik Chafik, with vivid description and poignant realism:

> Inspector Chafik followed the sergeant down the stairs and stood for a moment in the narrow doorway smelling the sourness of Al-Rashid Street, where desert Bedouins rubbed shoulders with sleek city effendis, and arabanas pulled by dying horses mingled with the taxis and fine new cars. The dirt of the street disturbed him, and for a fleeting moment he wondered how Baghdad had looked in the ancient days. It sprawled now, vast and brown and ugly, along the banks of the same Tigris, but the palaces and rose gardens were gone, and shabby modern houses smeared with the dust of sand storms crowded along the mean streets [11].

Counterbalancing this realistic and reflective portrayal of place and people are the often fantastic plot elements—sometimes clever "locked-room" murders and other impossible crimes. In "All the Birds of the Air" (1950) the gathering of birds to mourn the death of a fledgling and the jumping of a fish help Chafik "weave a pattern" and disclose an "impossible death" as an ingenious possible murder. In "The Invisible Killer" (1955) a corpse that had been dead for four thousand years is found with a knife in its back, but the murdered is much more recent, grabbed and strangled by an invisible force deep in the ground. Chafik turns the invisible visible and reveals a murderer of flesh and blood, though the corpse of the ancient remains unavenged.

Agatha Christie

In Christie's collection *Partners in Crime* (1929) the detective team of Tommy and Tuppence Beresford adopt the methods and play the parts of numerous famous fictional detectives, including Sherlock Holmes, Dr. Thorndyke, Hercule Poirot, the Old Man in the Corner, and Father Brown. In "The Man in the Mist" (1924) Tommy "Brown" encounters a case that, in true Chestertonian fashion, drips with the atmosphere of the fantastic—talk of ghosts, figures looming out of the mist, an impossible crime, and even an invisible man *a la* the classic Father Brown tale of that name. Ironically, the man who suddenly appears "as though materialized out of the fog.... One minute he was not there, the next minute he was" (Christie, 1984, 102), just as suddenly and completely disappears again, just in time to create the impossible in the impossible crime. Christie uses Chesterton's "The Invisible Man" motif again in a tale of Miss Marple, "Miss Marple Tells a Story" (1934) in which Miss Marple is the only one who sees the person (actually two people) who entered and left the "locked room."

One of Christie's lesser known detectives, Parker Pyne, in "The Regatta Mystery" (1929) encounters a locked-room diamond theft, complete with the disappearance of the jewel but not the departure of anyone in the room. Impossible? Not at all, as Pyne shows, for he recognizes the "fingerprints" of a gang specializing in using the appearance of the fantastic to camouflage very real crime.

G.D.H. and M.I. Cole

You probably wouldn't expect it of the methodical Superintendent Wilson (categorized by some critics as belonging to the "humdrum" school of detectives), but even he occasionally has a bit of the fantastic to apply his careful, somewhat plodding methods to solve. "In a Telephone Cabinet" (1928) involves Wilson in a bizarre case where the only possible solution to a locked-room mystery seems to be "a murderous gnome the size of a telephone, sitting on the shelf with a blunderbluss in his arms" (Penzler, 636). Appropriately, the natural explanation comes from careful analysis of clues, methodical reasoning, *and* a fantastic flash of inspiration from the wings of a fluttering owl.

Michael Collins (Dennis Lynds)

Although Collins' "No Way Out" (1963) is a fairly "standard" locked-room theft and murder ("a cockroach couldn't get into that room, and a germ couldn't get out," Ashley, 2000, 161), there are some interesting features that help it stand out: (1) it ridicules the lengths some impossible crime stories will go to (it cites one of Carr's least plausible solutions) for a "rational" solution that is more fantastic than most non-rational explanations—"You mean someone wants you to believe odds like that.... The guy who wrote that one drinks cheaper booze than you do" (157); (2) it humorously dismisses the non-rational solution—"It is a million to one against the guy being invisible. It's two million to one against him having wings" (163); and (3) it illustrates a novel and ingenious motive for murder and method of theft.

Joseph Commings

All of Commings' thirty-three stories of Senator Brooks U. Banner, including the fourteen collected in *Banner Deadlines* (2004), involve impossible crimes that at first appear to have no rational solution; some are intricate, intellectual puzzles where reason eventually supplants fantastic imaginings (e.g., in "The X Street Murders," 1962, where a man is shot by a gun sealed in an unbroken envelope and in "Murder Under Glass," 1947, where a man is stabbed inside a sealed glass dome), while others add a further touch of the fantastic by evoking the supernatural—vampires, phantoms, ghosts, spirits, even Death himself dancing at a masked ball. In the best of these stories, the puzzle is clever, the mood is ominous and exotic, and the fantastic and reason clutch in a mad embrace—"A night full of grand-guignolesque revelations, when the unreal became the real, and the real became the unreal" (191). Even with Banner himself, it's not always clear what is real and what is not, as he can be crude and insensitive but also deeply compassionate and humane.

Adrian Doyle and John Dickson Carr

In the collection of Sherlock Holmes pastiches, *The Exploits of Sherlock Holmes*, six of the stories were written jointly by Adrian Doyle, Arthur Conan Doyle's youngest son, and Carr, while the other six were the works of Doyle alone. One of the former, "The Adventure of the Sealed Room" (1954) is a locked-room tale, and although the presumed solution is suicide rather than something more "fantastic," the reader has doubts as the story, though taking place in an English country house, is immersed in an eerie atmosphere of death masks and other Indian antiquities and a rather ominous Indian servant—"There we lived almost as though we were at a hill-station in India, even to the white-clad figure of Chundra Lal, George's native butler, in a house full of strange gods and perhaps strange influences too" (155). The solution turns out to be neither suicide nor fantastic, but deviously clever, though certainly not clever enough to deceive Holmes.

Arthur Conan Doyle

Even the ultimate detective of reason and deduction, Sherlock Holmes, has a few encounters with the apparently fantastic ("Working as he did rather for the love of his art than for the acquirement of wealth, he refused to associate himself with any investigation which did not tend towards the unusual, and even the fantastic," Conan Doyle, 2005, 227), including the famous locked-room story, "The Adventure of the Speckled Band" (1892)—"I cannot recall any [cases] which presented more singular features" (227). Although at first Holmes' reasoning is misled to the wrong natural conclusion (the nearby gypsy camp), he, just in time, discovers the real solution, just as natural but certainly more fantastic!

But Holmes isn't the only Conan Doyle detective to encounter the apparently fantastic. "The Lost Special" (1898) is an impossible crime story in which "in broad daylight, upon a June afternoon in the most thickly inhabited portion of England, a train with its occupants had disappeared as completely as if some master of subtle chemistry had volatilized it into gas ... and some thought that supernatural, or, at least, preternatural agencies had been at work" (Davies, 2006, 249). One correspondent to *The Times*, "an amateur reasoner of some celebrity at that date [1890] attempts to deal with the matter in a critical and semi-scientific manner ... [citing] one of the elementary principles of practical reasoning that when the impossible has been eliminated the residuum, however improbably, must contain the truth" (249–250). Whether this amateur reasoner is the detective we suspect he is or not, reason does enter the case to temper the fantastic, though the ultimate solution comes about only because of a death-bed confession.

Vincent Cornier

Cornier is represented in several of the chapters of this monograph, as his stories of Barnabas Hildreth in *The Duel of Shadows* (2004) are filled with the bizarre, the incredible, and the fantastic, though almost always with a rational and possible (if implausible) explanation. Many of these fantastic qualities are evident in his earlier tales, for example the amazing impossible crime story, "The Flying Hat" (1929) in which the question lingers, "Trackless and invisible, that agent—entity—being, call it what you will; how had it struck and felled and gone from all men's knowing, within a few short minutes; out of a well-lighted quadrangle, alive with police officers and stirring people?" (Penzler, 301). As if the impossible shot that wasn't a shot wasn't enough, Cornier introduces rare gold coins in a beggar's pockets, an Egyptian wedding ring, Hungarian shepherds, dental wax, ice that isn't ice, and a man who isn't there! And most amazing of all is that in the midst of all this absurdity is precise and astonishing logical deduction and a rational explanation that would do Sherlock Holmes himself proud. Whether Barnabas Hildreth or Sir Richard Brantygham is the detective, whether *EQMM*, *The Story-teller*, or *Strange Stories* is the medium, Cornier's strange tales are effective illustrations of the detective and the fantastic working in synchrony—"Although some of the stories include mystical elements, the solutions are all based on scientific concepts.... Cornier, though, pushes the barriers to the very edge of scientific knowledge" (Ashley, Introduction, Cornier, 2011, 10), and, it might be added, the very edge of scientific possibility.

Edmund Crispin

Author of several novels and two collections of short stories about erudite detective Gervase Fen, Crispin specialized in intricate plots and literary prose and, from time to time, impossible crimes. In "Beware of the Trains" (1951) the driver of the train mysteriously disappears—"vanishes like a soap bubble," (Penzler, 382) with all station exits guarded, then reappears dead. All through the story, the poetically realistic ("Rain was falling indecisively. It tattooed in weak, petulant spasms against the station roof, and the wind on which it rode had a cutting edge," 382) jousts with the fantastic ("Fate had a conjuring trick in preparation," 382) until finally the latter falls. "The Name on the Window" (1953) is especially interesting as it first lightly satirizes the locked-room mystery by pooh-poohing several "standard" solutions (e.g., walking atop the footprints of the victim, shooting the knife from a gun, swinging on a rope above the floor), then concludes by illustrating one category of locked-room mysteries that Carr didn't include in his famous Dr. Fell lecture—"the locked-room mystery that isn't a locked-room mystery" (Crispin, 1953, 630)

Freeman Wills Crofts

From his first short story, "The Mystery of the Sleeping Car Express" (1921), Crofts establishes his trademark meticulous, detailed presentation, analysis, and explanation of the crime. Some might call this style "plodding" or "humdrum," while others, like Raymond Chandler, call Crofts the soundest builder of them all. In this first story, the double murder in the railway cabin seems fantastic—beyond all logical explanation (and Crofts presents and rejects pretty much *every* possibility)—but in the end, there is, of course, *one* more explanation, which, though not fantastic, seems a bit that way in contrast with the preceding pages and pages of fastidious reason, logic, and logistics.

David Stuart Davies

Davies' unofficial solver of riddles and artist, Luther Darke, not only "had a fascination for the unexplained and the unknown," but "took a great interest in the work of spiritualist mediums and in unsolved crimes" (Davies, 2006, 177)—a wonderful combination indeed for fantastic detective stories. When he isn't investigating cases with ancient curses (see Chapter Three), he is solving locked-room crimes as in "The Curzon Street Conundrum" (1999) in which his "artistic" vision and flair for the fantastic complement the completely rational approach of his Inspector friend—"Ah, we see the world from different hill tops, you and I, Edward. You are the professional, scientific detective with a demand for rationality and feasibility; whereas I am the amateur, an artist, doomed to view things from a different angle and able to see shifting and often unusual perspectives. We are two halves of the perfect whole" (177), just as, perhaps, the rational and the fantastic (in this case, the appearance of the fantastic) can be two halves of a perfect detective story.

Lillian de la Torre

De la Torre's tales of Dr. Samuel Johnson and his Boswell of 18th century Europe are rich with the scenes and events of that time. Of the thirty-one tales, several, though fastidiously researched and realistically written down to the last detail, have fantastic elements, including the locked-room murder "The Triple-Lock'd Room" (1952) in which it appears "the devil is flown through the triple-lock'd door" (de la Torre, 1952, 96), but instead it's a "mountebank rope-dancer, a seven-foot Abyssinian traveler, a 'strange knot of Jamaicans,' a pug and a paraqueet" (89), and a little touch of humanity. "Murder Lock'd In" (1980) is an especially interesting locked-room murder story, for Johnson concludes that "the devil did it indeed, but in human form" (de la Torre, 1980, 112), then provides a lengthy list of possible solutions (*a la* Carr in Dr. Fell's famous lecture), none of which will work ("I thank you, sir, for demonstrating how this strange feat was not accomplished," 109). How it was accomplished was not on Dr. Fell's list.

Lord Dunsany

Most readers of detective or fantasy or horror fiction are familiar with Dunsany's infamous story "The Two Bottles of Relish" (1932) in which an impossible murder is committed (the corpse completely disappears) and the detective Linley arrives at the solution, which is almost as fantastic as was the apparently impossible, but perhaps most readers are not aware that there are seven other detective stories about Linley in *The Little Tales of Smethers* (1952) one of which involves an impossible crime where the victim is shot to death without a bullet ("The Shooting of Constable Slugger," 1932). Dunsany, best known for his fanciful stories of the Edge of Beyond and the fabulous raconteur, Jorkens, is able in his few detective tales of Linley and Smethers, to immerse the detection in fancy and melt the fantastic with reason.

Stanley Ellin

Winner of numerous Edgars and other awards, Ellin included some impossible crimes among his many literate and intricate short mystery tales. "The Twelfth Statue" (1967) is a classic example in which a movie producer "walked out of the door of his office and vanished from the face of the earth as utterly and completely as if the devil had snatched him down to hell by the heels" (Penzler, 331). However, the police (and the reader) are "inclined to shrug off the devil and his works and look elsewhere for clues" (331), but here is where Ellin's ingenuity shows, for he sets us up to think we've discredited the fantastic and figured out the natural (though still rather fantastic) solution, then he jerks that solution away from us, then re-introduces it when we're not looking. We're always one step behind in this mad dance, as Ellin leads us by the nose with all the craft of an exquisitely skilled writer.

Kate Ellis

In "The Odor of Sanctity" (2000) the impossibility of the locked-room murder (in a small tower room) is enhanced by several even more fantastic elements—a possible ghost, a suit of armor with a bloody sword, and the victim of the stabbing apparently staggering around the room, letting out a scream, and falling out of the window to his death, all at least a half hour *after* he had already died! The solution is naturally ingenious, revealed by clever detection and the aroma of sanctity.

R. Austin Freeman

Even the "greatest of all scientific detectives" (Penzler, 136) does encounter, from time to time, what appear to be impossible mysteries that can only be explained by the fantastic. The juxtaposition of the seemingly inexplicable with the fastidious and detailed analysis and unarguable logic of Dr. Thorndyke makes the "impossible" seem all the more fantastic to the reader but not to Thorndyke—"The fact that he [the murderer] did get in, and that he is not here now, and therefore he must have got out; and therefore it must have been possible for him to get out; and, further, it must be possible to discover how he got out" (140–141). In "The Aluminum Dagger" (1909) this is just what Thorndyke does, though the rational and "scientific" explanation is almost as fantastic as the inexplicable, at least to the official police—"This is all very ingenious, but I say it is impossible and fantastic" (148). For Thorndyke neither exist, as everything that happens happens "naturally" and so is not only natural but explicable.

Jacques Futrelle

Many of Futrelle's classic cases of the Thinking Machine involve fantastic or even supernatural elements, but in many others the apparently fantastic is debunked by the Thinking Machine's impeccable and infallible logic. In his most famous case, "The Problem of Cell 13" (1908), the Thinking Machine shows the impossible escape from a locked room (security prison) to be far from impossible and to involve nothing more fantastic than some intelligent, or easily trained, creatures of nature. What makes this story unique is that the detective in this case, the Thinking Machine, "solves" the mystery by committing the "crime," so there is deception rather than detection, the perpetrator is liberated instead of apprehended, and though there is a crime of sorts (one agreed upon in advance), there is no criminal.

"The Mystery of the Scarlet Thread" (1908) is a more conventional locked-room impossible crime, for here there is a murder committed, and the Thinking Machine is out to solve it. Of course, we know that he will refute its impossibility, not only because the murder did occur and so was clearly possible, but also because the Thinking Machine's oft-repeated mantra is "Nothing is impossible. Don't say that. It annoys me exceedingly" (Futrelle, vol. 1, 2009, 219). For the Thinking Machine, two plus two always equals four, so there is no room for the fantastic in a world of precise and irrefutable logic, though he does acknowledge that imagination (but not the non-natural) is the hallmark of the great criminals and is a vital tool for detectives to fill in what logic may not know. In "The Problem of the Perfect Alibi" (1908) the murderer uses imagination to create a perfect alibi so it was impossible for him to have committed the crime, but the Thinking Machine uses logic to imagine how this alibi must have been contrived and so traps the criminal into confession—"under the exact circumstances, nothing else could have happened. The simplest rules of logic proved conclusively that this did happen ... [so] I tricked Mr. Chase into believing that I was an eye witness. That was the only way to make him confess" (421–422). "The Grip of Death" (1908) is a bit reminiscent of "The Problem of Cell 13," for although this locked-room mystery entails a murder and most definitely not an escape, the solution does involve non-human agencies.

Erle Stanley Gardner

Although Gardner is best known for his Perry Mason courtroom dramas, he created several other detectives including the folksy country sheriff Bill Eldon; and although he is certainly not known for impossible crime stories, "The Clue of the Runaway Blonde" (1971) is one case where the murder appears to be fantastic—a corpse in the middle of a freshly plowed field with no footprints going in or out. Eldon forgoes the sophisticated methods of technology, and even of focusing on clues, instead using his tried-and-true analysis of character and human nature, which eventually reveals the natural (and rather rural) solution.

Peter Godfrey

Of Godfrey's many fantasy and detective tales, the best known and probably the most intriguing are those of the South African detective Rolf le Roux, who often encounters bizarre situations, some deeply psychological, some utterly fantastic. In "Out of this World" (1954) a man is stabbed alone in a cable car on its way down a mountain, and there are strange beings "floating" around the story—a mystical creature from Mars visible only to the victim, gamma-ray robots, and Vernerian Swamp-slugs. Although, in the end, the solution is natural to some, to the killer (and perhaps to the reader) it remains with at least a touch of the fantastic—"My arm may have struck the blow ... but the Mighty Messenger from Mars [the Angel of Death] entered my body the better to punish the evil one who scoffed at holy death. The Messenger has been here, flashing through chaos from golden Mars to green earth, from green earth to Golden Mars. And from this place he has taken a soul" (Greene and Adey, 192). The two cable car stations, at the top and the bottom, are solidly on earth, while the journey on the cable between them is out of this world, so the actual commission of the murder is natural and "earthly" while its appearance and motive are fantastically unearthly. (It is interesting that in the version of this story called "The Flung-Back Lid" that appears in the Godfrey collection *The Newtonian Egg*, 2002, much of the fantastic is toned down, though the locked-room enigma remains.)

"The Newtonian Egg" (1951) that appears in the same collection is especially interesting because the locked room is one of the smallest in detective fiction (an egg), and because the "locked egg" mystery is surrounded by reference to other locked room classics—Futrelle's "The Problem of Cell 13" and Carr's novel *The Three Coffins*. In another le Roux impossible crime mystery, "A Dagger of the Mind" (1951) the room isn't locked until after the murder is committed, but then the killer is locked in, and it takes le Roux's understanding of the killer's mind to find the very real though invisible murder weapon.

Paul Halter

Halter is regarded by many as the heir apparent of John Dickson Carr, for his specialty is the carefully plotted impossible crime story, often with a touch of mythology or fairy tale to give it a further touch of the fantastic. In his collection *The Night of the Wolf* (2004) all but one of the tales are locked-room mysteries and all enhance Halter's reputation as an admirable successor of Carr. Whether it is singing and ribald shouts of laughter coming from the family vault ("The Dead Dance at Night," 2000), a man lured to his death by the Lorelei, the siren of German myth ("The Call of the Lorelei," 1998), or a man murdered by cognac and a charlatan spiritualist ("Murder in Cognac," 2000), the supernatural permeates these atmospheric tales that all resolve in the end into the logical solutions of renowned criminologist Dr. Alan Twist.

Michael Harrison

In the collection *The Exploits of the Chevalier Dupin* (1968) Harrison presents the "first 'new' Dupin stories in more than 120 years ... a Herculean task ... near to the original ... truly a 'tec tours de force'" (Queen Introduction, xi). And given that Poe is credited with the first detective story—"Murders in the Rue Morgue," 1841—and an impossible crime story at that, it is altogether fitting that some of the Harrison pastiches are themselves impossible crime tales. "The Fires in the Rue St. Honoré" (1967) is just that as fires are mysteriously starting within a "completely closed room—a sealed room—whose door has remained locked throughout and no person has broken in" (86). It is as much what Dupin doesn't see as what he does that leads him to replace the fantastic with "an infernal machine" (97). "The Murder in the Rue Royale" (1968) features a devilishly clever locked-room murder with a bullet that's not a bullet and a shot that's not a shot; ironically it is "facts" that aren't facts that reveal the "fantastic" to be not fantastic.

Edward D. Hoch

Hoch wrote hundreds of detective short stories over the years featuring quite a few different detectives, almost all of whom confront at least one or two impossible crimes, but Dr. Sam Hawthorne is far and away the impossible crime star—all sixty-eight of his cases (fifty-seven of which were written during our period of interest) are of that type:

> From the beginning I'd planned the Dr. Sam series as one frequently involving locked rooms and other impossible crimes. Fred Dannay thought the same way, and when I submitted the second story in the series, he suggested that all of them involve some sort of impossible crime. I was only too happy to oblige [Hoch, 2000, 9–10].

Part 1—The Apparently Fantastic Shown to Be Natural

The puzzles are always intriguing and perplexing (e.g., "a man drove his horse and buggy through the snow into a covered bridge, and never came out t'other end. All three vanished off the face of the earth, as if they never existed!," 11), but sometimes the solutions sag into implausibility or the mundane (after all, how many ways can an impossible crime be committed?). But in the best of these stories, the inventiveness of the rational solutions matches the ingenuity of the incredible puzzles, and they become brilliant illustrations of the sparkle and appeal that can derive from the integration of reason and the fantastic, or at least the appearance of the fantastic, as they always have logical explanations in the end. The contrast of the realistic—the detailed portrayal of everyday small-town life and Dr. Sam's precise observation of clues and logical deductions—with the wildly fantastic impossible crime situations engages readers and certainly kept *EQMM* interested (it published all sixty-eight stories). It also helped that Hoch was well versed in detective fiction, for his occasional references to impossible crime classics (e.g., Chesterton's "Invisible Man," Futrelle's "The Problem of Cell 13," Van Dine's *The Canary Murder*) lend a certain historical credence to his fantastic puzzles. Chesterton was a favorite of Hoch's, as he refers to the Father Brown stories, especially "The Invisible Man," in several of his tales, and Doyle is given tribute by Sam Hawthorne's initials.

The first twelve Sam Hawthorne stories (1974–1978) are collected in *Diagnosis Impossible: The Problems of Dr. Sam Hawthorne* (2000). There are several where the solutions are suicidal and somewhat disappointing, but in the best tales ("The Problem of the Covered Bridge," 1974, "The Problem of the Old Gristmill," 1975, "The Problem of the County Fair," 1978) the explanations, if mildly stretching plausibility, are ingenious, reasonable, and fulfilling, involving deceptions in appearance, identity, time, and space.

The next fifteen Hawthorne stories (1978–1983) are collected in *More Things Impossible: The Second Casebook of Dr. Sam Hawthorne* (2006). The best of these is probably the first one, "The Problem of the Revival Tent" (1978) where a revivalist preacher is stabbed with a ceremonial sword as "The Angel of Good Health" becomes the "Avenging Angel." There are other apparently fantastic murders including ones involving a whispering house and a dead man walking ("The Problem of the Whispering House," 1979), a poison dart gun and Cerberus, the three-headed dog of Hell ("The Problem of Boston Common," 1979), Lucifer and a fatal ball of flame ("The Problem of the Pilgrim's

Windmill," 1980), a gypsy curse and a bullet in the heart with no external wound ("The Problem of the Gypsy Camp," 1982), and a pilot stabbed in a small, flying "locked-room" ("The Problem of the Tin Goose," 1982). As the Sam Hawthorne saga continued to unfold, Hoch became even more a spokesman for the blend of the traditional and the apparently fantastic, as his impossible crime scenarios seem to get even more impossible, while the rational solutions, at least in a few of the stories, become more ingenious and even more plausible.

The next fifteen Hawthorne stories chronologically (1984–1991) appear in *Nothing is Impossible: Further Problems of Dr. Sam Hawthorne* (2014). As in the previous collections, the impossible crimes in most of the stories are fantastically intriguing (e.g., an acrobat disappearing from a trapeze in the middle of an act—"The Problem of the Invisible Acrobat," 1986; a murder in a locked "fortress" with an electrified fence, a vicious guard dog, and FBI surveillance—"The Problem of the Protected Farmhouse," 1990). Although the solutions don't always match the problems in ingenuity, in the best stories of the collection, "The Problem of the Crying Room" (1984) and "The Problem of the Thunder Room" (1988) not only are the explanations clever and plausible, but the plots are enlivened with fantastic "accessories"—a murderous nightmare premonition, a confession to a murder that hadn't yet happened but soon did, a bullet that found its home.

The fourth collection of Hawthorne tales (1991–1999) containing the next fifteen is *All but Impossible: The Impossible Files of Dr. Sam Hawthorne* (2017), which is one of the very best of the Hawthorne collections. There are several excellent stories in this collection, not only for the puzzling impossible crimes but also for the clever solutions that often match the ingenuity of the mysteries—the apparent ghost of a man in leather walking the countryside with Hawthorne but unseen by everyone else ("The Problem of the Leather Man," 1992); the room where a murder occurred but which can't be found in the house, almost driving Hawthorne to believe in the supernatural ("The Problem of the Phantom Parlor," 1993), a roadhouse that could appear for a brief time and then vanish leaving no trace except a dead man with a bullet in his head ("The Problem of the Missing Road House," 1994); the woman who murdered her husband two years after she died ("The Problem of the Country Mailbox," 1994); a fresh corpse found in a coffin buried for twenty years ("The Problem of the Crowded Cemetery," 1995); Herman Melville's ghost and the hunting of the whale ("The Problem of the Enchanted Terrace," 1997), and even an impossible shooting on the same covered bridge as in "The Problem of the Covered Bridge" written twenty four years previously ("The Second Problem of the Covered Bridge," 1998). It seems that Hoch improved with age as he juggled the fantastic with the rational with increasing expertise.

The last collection of Hawthorne tales (*Challenge the Impossible: The Final Problems of Dr. Sam Hawthorn*, 2000–2008) extends beyond our period of interest, but two of the impossible crime stories were written in 2000. The second one, "The Problem of the Potting Shed" (2000) has an interesting solution involving an alibi that is pregnant with possibilities.

Although the stories of Dr. Sam Hawthorne were Hoch's main venue for the impossible crime mysteries, he did write a few others with other detectives, including one extremely clever one featuring Cpt. Leopold—"The Leopold Locked Room" (1971) in *Leopold's Way* (1985)— in which the conventions of the impossible murder are turned on their head, for the impossible is designed to look not only possible but inevitable, to implicate rather than to exonerate, and, as a final fantastic touch, to turn Cpt. Leopold into not only detective but suspect. In the end, of course, the fantastic is shown to be quite possible and real though not the "possible" that the killer was hoping for.

Even Interpol becomes involved in an impossible crime in "The Case of the Musical Bullet" (1974) as Sebastian Blue and Laura Charme have to solve a mysterious shooting on an airplane with no one noticing and no apparent weapon. It turns out good French-Chinese relations is more impossible than the crime, which involved disguised identities and an even better disguised gun.

Even though Nick Velvet is a master thief, in some of his stories he has to become detective first before he can carry off the theft. "The Theft of the Venetian Window" (1975) is a particularly interesting locked-room crime because it appears that the only possible entrance and exit for the murderer was through a special Venetian mirror—not just any mirror, but a window connecting this universe with an alternative one, and so a pathway "Through the Looking Glass" for the killer to make the transition between universes! Of course, the solution is nowhere near so exotic and far less fantastic!

A clever non-series impossible crime story, "A Shower of Daggers" (1997) involves an amateur detective with no special abilities except for acute perception and clear thinking—"I'm no psychic. I don't pick up the killer's thoughts or visions. Sometimes I notice things that others have missed" (Ashley, 2007, 213). In this story of a puzzling stabbing in a shower with no one else present, the normal vanquishes the fantastic with a flourish of daggers and adhesive tape. "The Impossible Impossible Crime" (1968) is another non-series story where "Two men in northern Canada two hundred miles from civilization; one man is murdered, the other man is innocent. No possibility whatsoever of an outsider being involved" (Hoch, 1968, 140).

H. Edward Hunsberger

There are several fantastic elements in Hunsberger's droll "Eternally Yours" (1985)—not only a locked-room murder but postcards apparently written by the victim after his death. The skeptic amateur detective ("I don't believe in ghosts.... The whole notion of restless, prowling spirits strikes me as a waste of time. Even in the afterlife there must be better things to do than wandering around moaning and wailing, frightening poor mortals out of a good night's sleep," Ashley, 2007, 310) is a bit shaken by the fantastic nature of the man's death (although "people are always getting murdered behind locked doors in mysteries," 311–312) and his continuing stream of mail ("Was the late admiral carrying on a correspondence from beyond the grave? Was heaven a seedy resort hotel? And was I, nonbeliever in ghosts, being haunted, indirectly, by means of the U.S. Mail," 312). In the end his disbelief triumphs as the fantastic melts away in the tug on a rug.

H.R.F. Keating

Many of the stories of Inspector Ghote of the Bombay police, with their touches of Indian culture and religion, have elements of the fantastic; a few involve locked-room crimes, but the seeming impossibility in "The Legs that Walked" (2000) is not your standard "how did the murderer get in or out of the locked room," but a much more fantastic "how did the missing legs get out of the locked room." The title of the story tells it all, but the walking occurred years before—not as fantastic as it sounds.

Harry Kemelman

"Man on a Ladder" (1967) is one of the ingenious impossible crime stories of detective Nicky Welt collected in *The Nine Mile Walk* (1967) where the solution constantly lies just beneath the surface, where conversation is not what it appears, and where a whistle is a call to murder. The interplay of the fastidious, logical deduction and the fantastic impossibility, and the "coded conversation" between the surface material reality and the fantastic truth beneath it provide an infinity of appeal and fascination.

Gerald Kersh

"Open Verdict" (1959) is a murder not only in a locked-room but in a locked-house surrounding that room. The reference to Chesterton's classic impossible crime story "The Invisible Man" is done subtly but has unexpected significance, as in this brutal murder by knitting needle the killer is in a quite surprising way also invisible. The detective dispels the impossibility by careful observation and deduction but can't overcome the invisibility, so the case remains an "open verdict."

C. Daly King

Several of the stories from King's collection *The Complete Curious Mr. Tarrant* (2003), one of Crippen and Landru's issues in their "Lost Classic" series, incorporated aspects of the fantastic or the appearance of the fantastic, including two intricate and elaborate locked-room stories, "The Episode of the Nail and the Requiem" (1935) and "The Episode of the Little Girl Who Wasn't There" (1944). In the former tale, despite a seemingly impossible murder and disappearance (to the accompaniment of the Palestrina *Requiem*), Tarrant demonstrates the power of reason to restore order and natural law—"it brought out the unusual aptitude of the man to see clearly, to welcome all the facts, no matter how apparently contradictory, and to think his way through to the only possible solution by sheer logic, while everyone else boggled at impossibilities and sought to forget them" (48). While the impossible is by definition fantastic, the improbable can be quite natural if logic can peel away the camouflage. "The Episode of the Little Girl Who Wasn't There" is even more intricate and complex as the solution to an "impossible" disappearance ("We have a little puzzle. Rather an old and hackneyed one, I fear; the sealed room trick again—it keeps turning up regularly every so often," 171) turns out to be the farthest thing from hackneyed, so far that it amazes and puzzles even Tarrant's reason and logic—"He emitted an incredulous whistle and a moment later made clucking noises indicative of astonishment or chagrin, or both" (175). This locked-room story is reminiscent of the best detective tales of Anthony Berkeley or Christianna Brand or Helen McCloy, as reason is shown to falter before the fantastic before it eventually triumphs (several seemingly reasonable solutions are offered only to be disproved and discarded before the final explanation is given).

Rufus King

In King's "The Man Who Didn't Exist" (1925) the dilettante dandy detective Reginald de Puyster has to solve the impossible disappearance of Houdini Jake who has just stolen a valuable emerald. Though the tale is harshly realistic in its portrayal of character, it oozes with the aura of the fantastic in its oddly stilted prose and its eccentric descriptions—"He is built like a Dutch windmill, so long are his arms and so squat is his body, not from the fat of loose living, but tough as a table d'hote steak he is, to judge by the wallops he handed the Two Mitt Kid, who has more false teeth and black eyes to his credit than the bandits of the West have notches in their guns" (King, 1947, 86). Houdini Jake, the man who doesn't exist ("I mean a man who does and who doesn't," 86), in fact both does and doesn't in this somewhat tongue-in-cheek impossible crime tale of an old lady with a wicked left hook.

Stephen King

It might be surprising to see Stephen King's name here, but although he is most famous for his horror and supernatural stories, he did also author a short locked-room pastiche of Sherlock Holmes, not only a locked-room mystery but "the perfect locked room I've been looking for all my life" (Penzler, 159). In "The Doctor's Case" (1987) Holmes does refer to "The Adventure of the Speckled Band" as a locked-room but not a sealed-room mystery, as in that case there was a passageway to admit the murderer. In addition to the dissolving of the fantastic and the solving of the sealed-room murder in "The Doctor's Case," there is the added attraction of it being the only time Watson solved a crime before Holmes—maybe the most fantastic occurrence of all!

William Krohn

Inspired by the locked-room stories of John Dickson Carr, Krohn's "The Impossible Murder of Dr. Satanus" (1965) is rich with the spirit and atmosphere of magic, as the killer and the victim are both magicians ("a sorcerer ... a student of occult mysteries," Ashley, 2007, 400), and the impossible murder of the man alone in an elevator car has more than a touch of magic about it. But just as the magician's magic is misdirection, suggestion, and illusion, so too is this fantastic murder shown to be conjuring of the most ingenious and misleading kind—"all the work of a celestial Fifth Magician who stood back in the shadows, invisible and omniscient, pulling the strings" (412) but aided by a far-from-celestial puppet, the earthbound Fourth Magician with all the flaws and weaknesses of the flesh.

Conway Lonstar

In "The Weapon from Nowhere" (1970) a "psychic" predicts a murder in her house, which happens exactly as she prophesizes despite the presence of police and the press. The resulting impossible murder appears to be not only a case of psychic prophecy but psychokinesis as no one was near the victim when he was stabbed. Although the magician/detective Maitre Glenthier sees behind the misdirection and penetrates the impossible façade, a trace of the fantastic remains as the names of all the characters turn out to be anagrams—even the magician and the author are revealed to be not what they seem, as "Maitre Glenthier" re-arranges to reveal the famous magician/detective of Clayton Rawson.

Richard Lupoff

"The Second Drug" (2000) chronicles what appears to be a locked-room vampire murder—murder by a vampire of a vampire—for the victim, a Hungarian matinee idol playing a vampire on stage, seems to be drained of blood and has two marks on his neck. The more fantastic minded speculate that the vampire entered the room unobtrusively in human form, then after committing the murder "exited by flying through the window, first having taken the form of a bat" (Ashley, 2007, 424). No one takes this seriously, including the readers, but it does add a touch of the exotic to the already ironic. The solution, however, is neither—just a very human killing with a very human motive.

Ngaio Marsh

One of the few short stories featuring Marsh's familiar (in novels) detective, Roderick Alleyn, "I Can Find My Way Out" (1946) is interesting as an impossible-crime mystery primarily for its intricate juxtaposition of the fantastic and the real as the play "is the thing"—the action takes place both backstage and front stage at the theater, and it is sometimes difficult to tell which is real and which is fiction. Since all the actors are always in "disguise" pretending to be someone else, who are they really? And to add to the confusion, an assistant of Alleyn, in disguise, is mistaken for a key (real) character and contributes to the motives and the murder backstage. The no-nonsense Alleyn disparages the fantastic nature of the crime—"Don't let us have any nonsense about sealed rooms" (Greene and Adey, 90)—but this is a locked-room murder that seems to be a suicide until Alleyn "steps on the gas."

A.E. Martin

"Naked men dropping from the sky! Crying circus girls! Illiterate Cassanovas!" (Martin, 94): "The Flying Corpse" (1947) is as fantastic as its title would suggest as a corpse dressed with a bullet hole and nothing else is found, impossibly, in a field in the middle of nowhere with no surrounding footprints. There is, of course, a logical (if somewhat unlikely) explanation, and the fantastic aspects coexist comfortably with the realism of the circus, a love affair gone wrong, and a delightful "Thin-Man" sort of sleuth partnership between the "detective" and his wife.

Theodore Mathiesen

Among the many stories of Mathiesen in which historical figures play the part of detectives (e.g., Alexander the Great, Captain Cook, Cervantes, Galileo, Daniel Boone, Stanley and Livingstone), the story "Leonardo da Vinci, Detective" (1959) presents a "locked-amphitheater" puzzle of an impossible murder which da Vinci reveals to be quite possible thanks to a golden oriole, a Scottish tartan, and da Vinci's trust in the secret processes of his unconscious.

Augustus Muir

There is more than a touch of the fantastic in Muir's "The Kestar Diamond Case" (1935), for the solution to the locked-room murder and theft is, though natural, almost as fantastic as the impossibility of the murderer and the diamond escaping the locked room. In a unique solution, the locked room stays locked, and neither the victim, the murderer, nor the diamond ever leaves it.

Francis Nevins

In Nevins' "The Ironclad Alibi" (1974) the detective Loren Mensing has to solve an impossible crime where "the only person who could be the murderer was also the only person who couldn't possibly be the murderer" (Nevins, 72). With some clever ferreting and knowledge of movie making, Mensing penetrates the fantastic enigma to find another person who could be the murderer—this time one who didn't have the advantage of also being one who couldn't have committed the crime.

Nicholas Olde

Although Olde only wrote one collection of detective short stories, *The Incredible Adventures of Roland Hern* (1928), so many of these stories are memorable for their clever plots and fanciful or fantastic elements (see Chapters Three and Six). The solution to the impossible murder in "The Invisible Weapon" (1928) is not novel and has been used again elsewhere (e.g., see Dunsany's "The Shooting of Constable Slugger," 1952), but the interesting, and ironic twists here are that "There is only one man who could have done it—and he could not have done it" (131), and the only way the killer could establish his innocence was to remain at the scene of the crime. In "The Red Weed" (1928) an "impossible" disappearance is solved by a strange, red weed—*Barba sanguinea horrida*—whose barbarous Latin explains everything.

Stuart Palmer

Most of the cases of the irrepressible Hildegarde Withers are straightforward though clever clue-puzzle mysteries, but occasionally she encounters an impossible crime (e.g., "The Riddle of the Tired Bullet," 1948, in which a bullet is exhausted after a very short journey) or even one with hints of the bizarre and fantastic (e.g., "The Monkey Murder," 1947). This latter tale involves an exotic locked-room murder—"the Witch-Men dancing their ceremonial dance of death ... the vast looming statue of Hanuman, the monkey-god its tail moving like a sinuous, hairy snake, moving down slowly to wrap itself around the throat of the helpless girl" (Palmer, 1947, 77–78)—but Miss Withers not only explains the impossible and exposes the exotic, but ironically she does it by weaving her own fantastic tale.

Edgar Allan Poe

Although Poe's classic story, "Murder in the Rue Morgue" (1841), considered to be the very first detective short story, is in many ways a celebration of the power of pure reason and deduction to explain the seemingly fantastic (the manner and perpetrator of the locked-room murders); nonetheless, in its long, pedantic, philosophical introduction, it presents extreme rationality as itself verging on the fantastic:

> As the strong man exults in his physical ability, delighting in such exercises as call his muscles into action, so glories the analyst in that moral activity which disentangles.... He is fond of enigmas, of conundrums, hieroglyphics; exhibiting in his solutions of each a degree of acumen which appears to the ordinary apprehension praeternatural. His results, brought about by the very soul and essence of method, have, in truth, the whole air of intuition [Poe, 78].

And so the stage was set and the model was established not only for the classic clue-puzzle detective story that would burgeon and blossom in the decades to follow, but also for the dynamic dialogue between the rational and the fantastic, between the laws of nature and the supernatural or at least the appearance of the supernatural.

Arthur Porges

Porges was probably best known for his parodies and pastiches of Sherlock Holmes (his tales of Stately Homes) and the tales of his own detectives Celery Green and Cyriack Skinner Grey. In "Her Last Bow: An Adventure of Stately Homes" (1957) he manages to spoof not only Holmes and John Dickson Carr's obsession with impossible crimes, but locked-room mysteries themselves—"Who's dead in a hermetically sealed chamber now? Who's been stabbed in a locked bank vault behind four feet of reinforced concrete and no weapon to be found, or strangled in a sunken submarine under three hundred fathoms of icy water?"

(Porges, 1957, 27). The locked-room murder, the suspects (including Dr. Jekyll, Quasimodo, and Captain Ahab), and Stately Homes' solution in this Porges parody are even more fantastic than in any of the locked-room murder stories he spoofs!

The short tales of his scientist detective collected in *The Curious Cases of Cyriack Skinner Grey* (2009) are entertaining for their irony in regards to the fantastic, for in story after story Grey uses the phenomena of science—the ultimate hard-nosed facts—to show that the "impossible" is not only possible but real. In "The Scientist and the Vanished Weapon" (1966) a birdbath and the "super cool" turns the fantastic into "hard" reality; in "The Scientist and the Invisible Safe" (1967) Grey sees the light and a diamond glitters bright; in "The Scientist and the Time Bomb" (1974) a bomb with a fifteen-year fuse and 17-year locusts almost detonate an explosion from the grave, and in "The Scientist and the Stolen Rembrandt" (1975) the purloined is more than a letter.

Porges was also a prolific author of all sorts of non-series detective and mystery stories, some of which feature locked-room and other impossible crimes. "No Killer Has Wings" (1960) is one of the few stories in which the fantastic crime (a man clubbed to death while lying on a beach with no tracks of the killer) is solved by a sort of fantastic variation of reason—brainstorming ("throwing your rational mind out of gear, and letting its motor race. You give the wildest fancies free rein, hoping to find gold among the dross," Ashley, 2007, 350). Brainstorming itself is a perfect illustration of the co-operation between reason and the fantastic, as reason lets go of itself and invites the fantastic to arise as eventual fuel for reason's return. Despite the deference to John Dickson Carr and locked-room fiction ("Maybe Carr can make up and solve these locked room puzzles on paper, but this was too much for me," 351), Porges' amateur detective does manage, with the help of a wordless accomplice, to solve this "real" fictional puzzle.

In "Murder of a Priest" (1967) the premise for the "impossible" murder is much more interesting than the murder method itself, for in this story the "detective" has to make the impossible possible but not so as to solve or prevent the killing but rather so as to *commit* it.

Melville Davisson Post

"The Doomdorf Mystery," though probably the best known of the Uncle Abner tales in the collection *Uncle Abner: Master of Mysteries*

(1918), is not the only "locked-room" story in the Abner canon and is only one of many in which the atmosphere, if not the actuality, of the fantastic "co-stars" with Abner's careful observation and logical deductions. In "The Hidden Law" (1914) it appears that a witch must have stolen a miserly old man's gold from a locked room—"A thief cannot crawl through a keyhole, but there are things that can" (Post, 1977, 101)—and even Abner seems to confirm the fantastic much to the chagrin of his "Watson"—"You used to be a crag of common sense. The legends and theories of fools broke on you and went to pieces. Would you now testify to witches?" (102). In a beautiful merging of the rational and the fantastic, Abner shows the "witch" to be quite natural, yet still able to perform the apparently fantastic act of entering through the keyhole and hording the gold.

Although certainly not at all as well-known as Uncle Abner, Post's Sir Henry Marquis in the collection *The Sleuth of St. James' Square* (1920) also illustrates the encounter of detective reason and logic with aspects of the fantastic. In "The Thing on the Hearth" (1920) the inventor Rodman ("one of those gigantic human intelligences who sometimes appear in the world," 6) has made a discovery that will threaten the world's economy—he has created a method to manufacture "genuine" precious jewels cheaply and in unlimited numbers. Although Post tries to divest this marvelous discovery of its fantastic quality ("If you want to understand what I am printing here about Rodman, you must think of it as a scientific possibility and not as a fantastic notion," 6), the resulting murder of Rodman in a locked room by a spirit being who leaves the print of a woman's bare foot appears to be irrevocably supernatural. However, if we go along with Post and are willing to accept the "fantastic" gem-making process as natural, the rest of the fantastic murder dissolves into a reasonable and natural motive and method, so one "good turn" of discrediting the fantastic deserves another.

Post offers a different clever twist on the fantastic in "The Phantom Woman" (1920) in the *Bradmoor Murder* collection, for in this story both Marquis and the criminal know that the theft was of human origin, but Marquis with the aid of a high-powered magnifying glass and impeccable logic "proves" (and the criminal is forced to admit) that it was the act of no living person, but an intervention by the dead—"One enters this house through a window probably fastened, through a door probably locked, opens a drawer in a desk with a key which the dead woman had hidden, and removes its contents ... these slippers belonging to the dead countess have walked before the window but with only the weight of a phantom on them…. How shall we say that she has not been here?" (187). Post's ingenuity has somehow validated the fantastic at the same time as it has debunked it!

John Basye Price

Price's "Death and the Rope Trick" (1954) presents an utterly convincing "absolute proof of the genuineness of psychic phenomena" (Ashley, 2007, 173) with a fantastic Indian rope-trick, where a coiled rope elongates high into the air, a boy climbs it to the top, vanishes in a puff of smoke, then reappears miles away. Although the eventual natural explanation, arrived at by observation of clues and deduction, is convoluted, overly elaborate, and difficult to swallow, the trick itself is mesmerizing and fascinating, a truly fantastic piece of "performance art" by a brilliant, self-styled student of the occult and a "monomaniac with delusions of grandeur" (172) and an unquenchable lust for riches. Here is a story where the fantastic rings much truer than the rational, where the impossible is gloriously intriguing, but the possible is too contrived and implausible.

Bill Pronzini

Many of his stories about the nameless "pulp" private eye for which he is best known combine realistic detail about places and investigative methods with the seemingly fantastic events of impossible crimes. "Thin Air" (1979) is a fine example of this very effective combination, for the impossible disappearance then murder of a man contrasts starkly with the fastidious detail of the detection. Somehow the apparently fantastic elements, though eventually shown to be quite natural, seem more vividly and strikingly fantastic and linger longer in the reader's mind because of their juxtaposition with their almost ploddingly realistic context. "The Pulp Connection" (1978) is especially interesting because the murder victim is an avid collector of pulp magazines and, in his death throes in his locked pulp library, he creates a clue with the titles of three of his magazines—"*Clues*," "*Keyhole Mystery Magazine*," and "*Private Detective*." It will take a reader of a certain age, like the nameless private eye, to understand the clue and dispel the fantastic with a very real article of the commonplace.

In addition to his stories of the nameless private eye, Pronzini wrote several impossible crime stories none more outrageous than "Proof of Guilt" (1973). Even though the killer is the only one in the room with the victim at the time of the shooting, he can't be charged, for the weapon can't be found. The solution—"an answer that was at once fantastic and yet so simple you'd never even consider it" (Ashley, 2007, 494)—is paradoxically utterly fantastic and completely realistic at the same time, quite a trick of yin/yang and complementary opposites all hiding in a cast-iron vessel.

Although not as outrageous as "Proof of Guilt," the impossible crime story "Vanishing Act" (1975) written with Michael Kurland is more effective with its interweaving of "real" magic and the magically fantastic—after murdering a magician in the middle of his act (a murder the audience, at first, thinks is part of the act), the killer vanishes off the stage, a "real" act of magic, but ultimately is found out by another magician. The seemingly impossible crime is always a sort of magic act, but in this case it really is one, but as in all acts of "real" magic the fantastic turns out to be in the deception not in the reality. In "The Half-Invisible Man" (1974), written with Jeffrey Wallman, there is a bit of a twist on the usual locked-room murder—the killer seems to be completely invisible (though the weapon is found outside the locked-room); it's the detective who is only half-invisible.

Clayton Rawson

In Rawson's collection *The Great Merlini* (1979) several of the stories involve impossible crimes with a bit of supernatural added in. Whether it's UFOs, Mayan hieroglyphs, and a midget's three-toed footprints ("Nothing is Impossible," 1958) or a psychokinetic murder by "some malign and evil entity whose astral substance materialized momentarily then returned to the other world from which it came," (33) in "From Another World" (1948), the supernatural at first challenges but eventually succumbs to Merlini's magic and deductions.

Although less known than the Great Merlini, Rawson's other magician/detective Don Diavolo, the Scarlet Wizard, has to deal with even more apparently fantastic circumstances in the pulpish impossible crime stories collected in *The Magical Mysteries of Don Diavolo* (2004). In "Death out of Thin Air" (1941) Diavolo encounters Dr. Palgar's Invisibility Ray Projector, an invisible thief who's after Marie Antoinette's famous diamond necklace, a dwarf in a suitcase, and a large statue of Siva the destroyer. Incredibly, there are logical explanations for all of it, though the police are as skeptical as most readers will probably be. In "Ghost of the Undead" (1941) murder and theft are accomplished by, apparently, a vampire bat which flies in and out of windows of otherwise locked rooms, but the bat turns out, almost as fantastically, to be a bat but of the "acro" kind.

Mary Reed and Eric Mayer

Already with an exotic air of strangeness from the Mongolian locale, "Locked in Death" (2000) adds another layer of unreality with the circus setting and its touch of magic ("an unworldly air, reminding him of Prospero's island," Ashley, 2007, 47) that takes the reader and the detective to a land far away from their daily realities—"for a few hours the circus's dazzling lights, nimble performers and sideshows would free him from the dreariness of the vast grey desert and cramped grey offices of his official life" (54–55). And as if this weren't enough magic, a corpse apparently rises from the dead to strangle an enemy, an impossible crime that is attributed to the calling of the dead "back from the lower world" (44). The fantastic permeates every aspect of this story—the impossible locked-room plot, the eccentric characters, the magical setting and fairy-tale atmosphere—until it comes to seem normal and natural: "Up here ... it was easy to believe the impossible" (58). But, of course, in the end "it is all too fantastic, even for a circus" (58), and the fantastic is shown to be only slightly less so.

Max Rittenberg

In addition to the collected stories of the super-sensitive "Colour-Criminologist" detective, Dr. Xavier Wycherley (see Chapter Five), Rittenberg wrote a series of tales, never gathered in a Rittenberg collection, about the irascible scientist/detective Magnum ("He was in the midst of a highly complex calculation of a formula based on a crystallographic angles and axes, requiring quaternions and perfect quiet," Ashley, 2007, 241). In "The Mystery of the Sevenoaks Tunnel" (1913) a man's death alone in a railway car is an enigma as is the warning note "From the Earth, From the Water, From the Sky," but to the ultimate rationalist it is the facts that are the only weapon against the fantastic whether in the crime or in the detection, for the facts not only have an "unfortunate habit of contradicting the most ingenious and elegant theories" (247), but eventually penetrate the mysterious and for the detective of reason and natural law "fit together like the pieces of a jigsaw puzzle" (251).

Sax Rohmer

Rohmer's stories of the occult detective Moris Klaw collected in *The Dream-Detective* (1920) illustrate Klaw's beliefs in the Cycle of Crime and the impressions left by strong emotions in the "etheric atmosphere." As a "sensitive" to these impressions, Klaw solves crimes by "receiving" the images and thoughts of the criminal or the victim (see Chapter Five). Most of the crimes are thefts of sacred relics or related murders; in at least one episode ("Case of the Blue Rajah," 1913) the theft of a fabulous diamond is from a locked room. This is a case where the fantastic method and results of Klaw's "odic receptivity" are much more interesting than the natural solution to the crime—"I shall secure many alien impressions of horror at finding the Blue Rajah missing. That is unavoidable. But I hope, amongst all these, to find that other thought-thing, the fear of the robber at the critical moment of his crime! That should be a cogent and forceful thought, keener and therefore stronger to survive" (82).

Forrest Rosaire

An amazing, raucous, pulpy tale of Chinamen, vials of acid, death threats, cut-out tongues, abandoned babies, an impossible murder, and "ghouls hunched over dead bodies, their talons busy with dead flesh" (Ashley, 2007, 466), breathlessly told in a hardboiled manner with a Fu-Manchu flair, "The Poisoned Bowl" (1939) first hits with the hard fists of reality, then suffocates with the choking odor of the ominous and fantastic as reader and heroine alike "seem sucked out of reality, soul yawing and heeling over in blackness" (481). It all makes a melodramatic kind of sense in the end as the heroine and reason triumph, but the aroma of the fantastic still clings heavy to the pages and to the mind.

Georges Simenon

Although best known for his many atmospheric novels and short stories of Jules Maigret, Simenon created several other detectives, including Joseph LeBorgne. "The Little House at Croix-Rousse" (1947) is a short and tight little locked-room gem in which a man is inexplicably murdered with no weapon and no murderer and "no hocus-pocus. Nothing out of a mystery novel" (Penzler, 781). Ironically, only when LeBorgne's partner concludes that it is truly impossible, does LeBorgne's reason find the possibility and solve the mystery.

Joseph Skvorecky

In "The Case of the Horizontal Trajectory" (1966) collected in *The Mournful Demeanor of Lieutenant Buruvka* (1988) the Czech detective Lieutenant Buruvka solves the locked-room murder of a woman with a "dagger" in her eye. There is reference to Freeman's "The Aluminum Dagger" (see above) when a similar solution is offered (but rejected), but the most interesting part of this story is not the rather contrived mechanical solution but the fact that an open window is used to locate suspicion (falsely) *outside* the locked room. In "Death on Needlepoint" (1966) in the same collection an "impossible" murder is committed on a mountain pinnacle during a treacherous climb, and although with its wide-open spaces it seems to be the furthest thing from a locked-room crime, in actuality "it's just a variation of the Locked Room Mystery ... we did have a place which the murderer couldn't have reached and from which he couldn't have escaped, and yet he did get there, and he did get away from it. Just like a murderer who leaves the corpse in a room that's locked on the inside" (94). The vivid and detailed description of the climb makes the whole story seem fantastic—like a dream, or rather a nightmare. "A Tried and Proven Method" (1966), another "impossible" murder in a mountain setting, also has a fantastic atmosphere about it—"Opposite her a rugged rock, a stark mountain crest, loomed out of the surging, vaporous whiteness like a Gothic cathedral carved by Salvador Dali; a spray of sunbeams, straggling through a rent in the grey autumnal clouds, played upon it. The sinister, gilded Dragon's Peak with its twin towers, rising out of the grey-black mist resembled a mythical castle in an Arthurian legend" (142)—yet the sensitive portrayal of the characters and their interplay and the carefully unfolding plot with the natural solution bring solidity and stark realism to the nebulous and fantastic mist. "Falling Light" (1966) doesn't have the same fantastic aura surrounding it, but it does have a locked-room murder the "natural" solution to which involves a fountain of falling and flowing water.

Julian Symons

Symons wrote numerous short, short stories about Francis Quarles many collected in *Murder! Murder!* (1961), *Francis Quarles Investigates* (1965), *How to Trap a Crook and 12 Other Mysteries* (1975), and *The Detections of Francis Quarles* (2006). Most of his stories are of the classic, clue-puzzle type—"There are no humdrum murder cases, and no insoluble ones either. In every unsolved crime, there is always a human error, a clue which, if we could understand its meaning, would point straight to the murderer" (Symons, 2006, 10)—however, despite the emphasis on logic and deduction, from time to time elements of the fantastic intrude, at least as red herrings, as in the case of the apparently impossible crimes that are shown by Quarles to have completely rational explanations. "As if by Magic" (1961) is a tight little tale about a murder done in broad daylight in an amusement park but where the murderer vanishes in seconds and can't be found until Quarles takes the "last stand" with reason and ironically finds reality in child's play. In "The Impossible Theft" (1966) a theft of a string of pearls seems impossible as the pearls have vanished without an "escape route," but Quarles discovers their hiding place by figuring out why a man who wasn't Oswald and wasn't Australian was called "Ossie."

E. Charles Vivian

Cellini, Michaelangelo, Alexander Borgia, a not-so-blind Cupid, and hair not singed all have their parts to play in Vivian's locked-room murder "Locked In" (1926) in which the solution, reached by experiment, fingerprints, and logic, is nearly as fantastic as the puzzle—"Well, I'm damned" (Jakubowski, 47).

Manly Wade Wellman

Of his two stories of the Native American detective, David Return, whom Ellery Queen called "the first truly American detective to appear in print—even more authentically than Melville Davisson Post's Uncle Abner" (Queen, 1946, 3), his "Knife Between Brothers" (1947) is a locked-room mystery or perhaps more accurately a locked-hut mystery. The seemingly fantastic element ("Maybe an enemy ghost put a spell on me to make me do this thing [a stabbing]," Penzler, 181) is all the more striking because of its contrast with the gritty realism of the description—"Flat red-brown dryness stretched away to right and left, with occasional dimples where buffalo had wallowed long ago, and more distant clumps and stragglings of brushy willow or cottonwood scrub to mark scanty watercourses" (179). With the heavy atmosphere of Native American myth and culture, we are tempted to credit the fantastic, but eventually Return figures out the natural explanation—not ghosts, not myths, but murder with a long reach.

James Yaffe

Not only did Yaffe write several stories about his detective Paul Dawn solving impossible crimes, but he had Dawn be the head of a whole "Department of Impossible Crimes" (admittedly Dawn was its only member). In a series of stories, the teenage Yaffe creates some interesting cases in which the seemingly fantastic crimes are shown to be quite natural. The first step is to assume that they are not impossible, then logic will reveal the only possible solution—"In solving these impossible murders you've got to discount ghosts, or invisible men, or complicated contraptions operated by remote control. You've got to get it in your head that there's no such thing as an impossible crime" (Yaffe, 1943, 60). In the first Dawn story, "The Department of Impossible Crimes" (1943), a man is murdered in a sealed elevator in which he is the only passenger. While everyone else is marveling and puzzling over the fantastic impossibility of it, Dawn discards the impossible—"Pigs don't fly. Automobiles can't change into kangaroos. And murderers don't disappear up elevator shafts" (52)—leaving only the improbable, but natural. In this tale and in the later stories "The Seventh Drink" (1944) and "The Emperor's Mushrooms" (1945) the apparently impossible sets a fantastic stage on which the rational and reasonable eventually steals the scene, but the scene would have been nothing without the stage.

Two

Other Fantastic Scenarios

Although all impossible crime stories appear to be fantastic before the rational explanation is revealed, not all detective stories where the apparently fantastic is eventually shown to be rational involve locked rooms or impossible crimes. In this chapter we examine some of these other types of detective stories and see that, as with the impossible crime tales, the inclusion of the fantastic as atmosphere and red herring can add to the ingenuity and appeal of an otherwise traditional tale. There is something very satisfying and reassuring when what appears to be "hocus-pocus" resolves into reason and rationality, when what seems to be heading in one direction reverses course and settles into the comfortable zone of tradition. Perhaps, too, it comforts us to have an "enigma beyond reckoning" turn out to be compatible after all with the natural law that we so depend on and govern our lives by. It is probably not surprising, then, that some of the most engaging, ingenious, and popular detective short stories are those where the apparently fantastic or supernatural is unmasked to reveal "normal" human passions, depravities, and crimes.

Exemplars

Charles B. Child

"The Long, Thin Man" (1950) is a sensitive and deeply moving account of a military man who has created dysfunction by bringing a new wife into a "garden of remembrance, a place where a man must walk alone, where a new bride cannot enter" (Child, 1950, 93). His first wife is "a cherished ghost in the house" who haunts not only him but his young daughter of that first marriage, haunts her into apparent madness—an obsession with a long, shadowy, thin man who eventually murders. Chafik shows not only great insight but also great compassion for the daughter as he slowly, logically, dissolves the shadow, the terror, and the madness right before our eyes into flesh and blood and human suffering. The fantastic presence, though disembodied, continues to drive the story and haunt our thoughts even as it releases its hold on the terrorized girl.

Michael Innes

The author of so many droll, erudite, and intellectual detective stories of Inspector John Appleby, Innes wrote several where fancy goes frenetic (see Chapter Six) and a few where the supernatural takes center stage, at least for a while. "A Matter of Goblins" (1954) is one of those few, a wildly entertaining tale where rationality seems to be suspended in the ruins of an isolated country estate which has night-time visitations by bright lights and goblins or specters of times long past. Slowly the specters materialize in the hands of a master of illusions, and the play becomes the thing to revivify a dying man and his decaying estate. The last act is laughter from the Goblin King—"I knew at once that it was supernatural" (Innes, 2001b, 45)—before he disappears, "following darkness like a dream," and "what once or twice looked like crime proved to be comedy in the end" (45). The aura of the supernatural hangs like a ghost over this story well after it has dissipated into fact and reason.

Harold and Jerome Prince

The dance between the fantastic and the real begins early in the remarkable story "The Man in the Velvet Hat" (1944) as we discover that the journalist who will report the incredible story of Death appearing in the Velvet Hat previously wrote brilliant fantasies, describing "as Stevenson and Arthur Machen had once done the romance lurking just beyond the pavement; the unusual, the macabre which rubbed elbows with you in the Polo Grounds, on the B.M.T., along the Bowery, in the middle of Central Park" (Prince, 1944, 103). The fantastic still lives inside him although "as he, and his bank account, grew fatter, the rigid discipline which is necessary for the creation of the unreality which is real, was, after a small struggle, forgotten, and his poetry became facts, his dreams, articles" (103). But the line, for him and later for us, between poetry and facts becomes blurred, and the figure of Death is born—"he is a murderer such as the world has never known, or perhaps as the world has always known, but never seen.... Where he walks, Death walks—and this man may be Death itself" (106). The story is alive, but people, many people, die as Death walks the streets and through the pages of newsprint and a man's dreams. The rhythm of the prose, rushing like a torrent unleashed, inundates reality with a flood of images and fears, but behind it all in the calm reality of the detective's mind lies reason, triumphant in the end.

Ellery Queen

"The Lamp of God" (1935), thought by many to be the best long detective story ever written, is for a long time a tale of the fantastic, of the shattering of a man's (Queen's) faith in the natural and in reason—"When what happened happened, proper minds tottered on their foundations and porcelain beliefs threatened to shiver into shards. Before the whole fantastic and incomprehensible business was done, God Himself came into it" (Queen, 1967, 362). An entire house—"No walls. No chimney. No roof. No ruins, No debris. No house. Nothing. Nothing but empty space covered smoothly and warmly with snow" (397)—along with reason and sanity disappear overnight, but amazingly, as the detection comes to life, Queen, though shaken and in doubt, finds reason alive and well as we shake our heads in wonder.

Other Stories

Robert Barr

Best known by detective fiction connoisseurs for his much-anthologized tale "The Absent-Minded Coterie" Barr wrote several other rather droll stories of the arrogant French detective collected in *The Triumphs of Eugene Valmont* (1906) at least one of which, "The Ghost with the Club Foot" (1906), summons the supernatural in the form of "groans and shrieks and the measured beat of a club foot on the oaken floor" (Barr, 136) where no person is to be seen. Although in the end the ghost is dispelled—"I find it easier to believe in a living man than a dead man's ghost," (144)—it is not easy to believe in this living man or the highly implausible, though natural, solution. (It also is difficult to believe in the ruse typical of the early 1900s that pretends the collection of seven short stories is a novel with twenty-four chapters.)

Ernest Bramah

Although most of the cases of Max Carrados, the blind detective, are fantastic only in the remarkable abilities of Carrados to "see" the solutions to the mysteries, there are a few tales in which the truly fantastic or supernatural come or seem to come into play. "The Eastern Mystery" is an incredible case where no one is quite certain what is natural and what is not (see Chapter Eight), but in "The Ghost at Massingham Mansions" (1923) Carrados reveals that a "haunting" is only part of a renter's clever attempt for fair treatment from the landlord.

Fredric Brown

Brown, known for blending the fanciful with the darkly realistic, sometimes wrote more light-hearted tales which had more fancy than realism. "The Djinn Murder" (1944) is a good example, effectively combining the genie-in-the-bottle Arabian fairy tale, a touch of the occult (spirit rappings), and a romantic detective story; however, only the romance turns out to be true, as the bottle holds something altogether different, and the rappings have more to do with the flesh than the spirit.

G.K. Chesterton

In addition to the marvelous stories of Father Brown many of which have apparently fantastic elements that are revealed to be completely natural (if a bit outlandish), Chesterton also wrote stories of other detectives, some of which also reveal the seemingly fantastic to be (exotically) rational. In "The Finger of Stone" (1920) the detective (and poet) Gabriel Gale searches for the vanished body of the renowned evolutionist Boyg, eventually to find it in a stone tribute to creationism. Although its hiding place is revealed to be as natural as the earth, the message it sends is a fantastic fossil of philosophy.

Charles B. Child

Several of Child's Chafik Chafik stories involve elements of the fantastic, but in "The Man Who Wasn't There" (1969) there is an interesting twist as a murderer fabricates the appearance of an impossible crime to create a very possible one, but the detective, Chafik, outdoes him to create a fantastic killer with real and deadly consequences. "Death in the

Fourth Dimension" (1952) is an intriguing tale of the twice-murdered refusing to stay dead, possible telepathy, a drama staged to prove insanity, and a snake in the Garden of Eve. "Until now, murders have been three-dimensional. This one appears to have been activated on a fourth plain" (Child, 2002, 107), although the "fantastic" re-appearance of the dead turns out to belong to the three dimensions we know and has a rational though somewhat melodramatic explanation.

Manning Coles

"...ghost-breaking, the supernatural, mystery, horror, detection, secret service work, humor, hair-raising adventure, suspense, and a surprise ending in the final paragraph that will, or should, give you a terrific jolt" (Queen, Introduction, Coles, 5), "Handcuffs Don't Hold Ghosts" (1946) is a remarkable story of hauntings, ghost investigators, underground passageways, and impersonation. In the end, however, it illustrates the Chief Inspector's comment that "any ghosts I have hitherto encountered have always been the cover for nefarious enterprises" (6), in this case, a cover as interesting and entertaining as any actual supernatural ever could have been.

Arthur Conan Doyle

Sherlock Holmes, the ultimate advocate and practitioner of logic and deduction, is very clear about his dismissal of the supernatural—"This agency stands flat-footed upon the ground, and there it must remain. The world is big enough for us. No ghosts need apply" (Conan Doyle, 2005, 1558), and, to Watson, "I take it, in the first place, that neither of us is prepared to admit diabolical intrusions into the affairs of men" (1403). Although of course the Holmes canon is full of seemingly inexplicable mysteries, Holmes' fastidious observation of physical clues and his brilliant deductions solves them all (or nearly all)—resounding affirmation of the power of reason and rationality. However, this does not prevent Conan Doyle from occasionally introducing fantastic or supernatural elements into the cases—all the more opportunity for Holmes to demonstrate that the "natural" is all that is needed to deal with even the strangest of mysteries, although Holmes does admit (in "The Adventure of the Devil's Foot") that *if* there were supernatural occurrences, they would be beyond even his power to explain:

Part 1—The Apparently Fantastic Shown to Be Natural

"It is devilish, Mr. Holmes, devilish! It is not of this world. What human contrivance could do that?"

"I fear," said Mr. Holmes, "that if the matter is beyond humanity, it is certainly beyond me. Yet we must exhaust all natural explanations before we fall back upon such a theory as this" [1399].

And in a few cases (notably "The Adventure of the Devil's Foot," 1910, "The Adventure of the Creeping Man," 1923, and "The Adventure of the Sussex Vampire," 1924), Holmes does encounter bizarre, seemingly supernatural events, but only "seemingly," as his explanatory power is able to divest them of the "fantastic," revealing the very human agencies at work behind appearances.

It should be mentioned, however, that Watson refers to quite a few cases that Holmes could not solve, and these cases seemed to have fantastic elements:

Mr. James Phillimore, stepping back into his house to get his umbrella, was never more seen in this world ... the cutter Alicia, which sailed one spring morning into a small pocket of mist from which she never again emerged nor was anything further ever heard of herself or her crew.... Isador Persano, the well-known journalist and duelist, who was found stark staring mad with a match box in front of him which contained a remarkable worm said to be unknown to science [1603].

This hint of the fantastic in some of Holmes' cases—the cases he was *not* able to solve—is intriguing, for perhaps this was Conan Doyle's sly way, without challenging the conventions of the clue-puzzle detective story, to suggest that, as Hamlet stated, there truly are "more things in heaven and earth than are dreamt of in your philosophy," fantastic things that even Holmes could not reason away.

In one of his lesser known non–Holmes tales, "Selecting a Ghost" (1883), Conan Doyle pokes fun at the lovers of ghostly things, as the owner of a feudal mansion bemoans the mansion's lack of a resident ghost—the only thing missing "to round off the mediaevalism of my abode, and to render it symmetrically and completely antique" (Tyler, 84)—and fully intends to buy one—"It was a proud moment when I felt that a ghost was one of the luxuries which money might command" (84). His attempts to recruit such a specter for his mansion from a catalogue ("gems—gimlets—gas-pipes—gauntlets—guns—galleys. Ah, here we are. Ghosts. Volume nine, section six, page forty-one" [87])—result in an unrelenting parade of ghoulish guests and a mansion missing some of its most prized treasures. The "ghosts" have almost as much fun as Conan Doyle as they spoof as much as spook—"I am the invisible nonentity. I have affinities and I am subtle. I am electric, magnetic, and spiritualistic. I am the great ethereal sigh-heaver" (93).

Basil Copper

Not only did Copper complete the monumental task of editing August Derleth's sixty-eight tales of Solar Pons—brilliant pastiches of the classic Sherlock Holmes stories of Conan Doyle—culminating in the *Solar Pons Omnibus*, but he continued the Pons saga by authoring six further collections of wonderful pastiches of pastiches that evoke the times, settings, and atmosphere of not only Pons but of Holmes himself. And just as with Derleth and Conan Doyle, Copper occasionally intensifies the mood and the mystique by having his detective, the ultimate practitioner of observation and logical deduction, encounter apparently fantastic or supernatural occurrences. "In the Adventure of the Crawling Horror" (1979)—a "bizarre affair indeed" (Copper, 103) that is highly reminiscent in setting, atmosphere, and plot of Conan Doyle's *The Hound of the Baskerville*—Pons confronts a "corpse-like figure dragging itself from the edge of the marsh, all burning and writhing with bluish flame" (112). In typical determinedly rational fashion, Pons dismisses the fantastic—"Phantoms do not walk in my book, neither do the dead return to plague the living" (162)—and reveals the human agency disguised beneath. Copper (as Derleth and, of course, as Conan Doyle before him) wrote stories in tribute to the classical detective of reason, but also from time to time illustrates and celebrates the power and appeal of pitting that reason against at least the appearance of the fantastic.

Ray Cummings

Combining Cummings' interests and talents in science fiction and fantasy and in detective fiction are the series of science-fantastic detective tales collected in *Tales from the Scientific Crime Club* (1979), a club of "amateurs" with similarities to Asimov's Black Widowers and Christie's Tuesday Night Club. "The Confession of Rosa Vitelli" (1925) is especially interesting for its meticulous "scientific" descriptions juxtaposed with fantastic premises and methods. In this story a seemingly impossible murder is solved by the use of an instrument which can detect and record light waves from the past, a fantastic premise yet one based on widely accepted scientific "fact":

> The visual representation of every act ever performed is in existence at this present moment. Light does not go out, in the sense of being destroyed. It goes away. The light rays which shone upon the white sands of San Salvador when Columbus knelt there have not yet reached some of the distant stars. If you were on one of those stars, mechanically equipped to receive that image upon the retina of your eye, you could watch tonight and see Columbus discovering America [Penzler, 579].

In this fascinating interplay of scientific reality and the fantastic not only is the impossible crime revealed to be quite naturally accomplished but it is avowed that the fantastic methodology of capturing light waves from the past is not so fantastic either—"It is a hope of his that someday an apparatus such as I have described will be perfected. But for our ignorant present we had to use a [simulated] motion picture" (582). The members of the Scientific Crime Club have as much to confess as does the murderer.

August Derleth

Just as Conan Doyle occasionally required Sherlock Holmes to apply his deductive skills to an apparently supernatural mystery, Derleth did the same for Solar Pons in his acclaimed pastiches of the Sherlock Holmes canon. In "The Adventure of the Haunted Library" (1963) Pons unmasks a ghost and solves a murder with typical careful observation and precise reasoning as he explains the supernatural to be "phenomena which science as yet has not correctly explained or interpreted" (Derleth, 103). As with many of the stories discussed in this chapter, an otherwise rather ordinary tale is made much more interesting and engaging by the judicious "sprinkling" of the apparently fantastic. In "The Adventure of the Tottenham Werewolf" (1951) three victims have been viciously murdered with their throats torn out, apparently by a werewolf or a man with a werewolf compulsion—"the distressing habit of loping about on all fours on moonlit nights and baying at the moon" (1054). The habit is real, but Pons manages to see the actual killer behind the claws. In "The Adventure of the Devil's Footprints" (1958) a vanished vicar's footprints in the snow abruptly end where they are taken up by the tracks of some hooved creature, but "The real Devil's footprints were invisible" (523) as Pons looks to the trees for his tracks.

Jacques Futrelle

Futrelle's famous detective, Professor Van Dusen—The Thinking Machine—is best known for his brilliant displays of logic and deduction in the solving of numerous clue-puzzle enigmas; however, it isn't all that uncommon for him to encounter cases with at least touches, and sometimes more, of the fantastic or supernatural. In a few of these fantastic cases, his detection discloses human motive and machination behind the façade—ingenious, entertaining, and in some ways incredible, violating human, but not natural, law. In these clever, engaging, and well-written "debunking" tales Van Dusen is the spokesman for human free will, intervening to "try to disarrange the affairs of Fate … to throw the inevitable, the pre-ordained, I might say, out of gear" (Futrelle, vol. 1, 2009, 273). Whether a plot to show a man his own murder in a crystal ball ("The Problem of the Crystal Gazer," 1907), a ghostly car that disappears into the night ("The Phantom Motor," 1907), demoniacal laughter from a glowing, nine-foot tall ghost ("The Mystery of the Flaming Phantom," 1907), a scream in the dark, an ivory god, and a house that never was ("The Grinning God," 1907, written in partnership with his wife, Mary), the apparently inexplicable murders by absence of air in the lungs ("The Case of the Scientific Murderer," 1907), or a ghostly woman in white with a gun ("The Ghost Woman," 1907), Van Dusen penetrates the fantastic fog and reveals the reason hiding within. In Futrelle's most famous story—"The Problem of Cell 13" (1908)—the Thinking Machine also debunks the fantastic (an "impossible" escape from a prison), but does so by perpetrating the escape himself.

E. and H. Heron

Although Flaxman Low, the psychic investigator of the Herons, is best known for his encounters with the dangers and terrors of the genuinely supernatural (see Chapter Eight), in a few of the stories in *The Experiences of Flaxman Low* (1899) the detective discovers that the supernatural is actually horribly and humanly natural. "The Story of Konnor Old House" (1899) and "The Story of No. 1 Karma Crescent" (1899) are tales of hauntings—"a dark, evil, whispering face that lurked in dusky corners, met them in lonely rooms, or hung over beds, terrifying the awakened sleepers" (Heron and Heron, 127)—but hauntings, however terrifying, that are shown to be of human design.

Edward D. Hoch

Hoch is best known for his amazingly prolific writing and publishing history—at least one detective story in every issue of *Ellery Queen's*

Mystery Magazine for an astounding streak of over thirty consecutive years! Many of his tales (e.g., the Sam Hawthorne series, see Chapter One) are locked-room mysteries with puzzling, sometimes peculiar situations, but with completely natural solutions reached by observation and logic. However, Hoch did stretch into the fantastic and supernatural with Simon Ark, his "appraiser of irregular phenomena with special attention to the black arts and the occult" (Hoch, 1979, 6), who claims to be a 2,000-year-old Coptic priest in eternal combat with Satan. Ellery Queen wasn't particularly fond of this supernatural premise, maintaining the traditional view that fantasy and the supernatural weren't often compatible with legitimate detective fiction, so it wasn't until just a few years before Dannay's death that the first Simon Ark story was published in *EQMM*. Even then Queen was very careful to point out, "Though usually described as tales of the occult with Simon Ark generally referred to as a 'fantasy figure,' it should be made clear that the stories scrupulously avoid fantasy. True, there are 'suggestions' of fantasy [a 2,000-year-old Coptic priest!], but as a detective Simon Ark has no magical powers; his solutions to mysteries, however bizarre, are always based on deductive reasoning and logical inference" (*EQMM*, October 1978, 6). Despite this claim, some of the Ark stories involve him in encounters with supernatural forces; however, most of these tales only use the supernatural as a red herring, revealing a rational, natural explanation to account for the apparently occult. Even the narrator maintains a "healthy" and pragmatic skepticism when it comes to the supernatural—"I never really believed all that business about Simon being 2,000 years old ... [but] whether I believed his story or not, I realized his vast knowledge of the occult and the mystic arts could be put to good use" (7). Whether the killing of a werewolf ("The Man Who Shot a Werewolf," 1979), a sacrifice to Yemanja, Goddess of the Sea ("The Mummy from the Sea," 1979), or Satan's footprints in the snow ("Hoofs of Satan," 1956), the apparently fantastic ends up being merely tragic and ultimately human ("Oh, there were devils. Devils of the flesh and the more deadly devils of pride," Hoch, 1979, 24), but along the way the stories get a "fantastic" boost and a jolt of atmosphere and imagery.

W.H. Hodgson

Hodgson, the esteemed author of the chilling horror novels *House on the Borderland*, *The Boats of the "Glen Carrig," The Ghost Pirates*, and *The Night Land,* and of haunting short stories of the Sargasso Sea (e.g., "A Voice in the Night" and "A Thing in the Reeds"), also wrote the celebrated tales of *Carnacki, the Ghost Finder* (1913). The novels and most of the short stories, including most of those of Carnacki, pit the protagonists against ominous forces of evil and horror, sometimes of nature and sometimes of the supernatural (see Chapter Eight). However, in a few of the Carnacki tales (e.g., "The Thing Invisible," 1912, where a dagger haunts a chapel and stabs on its own, and "The House Among the Laurels," 1910, where a malevolent force blows out candles, opens doors, drips blood, and kills dogs) those forces are revealed to be at least partly human in origin and intent. In those cases, Carnacki's usual tools of pentacles, garlic, candles, human hair, and silver don't help—it's the camera that dispels the fantastic and reveals the human agency. Even for Carnacki, the truly supernatural is rare, for not only are there the cases of human intervention, but "ninety-nine cases in a hundred turn out to be sheer bosh and fancy" (Hodgson, 2011, 123). But that hundredth case! After all, Carnacki is the "Ghost Finder"!

Michael Innes

All of Innes' stories of Inspector John Appleby, including the many novels, are literary and erudite, filled with literary and cultural references, a deft turn of phrase, and impeccable language. Many are frenetic, dashing wildly from improbability to improbability, yet somehow detecting the reason behind it all (see Chapter Six). A few extend the improbability to the impossible and the supernatural—the dead walking into its own funeral ("The Memorial Service," 1973), the painting that predicts the future ("The Magic Painting," 1957), the Poltergeist with fine, but destructive, taste in china ("The Poltergeist," 1975), and the Stone Age alive in a British cave ("The Cave of Belarius," 1953). The most fantastic thing about these ingenious and provocative tales is that, in the end, they're not, as they all have rational explanations. Although this may satisfy the traditionalist fan of detective fiction, something may be lost in the process of giving up belief in the fantastic—"If you are superstitious, you may believe them [ancient caves] to be tenanted by ghosts of your remote ancestors who once inhabited them. If you are a scientist, you know that these ghosts do, at least, still haunt the inside of your own head; they are slumbering there, and special circumstances may at any time prompt them to wake up and walk about" (Innes, 2001a,

78)—for when the Stone Age is explained away, "How very dull the truth can be" (81).

H.R.F. Keating

Keating's Inspector Ganesh Ghote is a very practical, down-to-earth man with a highly rational, matter-of-fact approach to life and detection, though he has a deep respect for his Indian culture and its philosophical underpinnings. Although "fervid religion had always made him shrink inwardly" (van Thal, 89), he is not immune to occasional philosophical speculation. In "Inspector Ghote and the Miracle Baby" (1972) Keating treats the fantastic and its relationship with the rational with great delicacy, as Ghote is assigned to a case of supposed "virgin birth," which has already led to much expression of that very fervid religion that discomforts him so much—"'I am sorry Deputy Superintendent,' Ghote said, feeling obliged to be true to hard-won scientific principles, 'I am unable to believe in virgin birth'" (Van Thal, 88). However, when he discovers that the "miracle birth" is quite natural, "a deep smothering of disappointment floated down on Ghote. So it had been nothing miraculous after all. Just a sad case, to be cleared up painfully. He stared down at the bed" (93). So the man of reason and practicality was hoping for the miraculous, the fantastic, even if it challenged his most fundamental beliefs, and perhaps readers were feeling the same way. But in a beautiful final blending of the fantastic and the everyday, Ghote reminds us that the miraculous is at the heart of everyday life, and the laws of nature themselves are quite fantastic—"The tiny boy suckled energetically. And with a topsy-turvy welling up of rose-pink pleasure, Ghote saw that there had after all been a miracle. The daily, hourly, every-minute miracle of a new life, of a new flicker of hope in the tired world" (93).

C.D. King

Several of the stories in King's classic collection *The Curious Mr. Tarrant* (1935) weave the appearance of the fantastic in with the fastidiously rational detection of Tarrant. In "The Episode of the Tangible Illusion" (1935) it appears that an invisible phantom is responsible for haunting some stairs and repeatedly terrifying a woman climbing them, but Tarrant is able to show the malicious human plot behind the ghostly presence.

Clayre and Michel Lipman

"The Walking Corpse" (1950) is a wild and fantastic story involving a corpse who walked out of a morgue carrying his organs in a jar, a possible interplanetary visitor from Planet X, a herd of midget elephants, snow in Liberia, a Buddhist monk getting messages from the moon through a diamond, and, yes, murder. Amazingly, George Washington Neff, the detective, comes up with a rational solution which explains away all the fantastic as merely the incredible plot of a murderer to cover his tracks.

Ed McBain

The 87th Precinct police procedurals by McBain might be the last place you'd expect to find the fantastic, as they are known for their gritty, big-city realism. Not surprisingly "Nightshade" (1970) features a "mosaic of murder, vandalism, bombing, theft, missing persons, junkies, pushers, drunk-and-disorderlies, burglars, muggers—you name it" (McBain, 117), but very surprisingly ghosts as well. The officers called to the scene actually hear the ghosts—"The voices rose in volume now, carried on that same chill wind, louder, closer, until they seemed to overwhelm the room, clamoring to be released from whatever unearthly vault contained them" (139), but eventually discover the human agency and motive behind them. Ironically, the debunking of the ghosts actually reveals "real" ghosts hiding in plain sight—"the ghost of a proud man who was once a brilliant judge and who is now a gambler and a thief, and the ghost of a man who once could see, and who now trips and falls in the darkness" (159).

L.T. Meade and Robert Eustace

Although in the stories collected in *A Master of Mysteries* (1898) there are numerous ghostly and other supernatural occurrences, John Bell, ghost exposer, debunks them using the tools of the traditional detective, careful observation of clues and logical deduction—"To explain, by the application of science, phenomena attributed to spiritual agencies has been the work of my life" (Meade and Eustace, 2011, 219). "The Application of Science" is perhaps a bit questionable (other than knowledge of magnetism in "The Warder of the Door," 1898, of poisonous gasses in "The Mystery of the Felwyn Tunnel," 1898, and of the lifting power of air in "The Secret of Emu Plain," 1898), but Bell does use material clues and reason effectively to dispel the "taint" of "spiritualism, theosophy, and mahatmas, with all their attendant hocus-pocus" (301). The detection is legitimate, if rather ordinary, but the occurrences are sufficiently fantastic and the descriptions are sufficiently vivid to create interesting puzzles and to induce a shiver or two of apprehension—"It seized me, laying siege to my brain till I felt like a child in its power. It was as if I were slowly drowning in the great ocean of silence that enveloped us. Time itself seemed to have disappeared" (106).

James Powell

Powell's saga of the Ganelon family—generations of detectives operating in a fictitious Mediterranean principality—is full of the fanciful, the eccentric, the hilarious, and the downright incredible (see Chapter Six), in a few cases leaking over into the supernatural, or at least the apparently supernatural. Though "The Haunted Bookcase" (1982) and "Unquiet Graves" (1992) are both illustrations of the supernatural turning out to be quite natural, it's difficult to imagine two stories more different in mood or impact—the former a rather whimsical minor case of "the follies of youth and old age" (Powell, 2009, p. 51), the latter an eerie, intricate tale of grave-robbing, a desecrated corpse, the walking dead, and a body exchange by the Almighty himself, yet all with a completely natural explanation. "Unquiet Graves" is a classic illustration of reason making sense of the fantastic and the fantastic giving meaning to reason.

Bill Pronzini

Author of several impossible crime stories, many about his nameless private eye, Pronzini also wrote a wonderfully atmospheric "nameless" story haunted by a ghostly manifestation of a murdered red-headed man. In "Dead Man's Slough" (1980) eerie feelings and the legend of a haunting swirl around Pronzini's hard-edged realistic prose and the "impossible" disappearance of another red-head. Despite the private eye's terse dismissal of anything fantastic, the reader isn't quite so sure, as the man seems to have completely vanished.

Seabury Quinn

Although the vast majority of the ninety-three Jules de Grandin stories of Seabury Quinn involve Grandin in deadly combat with evil supernatural forces (see Chapter Eight) or "mad scientists" and other human miscreants in overt crime, several of these tales show the apparently supernatural unmasked to reveal human design and manipulation. In "Mephistopheles and Company, Ltd" (1928) in Volume 1 of *The Complete Tales of Jules de Grandin* (2017) a gang of extortionists terrify a young woman into believing that she is possessed by the devil, but de Grandin begins "to sniff the odor of deceased fish in this business" (356) and discovers that the terrifying visage of Mephistopheles and his scalding touch are comprised not of supernatural evil but of human deceit, a fake beard, glowing phosphorus, and a branding iron. "The Dark Angel" (1932) in Volume 3 of the *Complete Tale*s is a powerful and beautifully written story of a dangerous winged avenger, the Dark Angel of Death, wreaking havoc on the sinful:

> Across the eighteen-inch-wide sill it came, as quiet as a creeping snake; a great, black thing, the moonlight glinting evilly on the polished scales which overlaid its form. From its shoulders, right and left, spread great black wings, gleaming with a sort of horrid, half-dulled luster, and as they grasped the window-sill I caught a glimpse of long, curved talons, pitiless as those of any vulture, but larger and more cruel by far than those of any bird.... Through the pale mask of horror looked two brilliant, glaring eyes, like corpse-lights shining through the sockets of a fleshless skull and from the forehead reared a pair of curving, pointed horns [274].

De Grandin, avenger himself for justice and love, reveals the truth beneath the mask of piety—a fabricated monster bedecking a distorted and self-righteous soul.

Arthur Rees

In "The Finger of Death" (1926) Rees' detective Colwin Grey is forced to acknowledge that in some cases the standard arsenal of the detective—logic and reason—are insufficient to explain the mysteries of life or death:

> In crime, human reason can usually unravel any human folly or wickedness, provided always the facts are material, confined to human motives and feelings, human interests and acts. But occasionally one is confronted with a problem beyond the power of reason, because something beyond the human element is there— that incalculable factor which some call chance, destiny, or fate; and others the

intervention of a superior omnipotent being whom they designate God [Thwing, Volume IX, 167].

In this dark and moody story, the explanation for a death ("the greatest mystery of all in this world of ours," 169) shows how fantastic the natural can be—"Yet his confession, when it came, was of a nature hardly to be believed ... something outside the nature and experience of ordinary life as we know it: some explanation based on the supernatural, the fantastic, or the bizarre" (168). And yet, Grey's attention to detail and logical analysis manage to bring the fantastic back to the world we inhabit, if not the world we fully understand.

Arthur Reeve

You might not expect "the American Sherlock Holmes" (Herbert, 378)—Reeve's Craig Kennedy of the early 1900s—to be involved in any fantastic situations as he is known for his "scientific detection" (e.g., use of the lie detector, ballistic tests, psychoanalytic methods); however, some of the so-called "science" borders on, if not crosses into, the domain of the fantastic, e.g., in "The Invisible Ray" (1911) a mad chemist who uses ultraviolet light and his supposed ability to "make the transition from the inorganic to the organic, from inert matter to living protoplasm, and thence from living protoplasm to mind and what we call soul ... control over telepathy and even communication with the dead" (Davies, 2006, 757). Kennedy's cool logic and a bit of his own science reveals the charlatan, solves the mystery, and rescues the victim. Sometimes yesterday's fledgling science or science fiction becomes today's science; sometimes it remains fantastic. Only the future will tell, but in the meantime it can bring vitality and mystique to the otherwise traditional detective story.

Dorothy Sayers

Sayer's detective Lord Peter Wimsey is comfortable in society—high and low—and his tales are usually as much about that society as about his cases, but every now and then one of his cases enters the realm of the fantastic, though it always ends "naturally" enough. The bizarre case of his "elopement" with another man's wife is almost a horror fairy tale (see Chapter Six), and "the 4th dimension mystery" (Sayers, 292) of the man with amnesia and reversed organs, "The Image in the Mirror" (1933), borders on science fiction or the supernatural until the very end. Sayers must have chuckled at Wimsey's self-effacing reaction to the man's incredible tale—"You've told me a queerish story tonight. For some reason I believe you. Possibly it only shows what a silly ass I am" (288)—and, no doubt, imagines (and hopes) the reader will show the same kind of belief.

Edgar Wallace

Among Wallace's hundreds of detective novels and collections of short stories, there are a few tales with elements of the fantastic, or at least the appearance of the fantastic. In "The Ghost of John Holling" (1963) the ghost of a man who committed suicide at sea appears to be on board robbing passengers, but the detective Felix Jenks eventually reveals the true criminal to be of murderous flesh and blood.

Dennis Wheatley

In *Gunmen, Gallants, and Ghosts* (1943) there are several tales of Neils Orsen, psychic investigator, a character Wheatley based on an acquaintance who, according to Wheatley, had genuine psychic abilities. Some of these stories involve struggles with genuine supernatural entities, but "The Case of the Thing that Whimpered" (1943) and "The Case of the Haunted Chateau" (1943) involve faked, though still frightening, events that Orsen eventually exposes with his tools of the trade—cameras, trip-wires, pentacles, recording devices, and his logical deductions.

James Yaffe

After his several impossible crime tales of Paul Dawn and the Department of Impossible Crimes (see Chapter One), Yaffe wrote eight Mom stories from 1952 to 1968 and then one more in 2002, all of which were eventually collected in the updated volume *My Mother, the Detective* (2016). Mom, rich with Jewish culture and temperament and insightful with her knowledge of people, out-detects the detectives and solves these several puzzle-clue cases, mostly murder. "Mom and the Haunted Mink" (1967) is the only one of these Mom tales that involves the fantastic—in this case a mink coat that seems to have a life and will of its own—although Mom eventually shows that human emotions (avarice, fear, and even love and devotion) are the quite real forces behind the haunting and the killing.

Three

Superstitions, Prophecies and Curses

For most people, the easiest type of the non-rational to accept, or at least to understand, is superstition, for even the most down-to-earth, matter-of-fact rationalist has probably at some time at least been tempted to be superstitious—the classic "I don't really believe in it, but just in case, I'm going to wear that lucky shirt." Although there are some detective stories where superstition and curses are at the heart of the puzzle and its solution, much more frequent are the stories in which the crime appears to be explained by superstition or curses, but in the end turns out to have a completely rational explanation. As with the other types of stories discussed in Part 1, these tales illustrate one of the easiest, least controversial, and most effective ways to integrate the fantastic into the classic detective story, for the fantastic turns out to be not fantastic at all, but appearances contrived by the criminal to conceal the true enactment of the crime. The most memorable of these stories integrate the best of both worlds—the intellect and the emotion, the comfort of logic and the excitement of the inexplicable—while, in the end, offering the satisfaction of seeing superstition debunked and logic triumph.

Exemplars

G.K. Chesterton

Chesterton's Father Brown stories are regarded by many critics and readers to be, with Conan Doyle's stories of Sherlock Holmes and Poe's stories of Auguste Dupin, the finest detective tales ever written. But although these stories of all three authors involve puzzles, clues, and detection, the methods of detection and the attitude and approach to the "fantastic" are significantly different—"there is, in many ways, a marked difference between your own method of approach and that of Dupin with its fine links of logic ... and of Holmes with its observation of material details" (Chesterton, 1951, 425). Where Holmes is the classic "magnifying glass" analyzer of physical clues and both Holmes and Dupin fastidiously follow the path of logic and both state explicitly that there is no place for the supernatural or the irrational in detective work, Father Brown's whole method of detection is more internal than external, more psychological than mathematical, more non-rational than strictly rational—"I am always inside a man, moving his arms and legs; but I wait till I know I am inside a murderer, thinking his thoughts, wrestling with his passions; till I have bent myself into the posture of his hunched and peering hatred; till I see the world with his bloodshot and squinting eyes ... till I am really a murderer" (427).

The case can be made that the Father Brown stories are as much metaphysical "parables" as they are detective stories (see Blackwell's *The Metaphysical Mysteries of G.K. Chesterton: A Critical Study of the Father Brown Stories and Other Detection Fiction,* 2018), but even as "straight" detective fiction, they distinguish themselves from most of the Holmes and Dupin stories by their treatment of the fanciful and the fantastic. So many of these stories read like modern fairy tales with fabulous settings and wild and eccentric happenings, although the puzzle-clue aspects are never completely submerged. All eight of the stories in *The Incredulity of Father Brown* (1926) and a few from other volumes throw the rational into jarring juxtaposition with the irrational, specifically superstition and curses, and illustrate Chesterton's contention that in an increasingly materialistic world (which Chesterton viewed as spiritless and mundane) people are desperate to believe in something magical (superstition, curse, and other non-rational phenomena). But Father Brown with his religious faith has no such vulnerability and so can penetrate the supernatural fog to reveal the rational processes beneath. In "The Resurrection of Father Brown" (1926) Father Brown himself is tempted by villains to believe in the magical (his own fantastic resurrection from murder), but he shows his humility and adherence to the rational by rejecting the miracle and all the acclaim that would accompany it.

Vincent Cornier

Almost all the stories in Cornier's *The Duel of Shadows* (2011) have at least a touch of the fanciful, the fabulous, and the bizarre that linger in the air even after rational explanations are provided (see Chapter Six). In "The Throat of Green Jasper" (1934) and "The Tabasheeran Pearls" (1937) superstition and curse seem to be behind the crimes; in only the second of these tales does the rational explanation survive alone, vengeance and the laws of physical matter comprising the "curse." In the other (see Chapter Nine), uncertainty and ambiguity outlive the plot.

David Stuart Davies

Whereas Davies' Luther Darke murder case "The Curzon Street Conundrum" features the apparently fantastic in the form of a locked-room murder, "The Curse of the Griswold Phantom" (2000) involves that "unofficial solver of riddles" in a case of beheading by what appears to be a "tall, ghostly, faceless fiend, attired in wet, tattered rags who emerges at sunset carrying a glistening scythe" (Davies, 2006, 1028). The ominous setting, with "all the ghoulish charm of a Gothic tale by Bram Stoker" (1033), is perfect for the horribly fantastic phantom and his curse:

> With the darkness, the mist rises, seeping from the gurgling, slimy depths to wreathe the surface with white coils, which camouflage its treacherous surface. Luckless is the lonely wanderer who finds himself out by these marshes after sunset. One false step and he is sucked down, sucked down deep into the bottomless darkness. But, as the locals know, there is another reason to fear the mire at night. It is the haunt of the Griswold Phantom [1026].

Although, as Darke points out, "When dealing with the supposed supernatural, one usually dispenses with logic" (1054), neither he nor this atmospheric tale succumbs to this temptation, the result being a wonderful example of how the apparently fantastic can enliven and intensify an otherwise rational tale of successful detective deduction.

Nicholas Olde

The delightful stories in Olde's *The Incredible Adventures of Roland Hern* (1928) are indeed incredible, fanciful, and wildly unconventional filled with outrageous, implausible characters and events, but they never completely violate natural laws or what is possible no matter how implausible. One particularly outrageous story, "Potter" (see Chapter Eight) verges on the supernatural, but in most of the stories the crime and the detection are eventually shown to be rational. In "The Monstrous

Laugh" (1928) a town ripe with superstition ("They do really believe, for instance, that at certain times, the bells of the old church can be heard tolling beneath the sea; and they say that, when the bells toll, they toll to warn them of a coming storm," 108), is haunted by the "dreadful, mocking chuckle" of a dead man, whose laugh they all abhorred in life—"And, as I fled madly inland, leaving all my hopes behind me, that laughter followed me, in gusts of hateful, mocking mirth" (113). Although Hern discovers the rational explanation, the power of the supernatural persists as "the villagers still refuse absolutely to accept the true explanation of the laughter from the sea, still hold that open merriment will bring ill-luck and ban it from their midst" (118).

Melville Davisson Post

Post's short stories of Uncle Abner, collected in *Uncle Abner, Master of Mysteries* (1918) with four more tales added to comprise *The Complete Uncle Abner* (1977) are acknowledged by critics to be, along with the Dupin tales of Poe, the finest American detective stories, and, along with the Dupin tales, Conan Doyle's Sherlock Holmes tales, and G.K. Chesterton's stories of Father Brown, the best detective stories ever written. All of the Abner stories, including the classic locked-room story "The Doomdorf Mystery" are rich with the atmosphere of Jeffersonian Virginia, the instrument-of-God's-Justice character of Uncle Abner, and the careful analysis of clues and deductive reasoning of the traditional detective. Although the atmosphere of the fantastic in the form of God's inscrutable will and Abner's steadfast belief permeate all the stories, most of them adhere to logic and reason with only the atmosphere, not the actuality, of the fantastic present. However, in a few of the best tales—the locked-room mysteries of "The Doomdorf Mystery" and "The Hidden Law" (see Chapter One) and the remarkable long short story, "The Mystery at Hillhouse" (1928)—the fantastic enters in a more tangible form, in this last tale as superstition and curse.

"The Mystery at Hillhouse" is a tour de force, for from the start there is created a dynamic tension between the harsh reality of murder, with four valid suspects and a multitude of clues and deductions, and the curse of the ancient people's burial ground which the victim heedlessly violated. Reason and the processes of the law, represented by Abner's "Watson"—Squire Randolph—are pitted against the superstitions of some of the locals—"I mean the ancient people on the mountain ... old

Webster was crazy to violate their grave. Nobody with any sense would have dug into the burial mound of the ancient people and carried off the flat stones over their graves to pave his portico" (Post, 1977, 366). Although the spirit of the curse hovers over the story, as the plot unfolds, the reader is quite certain the murder was not due to the fantastic but to human avarice and passion. Post's narrative evokes a vivid picture of the four suspects and surrounds them with a suffocating cloud of evidence:

> But four lights were visible: a candle at a window in the trapper's house; a gleam in the manor in the valley; another to the west where the trader lived; and a fire, halfway up the mountain road, where the man from Maryland camped out with his cattle. Four lights, burning in a darkened world! By which one of these did the murderer sit, fearful of the morning? [368].

But as the story continues, one suspect after another is exonerated by the evidence and deduction, and the supernatural, as foreseen in a dying woman's visions, begins to seem more plausible—"And as she died she cried out that she saw a huge devil issue from the violated tomb, leap down in great bounds as on an iron hoof, slay Webster with a single blow, and disappear out of sight and hearing under the water of the river!" (394). Abner, in his role as bridge between the worlds of logical detection and the fantastic (the will and justice of God) stuns Randolph and the readers by conceding that "Only a demon from a tomb, only a demon like the one in the Gospel of Saint Mark with the Samson strength to pluck chains asunder could have dealt it.... I will show you the very marks in the baked earth where this avenging thing from the tomb of the ancient people on the mountain landed with an iron hoof as it leaped down on old Webster Patterson" (395). And just when we readers are unsure whether the "genuine" supernatural has somehow worked its way into these tales of logic and reason, the story twists once again as rationality, human intervention, the supernatural, and the natural all have their part to play.

Other Stories

A.M. Burrage

Although most of Burrage's stories of the detective Francis Chard involve investigation or serious confrontation with the supernatural (see Chapter Eight), a few of them turn out to be carefully contrived criminal plots. Of these, "The Third Visitation" (1927) involves a family tragedy and resulting curse on the men of the family that almost drives one of them to suicide. The story behind the curse is probably the most interesting part of this tale, as the detection is rather "light" and the ghost rather "pale."

G.K. Chesterton

The stories in *The Incredulity of Father Brown* are wonderfully satisfying illustrations of how touches of the fantastic and the strictly rational can co-exist and commingle charmingly and effectively as superstition and curses are defused by reason: an arrow from out of the blue ("The Arrow from Heaven," 1926), a man flying through the air to his death by hanging ("The Miracle of Moon Crescent," 1926), the curse of a tomb ("The Curse of the Golden Cross," 1925), a bat out of Hell ("The Dagger with Wings," 1924), a curse of the seventh generation ("The Doom of the Darnaways," 1925), a vengeful apparition ("The Ghost of Gideon Wise," 1926)—in the end, all explained by Father Brown to be "flesh-and-blood" crimes of reason.

In *The Scandal of Father Brown*, "The Blast of the Book" (1933) presents a terrible curse—"They that looked in this book/Them the flying terror took" (Chesterton, 1951, 577). It seems that anyone who opens this book disappears off the face of the Earth, but, of course (since this is Chesterton), it turns out to be not a curse at all but a moral lesson in respect and attention.

It's not only in Chesterton's Father Brown stories where crimes are initially attributed to superstition and the supernatural. One of the most interesting of his stories that involves another detective is "The Trees of Pride" (1922), one of the non–Horn Fisher tales in *The Man Who Knew Too Much* (1922), where a landscape of ghosts, witches, mythology, and superstition surround an apparent murder with a "fairy ring of nonsense" (166).

Agatha Christie

Stories by Christie will be found under several categories in this monograph, for though she is best known for her clever plots, red herrings, and surprise endings, she also brought touches of the fantastic in many guises, including the psychological and the mythological, into some of her most memorable stories. In a few of her Poirot tales superstition and curses, debunked at the end, play an important part. In "The Adventure of the Egyptian Tomb" (1923) Christie evokes the romance of ancient Egypt and an ancient curse as a possible explanation of the mysterious deaths of the members of an archaeological dig that disturbed the tomb of King Men-her-Ra. Poirot stuns Hastings (his "Watson"), and probably the readers too, by proclaiming that he believes "in the power of superstition, one of the greatest forces the world has ever known" (Christie, 2013, 156); however, Poirot's "credentials" as a rational detective (and Christie's as a "respectable" detective author) remain intact as it becomes clear that Poirot's belief is in the *power* of superstition, not in its validity—"Once get it firmly established that a series of deaths are supernatural, and you might almost stab a man in broad daylight, and it would still be put down to the curse, so strongly is the instinct of the supernatural implanted in the human race" (165). Poirot discovers that the killer himself shares this belief and used it to his advantage.

Another sort of curse (a family curse on the first-born sons) plays a key role in "The Lemesurier Inheritance" (1923), but the real curse turns out to be of a psychological nature. Although in both these stories the curse is never given credence by Poirot or the readers, it adds a touch of romance and mystique to the tales, providing an adversary for reason and a foil for the detection.

Harry Kemelman

The stories about Nicky Welt in Kemelman's collection *The Nine Mile Walk* (1967) are a revival of the classic clue-puzzle mysteries of a couple decades earlier, but in one of the stories, "Time and Time Again" (1962) this exercise in reason and deduction is nestled within a quite un-reasonable context of the supernatural effects of a curse. An advocate for the power of the supernatural explains an apparently accidental death which almost immediately followed a curse on the victim as a demonstration of such forces—"When supernatural forces are present, a mere wish, fervently expressed, may serve to focus them" (104)—but Welt scoffs at this explanation, demonstrating by pure logic that the death was no accident and the curse was a carefully planted red herring. The crime is ingenious and Welt's reasoning is even more so, but the counterpoint of logic and the supernatural is the real appeal of this hybrid tale.

C.D. King

Ellery Queen called the stories in *The Curious Mr. Tarrant* (1935) "the most imaginative detective stories of our time" (Tarrant, 2003) and persuaded King to write four more tales, which appeared first in *EQMM* and were then included in the later comprehensive collection *The Complete Curious Mr. Tarrant* (2003). Almost all of them are locked-room tales and most involve Tarrant's finding the natural explanation for what at first appears to be a supernatural occurrence, often involving superstition or curse, though one of the most powerful stories leaves us in limbo, not certain of the true nature of the case (see Chapter Nine). In both "The Episode of the Codex' Curse" (1935) and "The Episode of the Vanishing Harp" (1935) curses or prophecies seem to be operating to cause the disappearance of sacred relics—"Beware lest vengeance follow sacrilege.... The desecration of Light-Words is a heavy thing; in an unholy resting place the third night bringeth the Empty" (15), but Tarrant, with impeccable logic ("It's the only way it could have happened," 27), almost always finds the very material cause. Few detective stories mix impeccable logic and wild fancy so effectively; few surround a resolute rationality with such an atmosphere of fabulous exoticism.

Nicholas Olde

The Incredible Adventures of Roland Hern (1928) are indeed incredible, including impossible crimes (see Chapter One), the reincarnation of a murder victim as a vulture (see Chapter Six), a mysterious cuneiform message from the Lost City of Lak, and several fantastic tales of curses, superstition, and legend in which the "natural" explanation is nearly as fanciful or fantastic as any non-natural solution could ever be. In "Black and White" (1928) a mysteriously disappearing thief is said to have "eluded capture by jumping clean over the top of a house" and "making herself visible and invisible at will" (50). Though these legends are easily dismissed, the reality is just as strange, as the thief who "is not so black as she is painted" (57) is shot in the face by Hern "to improve her beauty" (57) and is given by Hern what she cannot steal.

Melville Davisson Post

Although much more known for his stories of Uncle Abner, Post created several other detectives, among them Sir Henry Marquis of

Scotland Yard. "The Bradmoor Murder" (1925) is a beautifully written tale of impossible murder involving a curse from a stone god on a mountain top in Africa, a god worshipped for thousands of years and with armfuls of rubies. The most remarkable aspect of this story is that it is an eloquent illustration of both the conflict between the fantastic and the rational *and* of their coming together in harmony. The conflict pervades the story from the beginning as Marquis is as adamant about the rational ("There is only one thing of which I am absolutely certain: the supernatural does not exist. Every problem has an explanation," Penzler, 716) as other characters are insistent on the power of curses and the supernatural ("What sinister power over events had the magicians of Pharaoh, the witch of Endor, the dead prophets of Yahweh," 728). But, in the end, careful observation of clues and logical reasoning show that the death has a natural, though fantastic, explanation; it wasn't the curse of the god—"His right hand shall be his enemy" (728)—and yet it was exactly that.

Seabury Quinn

While most of the scores and scores of short stories of Jules de Grandin pit him against supernatural monsters and monstrosities, a few involve ancient curses which lead to family tragedies, or at least they appear to be the cause until Grandin pulls back the curtain. "The Curse of the House of Phipps" (1930) is a fine example, for it is a "real" curse on the generations to follow of a violent ancestor who tortured and killed his young wife, but although the curse was "real," it wasn't causal, so for Grandin, "an exorcism turned to an execution [and he] made a real ghost where there was a make-believe one before" (Quinn, 2017b, 237). In the same volume, in "The Dust of Egypt" (1930) an ancient Egyptian curse in revenge for grave-robbing leads to several deaths, but it's not so much the curse itself that is fatal as it is fear of the curse in the mind—"the idea of a dreadful doom awaiting him who invaded that wicked old one's tomb was firmly lodged in his subconscious mind, and there it germinated, and grew into a monstrous thing even as the hookworm's eggs grow into the body of the victim" (297). In "The Black Orchid" (1935) a "man who had incurred the hatred of a native noblewoman who was also a priestess of a dark, malevolent religion, a noted sorceress ... lived beneath a curse pronounced upon him by this woman, and in this curse she foretold that he should be stricken with a malady which should cause his blood to waste away like little brooks in summer" (Quinn, 2018b,

199). Only when de Grandin kills the strange bloom of the vampirish black orchid is the true villain revealed and the man's mind is freed. Similarly in "Flames of Vengeance" (1937) a gang of villains is shown to be the acting force behind a family curse of death by fire.

Dorothy Sayers

Lord Peter Wimsey is known for his aristocratic manner and rather breezy but matter-of-fact approach to detection. In many of the tales (novels and short stories) the appeal is as much or more in the human engagements and the societal machinations as in the detection—things decidedly realistic though perhaps not always desirable. In a few of the Wimsey short stories, however, a much different mood is struck as touches of the fantastic, usually quite dark, color the story and tremble the plot. "The Incredible Elopement of Lord Peter Wimsey" (1933) is the most dramatic and striking of these as superstition, curses, bewitchment, and The Evil One intersect to stimulate the detective and to awaken the wizard in Wimsey, so he can cast his rational "spell."

Robert Somerlott

In "The Hair of a Widow" (1965) a local detective uses an old witch and the superstitions of the people of a primitive Mexican village to trap killers that otherwise he has no way to apprehend. The modern view that this is all "superstitious nonsense and quite useless" (Somerlott, 120) turns out to be at least half wrong, as the grit of everyday life and death in this small village is contrasted sharply with the luminescent beliefs in the fantastic power of the dead to avenge and ensnare.

Hake Talbot

Along with his celebrated impossible crime novels, *The Hangman's Handyman* (1942) and *The Rim of the Pit* (1944), two of the greatest illustrations of the interweaving of classic detection with the fantastic, Talbot's short story, "The Other Side" (1944) does the same on a much lesser scale as the curse of a strange guru seems to have gotten a man shot, but careful detection reveals a much more tangible cause. Even though the solution is arrived at rationally, getting the confession is a bit of fantastic and flamboyant showmanship.

Four

The Charlatan Occult Detective

In the first three chapters of Part 1 we have presented and discussed stories in which it seems initially that the only possible explanation of the crime is non-rational, but the detective eventually demonstrates that the crime has a completely natural solution. In most cases, the criminal has carefully contrived the crime to appear non-natural to help him/her escape detection. In Chapter Four, we examine the infrequent stories in which the detective, not the criminal, has called on the services of the fantastic to cloak his detection in fantastic or supernatural vestments to create an aura of intrigue and mystique. Hiding beneath this mystical veneer is a detective of mostly traditional methods—careful observation, logic, and deduction. So, as with all the stories in Part 1, these tales are quite traditional in method and explanation, while the fantastic is used to provide color, atmosphere, sometimes satire, and in many cases, red herrings.

Exemplars

Philip MacDonald

The story of the creation of Dr. Alcazar, MacDonald's rogue-detective, is almost as interesting as the two Alcazar stories themselves. MacDonald deliberately set out to create a "really new detective and a new technique" (MacDonald, 1948, 4) where, as Ellery Queen puts it, "this clairvoyant extraordinary, this Olympian-browed charlatan, blends completely those two perennial favorites—the deductive sleuth and the debonair rogue" (4). Although this is not an altogether new idea (Leblanc's famous rogue-detective Arsene Lupin being a prototype), in MacDonald's Alcazar its conception is highly original. As with Burgess' stories of Astro, Alcazar's techniques are actually quite traditional, but are hidden beneath supernatural trappings—"I am what is sometimes called a metaphysician, a sort of Professor of the Occult" (25)—although much of the fun is that we are allowed to see the "man behind the curtain" and even to hear his silent admonitions to himself about not laying it on too thick. "The Green-and-Gold String" (1948) is an entertaining story of fantastic pretense and deception of criminal and detective alike.

Other Stories

Gelett Burgess

In the twenty-four short stories in *The Master of Mysteries* (1912) Astro is an avowed mystic who dons robe and turban to solves crimes by palmistry, crystal gazing, trances, and sensing the "actinic and ultraviolet vibrations to which I am exceedingly susceptible" (Burgess, 2008, 33). He claims to have "an inner sense and an esoteric knowledge of life and its mysteries that is hidden from all who have not lived for cycles and eons in solitude and contemplation with the Mahatmas of the Himalayas" (33)—"I see the invisible, I hear the inaudible, I touch the intangible" (44). Burgess is not at all delicate in his satire of the "cult of the supernatural," as he says in the famous second cipher comprised of the last letters of the last words of the stories, "false to life and false to art," but nonetheless he stays true to the norms of the traditional detective story (except that the detective falls in love with his "Watson"), as Astro's hidden detective methods are the customary ones of careful observation ("His eyes did not appear to survey his client, but under his long lashes they were busy noting detail after detail," 18), gathering of clues, and logical deduction. As is stated in "The Assassin's Club" (1912), he is adept at "living in both worlds," the practical one of reason and logic and the mystic and mystical one of intuition and occult powers—"Sometimes he was the dreamy occult Seer, cryptic, mysterious; again he was the alert man of affairs, keen, logical, worldly" (165).

Although none of the stories is memorable for its plot or narrative or particularly effective as a detective story, they all are entertaining for their fantastic trappings and conspiracy of satire that we are invited to join. In "The Stolen Shakespeare" (1912) with one of his typical clients who has "a weakness for anything occult, anything full of folderol and fake" (30), Astro solves the case of the missing folio using traditional detective methods, but he claims otherwise—"I have had occasion at times to use certain powers which are—ah—supposed to be occult" (30). In finding the quite logical reason for a man's disappearance in "Missing John Hudson" (1912) he exuberantly celebrates his supposed use of psychic methods—"My crystals are certainly wonderful" (29), as indeed they are ... for his reputation and his pocketbook. What in so many of the occult detective stories of Burgess' time is presented seriously and a bit pretentiously is here said with a knowing wink in our direction—"It is my fortune to be sensitive to vibrations that most minds do not register. Where you see a body, I see a spirit, a life, an invisible color. All these esoteric laws have been known by the priestcraft of the occult for ages. Nothing is hidden from the Inner Eye" (67). And what's not hidden from ours is the not always so gentle prodding of the supernatural itself.

Philip MacDonald

MacDonald followed his classic tale of Dr. Alcazar, "The Green-and-Gold String," with another story of the rogue-detective, "Something to Hide" (1952), in which the fantastic charade continues as coloratura for readers and remuneration for the detective—"The business of Private Investigator ... you type a report and they give you a century [$100], but you look in the crystal and they give you ten grand" (MacDonald, 1952, 45)—but beyond the entertainment of these two Alcazar stories as illustrations of charlatan-in-disguise is their interest as genuine and clever detective tales with subtle clues and astute deduction.

PART 2

A Touch of the Fantastic

As we've seen in Part 1, to evoke the fantastic and then to discredit it with reason is one way to benefit from the excitement and mystique of the fantastic without threatening the traditional conventions of the detective story. In Part 2, we examine a somewhat more problematic way that detective story authors have brought the fantastic into their tales, a way that does not dismiss the fantastic at the end, but explains the events by non-rational causes. By calling upon the less "scientific" domains of psychology and mythology, where non-rational, but still "natural," events can occur—intuition, defense mechanisms, dreams, complexes, symbolism—and can have powerful effects on the perception of reality, motivation, and behavior, authors have brought the fantastic (or at least a touch of it) into the heart of their stories. A couple centuries ago, before Freud and Jung, the wonders of the unconscious would have been regarded as supernatural, and even today some view mythology as fantasy rather than as symbolic expression of material reality.

But for most readers of today, these touches of the fantastic ring true, so their incorporation into the traditional detective story is relatively uncontroversial for contemporary readers and critics alike. As can be seen from the large number of successful stories dealt with in this section, many authors have eagerly and successfully accepted the challenge.

Before exploring, in Chapter Six, the many stories which have integrated a touch of the fantastic in the form of psychology, mythology, or fancy into the detective story, we first, in Chapter Five, examine cases where the detective himself or herself utilizes at least a touch of non-rational abilities or methods to solve the mysteries.

Five

The Super-Sensitive Detective

An otherwise traditional detective story where the detective has an unexplainable intuition or finely tuned sensitivity to clues that are not observable to other characters or to the reader walks a fine line of potential "mumbo-jumbo," for the reader may dismiss the story as unfair if the truth can't be deduced from the evidence. This touch of the fantastic—an unexplained sense of the mystery and its solution—may indeed, in the wrong hands, invalidate the story for readers looking for puzzle and reason. It takes a fine writer to walk this line without falling, to feature a detective with a "special sense" which can be accepted by the reader as plausible, if not rational. If the author can create through vivid description an atmosphere of strangeness or menace that the reader can feel, the detective's sensitivity is more easily understood and accepted. However, the story, as detective story, may still fail unless within this atmosphere and sensitivity reason and rationality also exist and thrive. At the end of the tale, the reader needs to be able to say that the crime and its solution were both sensed and sensible, that the detective and the reader had to think as well as feel the solution.

Often the author is not up to the task and the story falls flat, for the detective's special sense seems a "hocus-pocus" sleight-of-hand which deprives us of the satisfaction of making sense of the puzzle and the solution. But this doesn't mean it can't be done; in fact, there are a considerable number of highly successful examples where the inexplicable sensitivity either isn't so inexplicable after all, or the inexplicable forms a smooth and effective partnership with the rational and "every day," where the detective's special sensitivity directs his/her attention to clues that otherwise wouldn't have been noticed that then leads to reason and logical deduction. If we can feel what the detective feels as well as understand what the detective thinks, the touch of the fantastic can become an enhancement rather than an obstacle. Such stories can be extremely effective and even more gripping and engaging than a purely intellectual puzzle.

Exemplars

Mignon Eberhart

Eberhart's detective Susan Dare is a mystery writer herself, but her greatest tool is her extreme sensitivity to mood, atmosphere, and menace. In the six stories in *The Cases of Susan Dare* (1934) as well as in a couple more stories in *EQMM* she frequently has sudden feelings—"the small telegram of warning that ran along her nerves" (85)—that alert her to danger, and sometimes point her toward a solution. They are subtle and barely perceptible—"It was just there, that from somewhere, stealthily, cautiously, scarcely observed, there crept into the situation a strange sense of tension, of foreshadowing" (Eberhart, 1948, 40). Although they aren't quite the female intuition dreaded and scorned by detective story traditionalists—"...of the blind little tentacles of something that was so dangerously like intuition and yet was not quite that either" (Eberhart, 1934, p. 227)—they run the risk of seeming just as inexplicable and non-rational. However, Eberhart is so adept as an author at creating situations with ominous undercurrents and dark forebodings that elicit a tingle of apprehension and suspicion in the reader, that we can understand and accept Dare's sense of danger ("like a small red signal," Eberhart, 1944, 33) as, if non-rational, nonetheless genuine. And what really saves these stories as detective stories from the charge of "hocus-pocus" is that Dare herself realizes that her feelings are not enough, they are just the stimulus and the impetus to the detection: "She must confirm instinct—if that is what it was—with reason. With clues. With definite evidence" (Eberhart, 1934, 225); "She must confirm with hard fact the findings of the queer divining rod of her own consciousness" (227). Her feelings put her on the alert and guide her attention, but what follows in every story is analysis of clues and logical deduction. The stories, then, are interesting and satisfying as traditional clue-puzzle detective stories, and are also intriguing and engaging emotionally as we not only are challenged to solve the mystery but we are "Dared" to feel.

In "Easter Devil" (1934) a carved figure from Easter Island triggers Dare's sense of evil and her alertness to physical and emotional clues—"the air of strange and secret sentience that somehow managed to surround the small figure. There was a hint of something decadent, something faintly macabre, something incredibly and hideously wise. It was intangible: it was not sensible. But, nevertheless, it was there" (111). Although there were at first only her own feelings, when she assembles them and analyzes them, a pattern emerges though no proof. As in so many of her cases, she has to put herself in jeopardy to draw the murderer forth and elicit tangible evidence.

F. Tennyson Jesse

In the collection *The Solange Stories* (1931) Solange is a detective who "had been gifted by nature with an extra spiritual sense that warned her of evil" (xv). In the wrong authorial hands this premise could be fatal to the effectiveness and "validity" of a detective story, but Jesse abates this jeopardy first by giving plausibility to such a sense, and, second, by using it not to solve the crime but to lead Solange to seek out other clues and to draw conclusions from them—"her own strange gift, that delicate sense of hers which warned her of hidden evil.... It was a sort of animal intuition or perhaps, rather, a spiritual intuition. When she felt it, she then brought her reasoning powers into play" (7–8). Although Solange's sensitivity is extreme, Jesse points out that it isn't so unusual—"I myself have occasionally had, as which of us has not, and far more keenly and purely in childhood and extreme youth than would be possible in later life, a sudden warning of the nerves that has told me correctly, facts about some human being I had perhaps only met for half an hour, and with whom I had barely exchanged a word" (xv). Nonetheless, the intensity of Solange's "intuition" goes beyond most of our experience, as, for example, in "Lot's Wife" (1929)—"Now, as she stood on the stairs, her every nerve warned her of danger, some dreadful danger that was imminent ... wrapped up in the very fabric of that house" (136). She fears that the flesh and bones of the dead "that had housed so much malice in life" (139) still radiate their evil out into the world of the living. Some might dismiss this as "hocus-pocus" melodrama that disqualifies the stories from being taken seriously as detective tales, but in the hands of Jesse this incipient melodrama becomes instead grist for Solange's reasoning and deduction and lubrication for the coalescing of all the clues into a logical solution. It helps us to accept her "delicate extra sense" that Solange herself, with her scientific training, is skeptical and even scornful

of the trappings of the spirit world while believing in her "sense"—
"I certainly believe in nothing I saw or heard at my séances, and yet I
had the best séances, in the best houses, with the best mediums, or so
I was assured.... But there are strange things that we cannot explain.
Yes, I think I believe that" (6–7). Her hesitancy in believing anything
beyond the rational helps us suspend any "knee-jerk" disbelief we might
have in the fantastic beyond the ordinary—"And back in the ordinary
'now,' that tiny moving field of consciousness so roughly and crudely
called 'the present,' she stood looking at the garden and wondered
whether there weren't 'something in it' after all. Not in the inane accep-
tances of Miss Pratt and her séances, but nonetheless something big, the
visible world" (21–22). Jesse walks a fine line in these Solange stories,
but manages to keep her balance as that touch of the fantastic sears the
stories—their atmosphere, their mysteries, and their detection—into
our memories.

Sax Rohmer

For Rohmer's occult detective, Moris Klaw, appearing in the short
stories in *The Dream-Detective* (1920), the touch of the fantastic is more
of an embrace than a touch, as Klaw's detections embody his extraordinary theories of the indestructibility of thought and of the validity of odic photography—"What is it but the odic force, the ether—say
it how you please—which carries the wireless message, the lightning?
It is a huge, subtle, sensitive plate.... The supreme thought preceding
death is imprinted on the surrounding atmosphere like a photograph"
(8). Whether the "thought-forms" are of the criminal or of the victim,
Klaw has trained himself to be able to receive and "record" those pho-
tographs in his brain (when he sleeps on an "odically sterilized" cushion
at the scene of the crime). The criminal may be thorough in erasing the
material evidence of his crime, but it's impossible to destroy or hide the
thought impression from Klaw's "photographic plate":

> They destroy the clumsy tools of their crime; they hide away the knife, the blud-
> geon; they sop up the blood, they throw it, the jemmy, the dead man, the suffocated
> poor infant, into the ditch, the pool—and they leave intact the odic negative, the
> photograph of their sin, the thought-thing in the air. Here upon this sensitive plate
> [his yellow brow] I reproduce it, the hanging evidence! The headless child is buried
> in the garden, but the thought of the beheader is left to lie about. I pick it up. Poof!
> He swings—that child slayer. I triumph. He is a dead man. What an art is the art of
> the odic photograph [107].

All this could be easily dismissed as "mumbo-jumbo," but somehow these exotic stories through intricacy of plot and exuberance of narration (with a little rational detection mixed in) not only capture our imagination but somehow lead us to accept their premises as at least partly plausible. Although some of the solutions have at least a touch of the supernatural, most of them turn out to be perfectly natural, the supernatural ("if not supernatural, at any rate supernormal," 164) element being Klaw's "psychic" method of detection. "The Case of the Ivory Statue" (1920) is perhaps the best tale in the collection where the "developed negative" of the persistent thought reveals that the mystery, though strange, lies within the realm of "natural" psychology and human intervention.

Other Stories

Harold Begbie

Although Begbie's detective Andrew Lattner thinks of his investigative methods as rational and scientific, they demonstrate special abilities that go beyond those of even the most astute and brilliant traditional detective. Lattner is able to program his dreams to reveal how crimes were committed and who committed them, sometimes even projecting into the future, after which apprehending the criminal is just a matter of routine police work. This "psychic" method does eliminate the "meat" of most detective stories, as analysis of clues and logical deduction are supplanted by "dream vision," but the six stories, first published in *London Magazine* in 1904 then collected in *The Amazing Dreams of Andrew Lattner* (2002) still manage to hold our interest as we try to figure out the "how" and the "why" even after we know the "what" (e.g., a kidnapping and imposture of a Duke to send the world to war, "The Affair of the Duke of Nottingham," 1904; the torture of a cat and a man, "The Flying Blindness," 1904; a false charge of forgery to ruin a man's life, "The Charge against Lord William Grace," 1904) before Lattner dreams it. Although this "dream detection" may require some "suspension of disbelief," Begbie does offer some interesting philosophical and psychological justification that makes it a little more plausible when he suggests that events, both past and future, are in some sense existent always, and it may be that we are arriving at them instead of that they are happening to us in some particular order and rate.

Agatha Christie

Although Christie is best known for the "traditional" detections of Hercule Poirot and Miss Jane Marple, both these detectives supplement their logical approach with a touch of something a little less direct—Poirot with understanding the psychology of the crime and the criminal and Marple with drawing rather obscure analogies to her life experience. But the Christie detective who most strongly embraces a touch of the fantastic is Mr. Harley Quin, whose stories appear in *The Mysterious Mr. Quin* (1930) with one "lost" story ("At the Crossroads" in *Flynn's Weekly*, 1926) and one much later addition ("The Harlequin Tea Set," 1971). Quin is a strange, enigmatic character, who appears and disappears in cases at will and whose detections seem to be informed by and to serve the dead—"You believe in a life after death, do you not? And who are you to say that the same wishes, the same desires, may not operate in that other life? If the desire is strong enough, a messenger may be found" (Christie, 1986, 212). And Quin is that messenger, the advocate for the dead, the unraveller of mysteries by opening others' eyes to patterns they have seen but didn't know they had seen:

> I am not a magician. I'm not even a criminologist, but I believe in the value of impressions [34].
> But he has a power—an almost uncanny power—of showing you what you have seen with your own eyes, of making clear to you what you have heard with your own ears [33].

In story after story he is the catalyst for understanding through his sense of history, his pointing out details others have perceived but forgotten, and his "wide-angle" perspective, apparently including the perspective of the dead. In some of these stories (e.g., "The Shadow on the Glass," 1924, "At the Bells and Motley," 1925, "The Dead Harlequin," 1929) Quin uses elements of traditional detective tales (clues and deductions) to lead others to the solution of a crime, while in others ("The Man from the Sea," 1929, "Harlequin's Lane," 1927) he seems to be more of a metaphysical force addressing existential injustices; but in all of these remarkable tales Christie achieves an intricate and poignant tapestry of the traditional and the fantastic, as Quin's detection is a fascinating commingling of worldly logic and unworldly knowing.

Rose Champion de Crespigny

Norton Vyse, de Crespigny's psychic detective in the collection *Norton Vyse: Psychic* (1919), calls himself a "psychometrician"—one who is able to read the history of an object through sensing the vibrations recorded by it. Vyse's investigations are intriguing for what he encounters (some supernatural, or as he calls them, "superphysical," and some not)—a disembodied hand seeking out victims ("The Villa on the Borderive Road," 1919), an altar-stone in the woods with a violent history ("The Witness in the Wood," 1919), an invisible thread connecting a man to his possible death ("The Shears of Atropos," 1919), a suitor with a hidden criminal past ("The Moving Finger," 1919), a premonitory voice from the dead ("The Voice," 1919); but there isn't much actual detection in these tales beyond his special sensitivity, so their main appeal is in the lengthy discussions of how "everything automatically records its own history [by storing] the vibrations it's come into contact with," and how the specially tuned observer can tap into this information—"To one whose finer senses had reached so advanced a state of development it was difficult to realize the coarseness of the fiber of which the nervous tissues of the general run of humanity is composed" (de Crespigny, 1999, 235), for "Clear, sharply defined thought resulting in vibratory emanations from the brain cells will crystallize into form perceptible to those who can 'see'" (248). Despite the quality writing and the thought-provoking speculations on the "vibrational plane," the lack of "serious" detection (as in many of the supernatural stories in Part 3), prevents these tales from being as interesting and satisfying as detective tales as they are as explorations of fantastic skills in detection.

Harold Daniels

Although the shed in "The Haunted Woodshed" (1961) isn't exactly haunted, its new owner has a very bad feeling every time she enters it—"When she stepped from the brilliant sunshine into the gloom of the woodshed, she was almost overwhelmed by a feeling of melancholy so tangible that it was almost like a blow" (Daniels, 111). Perhaps this could be partly attributed to the actual gloom inside the shed, but her sense of "overpowering, lurking evil" (112) is a bit harder to explain logically. Her eventual solving of a murder and discovery of the source of her "bad feelings" about the woodshed are as much due to accident as to her observation and reasoning, but there is enough of the latter and of actual evil to divest her "inexplicable" sense of most of its taste of hocus-pocus.

Mignon Eberhart

Other than "The Easter Devil" discussed above, "Spider" (1934) may provide the most dramatic illustration of the effectiveness of Dare's special sensitivity to evil, as her sensing of "an enormous black female spider waiting in a web of shadows" (58) and "a queer kind of menace ... somewhere, somehow in this house, horribly alive" (75) directs her to the key clue that penetrates the dark and the dread and solves the crime. "Postiche" (1944) is another brilliant example of the "legitimate" and effective use of an intuitive detective ("And intuition with her was actually a matter of subconscious reasoning. And subconscious reasoning was far better than conscious, rule-of-thumb reasoning," 134), for although her sensitivity puts her on the alert, it is her careful attention to clues and deductions from them and her gathering of evidence that leads her to solve the puzzling poisoning (and, as usual, to put herself in peril in the process).

J.U. Giesy and Junius B. Smith

In the early 1900s, the long short stories of Semi Dual, the "occult detector," that appeared in *The Cavalier Magazine* were extremely popular. From 1912–1934, thirty-two Semi Dual stories were published in a variety of magazines, varying from one-installment to six. What makes these tales especially interesting for readers and for our study of the fantastic in detective stories is that they seamlessly blend rational and fantastic detection. Although Semi Dual believes in "anything which is capable of scientific demonstration" (Giesy and Smith, 31) and works with "mathematical formulas and geometric figures" (37), and he avows "there is nothing mystical in all the universe of worlds. Everything obeys a general law" (37); nonetheless, he is blessed with the ability to read personality and actions from handwriting and astrology ("I am sure, for the stars do not lie. To him who can read, they are an open book," 66) and demonstrates uncanny knowledge of the past and the future with no apparent rational evidence. He is a sort of psychic armchair detective, for he usually uses a newspaper man, Mr. Glace, to do his legwork, while he sits in his tower suite "tearing aside mere human veils and leaving man's soul bare" (60). In "The Occult Detector" (1912) a murder involving shady business dealings and blackmail is solved partly by Glace's astute fact-gathering and deductions and partly by Semi Dual's fantastic insight into the past and the future. Semi Dual appears to have known the outcome well beforehand, but uses Glace's gathering of evidence for courtroom proof. As Dual explains in the forgery case "The Sign of the High 'D'" (1912), he needs logic to prove his more fantastic methods of hypnotism, star-reading, analysis of handwriting, and mind-reading—"Modern courts of law do not recognize the evidence of trance mediums or astrologers as being of value" (121). In "The Wistaria Scarf" (1912), an abduction case which leads Dual and Glace all the way back to Dual's ancestral palace in Persia, Dual, "a sort of combination of an East Indian fakir and Sherlock Holmes" (166), complements rational detection with telepathy, mind-reading, and sensing karmic vibration. He expresses a view quite similar to Sax Rohmer's Moris Klaw when he avows that "thoughts are really things and live until they are received by some other brain. One who knows how can read them long after they are born" (192), and, of course, Dual can "see thy thoughts as a man sees the pebbles in a clear pool" (211).

William Le Queux

Dr. John Durston, Chair of Psychology and the "Colour-Criminologist" in *The Rainbow Mystery: Chronicles of a Colour-Criminologist Recorded by his Secretary* (1917), is said to be "the greatest authority on the psychology of crime in the world" (Le Queux, 11), but his methodology is quite unconventional, to say the least—he believes that:

> every action, every thought, every movement of man, either consciously or otherwise, has its origin in a latent moral colour image, and I have proved that the chromatic centre of ideation that is properly trained is capable of recording the thoughts and actions—that is, the vibrations and their results—of any number of other centres which are not trained to resist the superior force ... and the most powerful emanations arise from centres in which there is colour conflict resulting in criminal acts [15–16].

The practical consequences of this rather odd though intriguing theory is that Durston (and his assistant and narrator) can see what other "brains" see even if they are miles away—colour telepathy—including crimes planned or committed. It is certainly a fantastic premise, but most of the stories balance the fantastic with the plausible as logical detective work either precedes or follows the "thought materialization" in the solving of the mystery. In "The Song That Was Never There" (1917) Durston hears singing and sees a reflection of a hideous hag that are projections from the brain of a lunatic, while "acting upon the advice he [Durston] was able to give them, the authorities themselves solved one of the most baffling mysteries in the annals of Scotland Yard" (39). In all these stories Durston is a sort of fantastic armchair detective, as he "unraveled more mysteries and prevented more crimes than any man living, and that by the apparently impossible process of sitting home and watching things happen [on his mental screen]" (88). In "The Raven of Dinstonley" (1917) his vision of an injured raven chained up leads him to the criminal who is using an exotic African poison for his murders. Eventually (in "The Unbound Book," 1917) his enemies—the Gang of the Broken Cup—use some of his own skills against him, almost killing him by thought transference, but he recovers though he is forced to give up his special skills.

L.T. Meade and Robert Eustace

Diana Marburg, professional palm reader, has gained quite a reputation for her success at solving mysteries by palmistry and other acts of clairvoyance. In the three stories in which she is featured, she receives strong impressions about people and about crimes from "reading" palms—"Call her power what you will, she was guided by something too wonderful for explanation" (Prasil, 202). Although her powers arouse her suspicions and often point to the criminal, she does have to follow up with some reasoning and deduction to determine how the crimes were committed; however, the "detection" is not particularly noteworthy, leaving the stories with the definite taste of "hocus pocus." Even in the most interesting and effective of these stories, "The Dead Hand" (1902), in which her palmistry tells her who—"You are about to commit a murder and will suffer a shameful death on the scaffold" (189)—but not how, her detective work is minimal and unconvincing, so the Marburg stories, though mildly interesting, are not effective examples of the blending of the detective and the fantastic, for the fantastic remains unexplained, and the detection lacks significant clues or clear reasoning. This is not surprising as the "detective mystery" collaborations of Meade and Eustace (e.g., *Sorceress of the Strand*, *The Brotherhood of the Seven Kings*) are much more notable for their fabulous atmosphere and exotic crime than they are for convincing detection.

However, the stories by Meade and Eustace in *John Bell: Ghost Exposer* (see Chapter Two) are more successful in bringing together the fantastic and the detective, but this is because the traditional detective methods of Bell reveal that the "supernatural" phenomena are "naturally" the result of human agency.

Douglas Newton

Although Newton's detective Paul Toft "acted on intuition and instinct rather than hard facts and deduction" (Ashley, 128), and Toft (in "Contrary to Evidence," 1936) senses murder when all the evidence seems to point to accident—"I don't know, I feel that unmistakable sign that his queer mind had sensed crime," (133)—the story is saved from "hocus-pocus" by the presence of reasonable, though very subtle, clues. Toft's sense of crime doesn't offer him a solution, but rather leads him to observe and interpret behaviors which others have ignored or thought inconsequential, but have been lurking there in plain sight all along. In "Contrary to Evidence," Toft's suspicion of crime results in his noticing a man's making a little too much effort to keep his distance from a victim having a "heart attack" and to be sure a witness was present to observe that distance. The police no longer scoff at Toft's special sensitivity to crime because he had "proved these extraordinary 'feelings' of his too often" (134), and the reader too can take them seriously because there are events and behaviors, hidden from our attention until illuminated by Toft's suspicion, that upon re-inspection and re-interpretation confirm that suspicion. We're not certain where Toft's special sensitivity to crime comes from, but when we are forced to attend to the clues that Toft has seen, his sensitivity is reasonable, if not entirely explicable.

Max Rittenberg

Although Rittenberg's Dr. Wycherley is more an esoteric psychologist, hypnotist, and mind-reader than a detective, a few of the stories in *The Mind Reader: Being Some Pages from the Strange Life of Dr. Xavier Wycherley* (1913) involve him in detective work where he uses his "lifelong training in the judging of the unseen and the intangible" (Rittenberg, 1913b, 418) in combination with careful observation and deduction to solve the crimes. He dismisses the notion that his abilities are psychic—"People weave fairytales around my powers. There is nothing supernatural about them" (497)—but he does have a highly developed sensitivity to the "ghosts of thoughts" (538), not unlike that of Sax Rohmer's Moris Klaw:

> The professor has worked in this room for years past, and some faint echo of his thoughts and feelings might linger—might still make itself evident to the consciousness of the mental healer as the characteristic scent of a man might still make itself felt to the keen nose of a hound [498].
>
> I was alone in his room for half-an-hour today, and the thoughts of the dead man were still surging and echoing in it. A tangled maze of thoughts coloured with what I recognize as dangerous abnormality [302].

In "Accident or Murder" (1911) Wycherley's "keen nose" picks up the "scent" of insanity at a murder scene, which tells him "who," but his discernment of clues and deductive powers are needed to reveal the "how" and the "why" and sometimes even to interpret the "who"—"My psychic gift is a very rough and imperfect human spectroscope, and I am still at work on the meanings of the lines and bands" (447). The emphasis in this collection is certainly on psychology, hypnosis, and mind-reading in the service of treatment and healing, but the occasional detective story shows an easy and effective partnership between Wycherley's rather fantastic sensitivity and his very down-to-earth skills of deduction.

Sax Rohmer

All of Klaw's cases, whether murder by battle axe of the Crusades ("Case of the Crusader's Axe," 1913), sleep-walking and a poisoned harp ("Case of the Tragedies in the Greek Room," 1913), or the whispering trees on the grounds of a haunted house ("Case of the Whispering Poplars," 1913), illustrate Klaw's theory of the cycles of crime and the enduring imprint of thought on the surrounding "ether" to which Klaw is extraordinarily sensitive. There is some following of clues and deduction by Klaw, but it is his special sensitivity (which requires the reader's acceptance of the immortality of thought and its imprinting on the "atmosphere" of the crime) which permits and empowers the detection.

Ella Scrymsour

Sheila Crerar, as her advertisement proclaimed, is "A lady of gentle birth. Scottish, young, penniless, possessing strong psychic powers, [who] will devote her services to the solving of uncanny mysteries or 'the laying of ghosts'" (Scrymsour, 15). The six stories in *Sheila Crerar*, previously published in *The Blue Magazine* in 1920, show Sheila using her "most wonderful gift of sight" (15)—an extreme sensitivity to the restless spirits of the dead and their manifestations—and "detecting" through research of family histories, sensing the spirits, and suffering their torment. Although the visions entail such fantastic things as a werewolf on a killing spree ("The Werewolf of Rannoch," 1920), the revenge of a wronged man dead for two hundred years in a marriage ceremony in which the living are united to the dead ("The Phantom Isle," 1920), the attack of an elemental through a foul and slimy vapor ("The Death Vapor," 1920), and the haunting energy of a long-past torture chamber ("The Room of Fear," 1920), Crerar's sensitivity is handled tastefully and plausibly, aided by a charming love story, more "egalitarian" than would be expected for the times. She is much more believable because she is by no means infallible or invulnerable, her sensitivity to the emotions and the suffering of the spirits leading her to feel as well as understand their pain.

Six

The Fanciful, the Fabled
and the Psychological

As will be seen in many of the stories in this chapter, touches of the fanciful and the fantastic can be incorporated in an otherwise conventional detective story to deepen the mystery and add to the intrigue without weakening the traditional clue-puzzle structure and conventions. In these stories, the detectives don't use occult methods although they may use psychological ones, but they predominantly use the traditional, the tried, and the true—observation, logic, and deduction are still the modus operandi, and the explanation of the mystery or crime, though sometimes eccentric or bizarre, stays within the parameters of reason and the possible in the world as we know it.

One lively source for the fantastic in motive or method or outcome is the psychological, especially the sometimes strange workings of the unconscious. That which would have been viewed as supernatural (e.g., possession by demons) a couple centuries ago, has come to be understood by many since Freud and Jung in the early and mid–20th century as psychological reality, not necessarily rational but "real," not supernatural but "psyche-natural"—natural to the inner world of the psyche. That inner world is still puzzling enough and "fantastic" enough to add mystery and surprise to a detective story, but without violating "reasonable" explanation—"reasonable" as we now conceive it.

Another potentially rich source for a touch of the fantastic is legend and myth, which can be viewed as metaphorical descriptions of natural events or scientific facts. These stories tap into our fascination with culture and imagination and symbolism, expanding the reach of the detective tale beyond the immediate cultural and historical context and deepening "fact" with metaphorical associations.

Although science fiction tales in which a science fiction solution is "tacked on" to an otherwise rational detective story are excluded from this monograph, there are a few detective tales included which have science fiction elements (e.g., a time machine) that are integral to the plot from the beginning and form part of the parameters within which logical detection proceeds.

And finally, there is the fanciful, the outrageous, and the downright absurd, which though difficult to believe or to take seriously, could in fact actually happen in the world as we understand it. These tales may stretch the limits of credibility, but not of possibility, and usually evoke an appreciative gasp and a chuckle in the reader rather than outrage at being cheated or duped.

Exemplars

Agatha Christie

Although "Idol House of Astarte" (1928) turns out to be a conventional (though clever) clue-puzzle mystery, it is steeped in the atmosphere of the fantastic—emotional, psychological, and mythological, as a man is murdered apparently by a Phoenician goddess, and the only weapon is a threat—"I am the Priestess of Astarte. Beware of how you approach me, for I hold death in my hand" (Christie, 2011, 24). The night is dark, the place is ominous (an ancient grove where evil rites were performed), and the mood is malignant ("Something stronger than myself seemed to be holding me back and urging me not to enter. I felt more definitely convinced than ever of the essential evilness of the spot," 23). The victim is stabbed to death in front of several other members of his party, but while everyone saw the death, no one saw the murder, and no weapon can be found. Christie adroitly weaves a spell of Stone Age myth and peril that kills without reason or explanation—"A man can't be killed like that. It's against Nature" (25).

What makes the touch of the fantastic so effective in Christie's hands is her skill in juxtaposing it with the natural and reliable—"the house itself was unremarkable, a good solid house built of Devonshire granite," but right in its backyard are barrows and hut circles and carvings and traces of ancient rites from the late Stone Age permeated by a feeling of "desolation and horror" (19). The murder is mysterious enough without all the fantastic atmosphere, but the myth surrounds it with a heavy sense of irrational dread—an "awe and horror of that terrible moment when I saw a man stricken to death by apparently no mortal agency" (16). What would have been, without the touch of the fantastic, an interesting intellectual puzzle, with it becomes a haunting mystery and a challenge to our beliefs in the rational and the reliable. Only after her touch of the fantastic does Christie (in the person of Miss Marple, the detective of logic and deduction and a bit of intuition) restore the order and reason that was hidden behind "all the atmosphere of heathen goddesses" (32) and in the process restore our faith in that very reason.

H.F. Heard

In "The Adventure of Mr. Montalba, Obsequist" (1945) the ultimate criminal strategy of escaping arrest hovers on the edge of fantasy (though the author objects to this label, as he claims all the events in the story are realistic). The only thing arrested in this ingenious story is Time itself, as death becomes a partner in crime, and a master criminal escapes its clutches, briefly, by the latest technological "undertaking" of "permanenting" the dead—"Why leave him in the tomb when you may have him home at the table?" (100). Why indeed, and why force a criminal to pay for his crimes when he can be dead for the law and alive for the crime? As fantastic as the premise of this story may be, the detective (Mr. Mycroft) is careful, logical, and precise in his methods, demonstrating that the "real" and the "unreal" may at times be happy bedfellows.

Michael Innes

"Lesson in Anatomy" (1946) is not only a lesson in the human anatomy but also in the anatomy of the fantastic detective story, for it is a traditional clue-puzzle mystery embellished with "a sheer piece of macabre drama, possibly conceived and executed by a lunatic," (Innes, 2001a, 110). A public lecture on anatomy illustrated by a fresh corpse is punctuated by "lowering skeletons from the rafters, and releasing various improbable living creatures—lemus and echidnas, and opposums—to roam the bench" (101), fanfares of trumpets, the chanting of "It tolls for Thee," a vulture swooping from the rafters, the hall plunged into darkness, and the corpse disappearing then reappearing as an entirely different person. It is insanity, mania, and the "Keystone Cops," but amidst it all, like the eye of the hurricane, is Inspector Appleby and his calm, logical solution making sense of the madness. What would have been an interesting puzzle without the fantastic touch is transformed into a madcap, frenzied, fascinating entertainment.

Helen McCloy

"Through a Glass Darkly" (1948), which was eventually expanded into a less effective novel, is an intriguing psychological story where aspects of the unconscious psyche play major roles in the commission and explanation of the crimes. Even in these days when the dynamics of the unconscious are widely acknowledged as inner realities which influence or even direct motivation, thought, and action, this tale in many ways seems fantastic, and yet it is so well-written and cleverly plotted that the psychology becomes an active character with its own logic and reason.

Throughout the story McCloy brilliantly interweaves classic clue-puzzle plotting and detective methods (of the psychologist/detective Basil Willing) with the dark recesses of irrational fear and psychological torment. In what must be one of the most darkly clever criminal plots in the detective short story genre and one of the most insidious murders by psychological torment and obsession in fiction, McCloy creates a haunting exemplar of the seamless interweaving of traditional detective story and searing psychological case study. The methods of committing the crime and of detecting it are well within the detective story tradition, but the criminal's cultivation of the hidden corners of the psyche add a disturbing touch of the fantastic to the story's atmosphere, plot, and puzzle. As one character puts it, "Was a practical woman ever confronted with such a fantastic problem?" (McCloy, 18). The author uses knowledge of the structure and functioning of the unconscious as well as fastidious detail in description of the psychic and mythic reality (of the doppelganger) to create a crime and its explanation that, though reasonable, are highly provocative. Though such things do happen in the world we know (just talk to a therapist), this tale challenges our credibility. Adding to this touch of the fantastic is the fact that the victim's fear of the fantastic is a crucial part of the murderer's arsenal.

Other Stories

Samuel Hopkins Adams

In "The Flying Death" (1903) the legendary roc ("the billion-year-old Pteranodon, with its twenty-foot spread of bat-like wings and its four-foot bayonet beak," Adams, 66) strikes terror and death on a Long

Island beach, but reason carries the day and in the process demonstrates that the line between fact and the fantastic is a fine one, for "a scientific assumption is a mere makeshift, useful only until it is overthrown by new facts" (74).

Alexander Agis

In Agis' tale of the future "The Science of Anticipation" (1974) the Crime Analysis Station Enforcement Section (CASES) uses computers to document, analyze, and project crimes so that future crimes can be anticipated and prevented. It might sound promising in concept and benevolent in intention, but the reality is fraught with ethical ramifications and unanticipated outcomes. When a currently innocent man ("I haven't done anything yet," Agis, 30) who has been contemplating a robbery is shot, we all might be grateful this "science of anticipation" is to date fantastic, for, after all, we all know with what "the road to Hell" is paved!

Poul Anderson

"The Martian Crown Jewels" (1958) is a good example of a science fiction detective story where the science fiction just provides an unreal (at least at this phase of interplanetary travel) setting for a natural crime (theft of priceless Martian jewels) and rational detection, though the Martian detective, Syaloch, is fantastic enough—a "seven-foot biped of vaguely stork-like appearance, but the lean, crested, red-beaked head at the end of the sinuous neck was too large, the yellow eyes too deep, the white feathers were more like a penguin's than a flying bird's, save at the blue-plumed tail; instead of wings there were skinny red arms ending in four-fingered hands" (Anderson, 170). Though since it is "the brain that counts, not whether it is covered by feathers or hair or bony plates" (170), it is not surprising when Syaloch mimics his Terrestrial predecessor in announcing "the game's afoot" and solves the problem by eliminating the impossible, leaving only the improbable.

Issac Asimov

In defending his assertion that "the science fiction mystery is a thoroughly acceptable literary form" (Asimov, xi), Asimov sets the same parameters for the legitimate use of science fiction in the detective story that we have described in the introduction to this chapter—"You don't spring new devices on the reader and solve the mystery with them. You don't take advantage of future history to introduce *ad hoc* phenomena. In fact, you carefully explain all facets of the future background well in advance so the reader may have a decent chance to see the solution" (x).

In his collection *Asimov's Mysteries* (1968) there are several stories that illustrate the abiding by these parameters, stories which carefully describe the nature of the future world and its devices within which the mystery will play out and the detective will function. In "The Singing Bell" (1954) a murder is done on the moon aided by a rocket ship, a blaster, and an explosive micropile, while the extraterrologist and detective Wendell Urth has available a psychoprobe to assess guilt, but there are constraints on its use, so the actual detection is accomplished by the old standbys—analysis of clues, logic, and deduction, though in this case the vital clue is a matter of the utmost "gravity." In "The Dying Night" (1956) the ability to transfer matter instantly through space is at the heart of the crime, while the peculiarities of planetary night-and-day provide the clues that Urth uses to identify the criminal. In "The Key" (1966) a mind-controlling device from an ancient race is found on the moon that in the wrong hands could lead to totalitarianism and extermination of much of the Earth's population. As with the other stories of Wendell Urth, the context and the clues are "out of this world," but the detection is decidedly earthbound.

George Baxt

"Clap Hands, There Goes Charlie" (1982) is interesting primarily because it's not quite certain just what the touch of the fantastic entails—is it purely psychological, or is it genuinely supernatural? Whichever it is, it is fantastic and it brings intrigue and mystery, for the voice that comes through the medium is certainly of the dead but not of the intended or expected, and it may well be that the murderer is murdered by the victim after the victim's murder, and "if there's an afterlife, then they're [the murderer and the murdered] together" (Baxt, 623). It is conceivable that all this can be explained by psychological states, but in any case the boundaries of the natural world we know are severely stretched if not broken.

Lloyd Biggle, Jr.

In "Department of Future Crime" (1966) the fantastic takes the form of a machine that can show future crimes taking place, but the sleuthing strategies are the realistic and traditional—clue interpretation and logical deduction. The juxtaposition of the fantastic premise and the traditional methods is fascinating as, of course, are the usual "Greek tragedy" sort of philosophical questions—can knowing the future allow you to change it, and if you change it, how can the machine show you the "unchanged" future? The fantastic in this story rings true and allows these questions to be addressed, but the attempt at a "realistic" answer, though emotionally satisfying, isn't as convincing.

Anthony Boucher

Boucher was a renowned literary critic and author of numerous detective short stories. A few of his tales, including "Elsewhen" (1943) were published in *The Magazine of Science Fiction and Fantasy* and delved into the science fiction genre. In the Introduction to "Elsewhen" in the anthology *Death Locked In*, 1987, the editors make an interesting point—"Most of the time it would be cheating to combine a locked-room murder with a science-fictional device like a time machine, but not when it's done by Anthony Boucher" (Greene and Adey, 521). This statement reflects the objection to "hocus-pocus" in detective stories—abruptly imposing a "science fiction" solution onto a detective plot that until the end follows reason and logic—but also demonstrates the trust that, in sensitive hands, it can be done legitimately. In this Boucher story the science fiction element (a time machine) is an integral part of the plot introduced from the beginning, and the deductions from clues by the detective (Fergus O'Breen) proceed "naturally" (and cleverly) from this premise. The story turns out to be not only an interesting illustration of straightforward detection but also an intriguing speculation on time and its consequences.

"The Pink Caterpillar" (1945) is another fantastic Boucher story involving murder, time-travel, and the fastidious, logical detecting of Fergus O'Breen. In this tale O'Breen has to figure out why the burning of a man's skeleton causes that man to return to life while his murderer dies, and what really are the "pink caterpillars" that crawl after the murderer. Both of the Boucher stories certainly illustrate O'Breen's disagreement with the cliché that "detectives are hardheaded realists. Didn't you ever stop to think that there's hardly another profession outside the clergy that's so apt to run up against the things beyond realism?" (Boucher, 1969, 63). And the "beyond realism" works well in both these detective tales, especially in its dramatic contrast to the traditional detective methods employed to bring it back "to earth."

"The Anomaly of the Empty Man" (1952) is a strange story combining a sort of Sherlock Holmes pastiche (even the Holmesian adage, "Discard the impossible, and whatever remains, no matter how improbable, must be true" is modified to "Discard the impossible; then if nothing remains, some part of the 'impossible' must be possible," Boucher, 1955, 13) with a touch of science fiction—arias played backwards somehow sucking bodies out of their still-carefully-arranged clothes. As with the other two science-fiction-ish detective stories described above, traditional detective methods provide the reader with something solid to hold onto as he is reeling from the realization of what part of the "impossible" must be possible. The final "nema," though backwards, provides a bit of sanity and a hint of resolution.

Thomas Burke

Author of the acclaimed and terrifying horror story, "The Hands of Mr. Ottermole," Burke also wrote a deeply troubling tale ("The Bloomsbury Wonder," 1929) of a horrific multiple murder with a motive so fantastic that no detection can understand it until the murderer purges his dark psychology—"neither hate nor lust nor the morbid vanity that sometimes leads stupid people to the committal of enormous crimes.... He committed more than a crime; he committed a sin. And meant to" (Burke, 60). His possession by evil is so dark that it verges on the supernatural in its malevolence and its power to drive him to frenzied crime; his desperate need to sin in order to cleanse goes beyond the pale of reason and the natural and yet makes a strange sort of "natural law":

> There's something in these people, some awful essence of the world's beginning. Perhaps strange sins, projected in the cold hearts of creatures centuries dead, projected but never given substance, take on a ghost-essence and wander through the hearts of men as cells of evil. And wander from heart to heart, poisoning as they go, until at last they come to life in a positive sin, and, having lived, can die [p. 61].

Here is a tale where the touch of the fantastic overwhelms reason and hides from detection until the psychological finally detects itself and fact dispels fantasy—"It's useless to tell me that this couldn't have happened. I can only say that it did" (62).

Lilian Jackson Braun

"SuSu and the 8:30 Ghost" (1964) is a delightful tale with a couple fantastic twists—the detective is a cat, and the murder victim used to be one ("I was-s-s a cat myself in a former existence," Braun, 36). With their feline affinity, it isn't quite so fantastic that the former solved the murder of the latter (with a little help from two incredulous old ladies).

G. K. Chesterton

In all the stories in *The Incredulity of Father Brown* (1926) and in a few stories in the other Father Brown books, superstitions or curses seem to defy reason and be at the heart of the mystery (see Chapter Three), but Father Brown, despite his religious beliefs, is always incredulous and skeptical of these attributions and manages to find the true crime lurking beneath the "fantastic" façade; nonetheless the façade is indeed fantastic, much to the benefit and intrigue of the story. Although there are many Father Brown stories where the atmosphere is romantic or poetic and the crimes appear to be impossible, there is always a rational, though sometimes paradoxical, explanation. This is also true for most of the non–Father Brown stories, but there are several where the fanciful runs wild, creating events that, though possible in the "real" world, are extremely implausible, despite the rational explanation. Two of the most engaging are pre–Father Brown, both in *The Club of Queer Trades* (1905)—"The Noticeable Conduct of Professor Chadd" (1905) and "The Tremendous Adventures of Major Brown" (1903)—in which the professor stands for hours on one leg and flaps like a bird, and the major repeatedly has his life threatened by alphabetical flowers, an apparently decapitated head in a coal cellar, and a lady in green, all under the auspices of The Adventure and Romance Agency. The explanations restore sanity and reason, but not before fancy, whimsy, and the eccentric have their due, and along the way are championed as of a higher order than strict adherence to the factual and rational—"Logic like that's not what is really wanted. It's a question of spiritual atmosphere. Facts, how facts obscure the truth" (28–29).

The one Father Brown story that provides a touch of the fantastic—where the events are not supernatural or impossible but "seem to have slight relationship to the real world because of their strangeness or extravagance" (thank goodness!)—is "The Sign of the Broken Sword" (1911) in *The Innocence of Father Brown*. The aura of the fantastic is established early—"The thousand arms of the forest were grey, and its million fingers silver. In a sky of dark green-blue-like slate the stars were bleak and brilliant like splintered ice" (Chesterton, 1951, 127). The horror comes later—"Where would a wise man hide a leaf? In a forest. And if there were no forest, he would make a forest. And if he wished to hide a dead leaf, he would make a dead forest" (135). Father Brown's logic penetrates the gloom and finds, tragically, the dead forest is all too human, and the crime is, hopefully, at least a bit fantastic.

Agatha Christie

In addition to the Miss Marple tale "Idol House of Astarte" Christie wrote several Hercule Poirot stories that illustrate a touch of the psychological fantastic. In "The Dream" (1937) a typically ingenious Christie twist reveals a recurring, apparently prophetic dream of suicide to be instead a cleverly disguised murder plot, while in "The Tragedy at Marsden Manor" (1923) Poirot uses a word association test, the ghost of a murdered man, and subconscious guilt to catch the killer.

Arthur Conan Doyle

Although Conan Doyle is, of course, best known for his short stories and novels of Sherlock Holmes, who dismisses the fantastic and supernatural as irrational and unworthy of consideration, Conan Doyle personally became deeply interested in spiritualism and wrote several non–Holmes short stories, some with a detective, where the supernatural played a central role. In "The Leather Funnel" (1902) the detective, Lionel Dacre, is a learned man and serious student of the occult:

> He had spent much of his life and fortune in gathering together what was said to be a unique collection of Talmudic, cabalistic, and magical works, many of them of great rarity and value. His tastes leaned toward the marvelous and the monstrous, and I have heard that his experiments in the direction of the unknown have passed all the bounds of civilization and decorum [Conan Doyle, 1902, 98].

Dacre is a staunch defender of the exploration of the non-rational and of those who investigate it, protesting the charge of "charlatan"—"The charlatan is always the pioneer. The quack of yesterday is the professor of tomorrow" (101)—and uses dream psychology and his theory of the lingering traces of intense emotion on objects associated with emotional experiences (very similar to Moris Klaw's theory of mental negatives and odic photography) to aid his investigations. In "The Leather Funnel" these psychic techniques reveal the funnel's agonizing and horrifying history.

Vincent Cornier

It's surprising that in the late 1940s, Ellery Queen called Cornier's series of detective stories about Barnabas Hildreth (most first published in *Pearson's Magazine* in the 1930s and over sixty years later collected in *The Duel of Shadows*, 2011) "one of the great series of modern detective stories" (*EQMM*, July 1947, 115), and in a later issue of *EQMM* (September 1947, 115) praised the stories after using the words "amazing" and "extraordinary" to describe them. Since Queen was a severe skeptic when it came to mixing the supernatural or even the fantastic with the detective tale (see Queen's comment from *EQMM*, September 1945, in the introduction to this monograph), his praise is very revealing about the quality and effectiveness of these highly unusual tales. Although they are not supernatural, they definitely have a touch (in some case, a heavy touch) of the fantastic, seldom completely violating natural law as we know it, but almost always pushing it to the very limit of plausibility. Murder by a poisoned goblet activated by "a damned ass" ("The Stone Ear," 1933), a death by instant petrification that no man had ever died since earth began ("The Catastrophe in Clay," 1935), a golden death by chain mail of rippling laughter ("The Mantle that Laughed," 1935), and serious injury from a bullet fired over 232 years earlier ("The Duel of Shadows," 1934)—surely, as Queen says, "even after all these years there is still nothing else like them in the annals of mystery fiction" (Cornier, 2011, 13). But despite all the incredible events in these tales, the detection is profoundly logical and steadfastly reasonable (and even, in the case of "The Duel of Shadows" includes an explanatory diagram), so even Queen appreciated the pairing of such strange bedfellows.

In an only slightly milder touch of the fantastic, "The Courtyard of the Fly" (1937), published only in magazine and anthology, presents a large, hissing, stinging, orange-and-black fly ("It was loathsome and it looked deadly, as though it carried venom," Cornier, 1937, 33–34) as a thief of a priceless string of pearls. It wasn't until thirty-seven years later in the story that the "fly" and the fantastic were finally "grounded."

Aleister Crowley

Crowley's stories featuring the "mystic-magician-philosopher-psy-choanalyst-detective" Simon Iff (Crowley, back cover) are as unique and strange as Crowley's own life. In "Sterilized Stephen" (1918) Iff uses psychological weapons masterfully to induce in the criminal a fatalistic and ironic belief in supernatural retribution—"Hobbs had never believed in the supernatural, but now it seemed to him as the only rational explanation—a dead man was somehow able to revenge himself by throwing the mental machinery of his murderer out of gear" (414). Iff's use of psychology and its consequences have definite touches of the fantastic as does Iff's (and Crowley's) underlying philosophy of our material existence—"We are all really sorts of gods who have disguised ourselves as men and women for the sake of the experience; and life on earth is always so painful and hideous that we are all first-class heroes simply for getting ourselves born" (393). Although Iff grudgingly intervenes in several cases (e.g., "The Artistic Temperament," 1917) with psychological (and sometimes metaphysical) insight and strategies, he has a low opinion of this material life and prefers the even more fantastic world of "ultimate reality"—"I retire, whenever I am able, from this nightmare illusion of matter to a world of reality" (Crowley, 45).

August Derleth

Although Derleth's Solar Pons in many ways emulates Sherlock Holmes, including the occasional case where the apparently supernatural is revealed to be the "natural" machinations of a human criminal, from time to time Pons, unlike Holmes, encounters a genuine touch of the fantastic. In "The Adventure of the Ball of Nostradamus" (1982) the keen, analytic skills of Pons encounter the fantastic crystal ball of Nostradamus and the crystal gazer's vision into the future. Even Pons, the ultimate rationalist and skeptic of the psychic, gives some grudging credence to the historical crystal gazer—"The fulfillment of prophecies, like beauty, is too often only in the eye of the beholder, but I concede that the French physician offers as nearly adequate evidence for pre-vision as I know" (Derleth, 1303). This possible credence creates a bit of a moral dilemma for the reader, if not for Pons, for the visions show several youngsters to be dictators-in-the-making. Should murder be done to save a world from tyranny and misery? With the logic of Pons, the vision of Nostradamus, stern reason, and a fantastic view into the future, it's quite a potent brew but leaves so much undetermined—"Only the future will tell, Parker" (1306). "The Adventure of the Snitch in Time" (1982) is a clever tale with several fantastic elements—time travelers (including Moriarty) and alternative universes—threatening the "real" fictional world of Pons and his "Watson," Parker. The fantastic twists in on itself, as the time traveler tells Pons that in one of the alternative universes he's visited, Pons and Parker are fictional characters. At this, Parker, of course, is incredulous and we readers of the fiction shake our heads not sure what to think, but Pons cautions all of us not to "dismiss the incredible solely because it is incredible to us" (1294).

Paul Fairman

"Recollection of the Future" (1959) is an intriguing story with a fantastic touch of Oedipus-like classic Greek tragedy. A man who can see the future kills to prevent it, but in the very act creates it, and that future is murder. We and the psychologist listening to the killer's tale are more than ready to dismiss his precognition as fantasy or delusion, but as the pre-envisioned fate takes its course despite (and because of) everything the man does to prevent it, our easy belief in reason and will is shaken, for it is the heavy touch of the fantastic that here creates the real.

Robert L. Fish

All Fish's hilarious spoofs of Sherlock Holmes and his deductive brilliance collected in *Schlock Homes: The Complete Bagel Street Saga* (1990) are filled with wild puns and fanciful parody, but some go more over the top than others. In "The Adam Bomb" (1960) there is so much riotous absurdity that we give up any semblance of belief and join the ranks of the fantastic as Homes unintentionally sets off the detonation of a powerful bomb without knowing it—"A rather curious disappearance in the north ... the whole of Northumberland County disappeared" (27). We can only laugh when Homes responds to this disconcerting information, "Ah, well, at least there should be no need for us to become involved. Northumberland County is of sufficient size that even the police should be able to discover it" (27).

Jacques Futrelle

In many ways the famous stories of the Thinking Machine (Professor Van Dusen) are testimonies to the power of rationality and logic, as in so many tales Van Dusen calmly (and somewhat scornfully) reasons his way to the truth, which is hidden for everyone else behind the veil of appearance and red herrings. As he asserts, "Two and two make four, not sometimes but all the time" (Futrelle, vol. 1, 2009, 11); however, occasionally Futrelle (and the Thinking Machine) surprise us with a tale tinged with the supernatural or the fantastic (see Chapters Three and Nine). "The Roswell Tiara" (1908) is a story of impossible theft revealed to have a strange psychological and zoological explanation, although not so strange for those familiar with Wilkie Collins' *The Moonstone* and E.C. Bentley's "The Clever Cockatoo."

Futrelle also wrote a haunting non–Thinking Machine psychological tale of murder, "The Statement of the Accused" (1910), where a man's insanity battles the evidence, and the detective (Garron) and the reader must determine what is real and what is not. With touches of Poe's "The Telltale Heart" and Shakespeare's *Macbeth*, this dark, gripping story leads us to ponder the relation between perception and reality and between truth and fact and to question our assumptions about the inevitable success of rational detection.

Peter Godfrey

Many of the stories of the detections of Rolf le Roux in Godfrey's collection *The Newtonian Egg* (2002) are of impossible crimes with a psychological element or explanation (see Chapter One). "And Turn the Hour" (1952) is an especially taut tale of repression, amnesia, a cinema ticket, a white lily, and fifty-two missing minutes. Le Roux uses hypnosis and free-association, to say nothing of poetry—"Take the flower and turn the hour, and kiss your love again" (59)—but ultimately it is logic (with psychological understanding) and close observation that solves the case. The disappearance of fifty-two minutes from consciousness would have seemed supernatural a hundred and fifty years ago in violation of all natural law, but Freudian psychology has revealed a new code of "laws," so this fantastic occurrence, though still strange and haunting, is now viewed by many as natural (though not rational).

H.F. Heard

In addition to the fanciful tale "The Adventure of Mr. Montalba, Obsequist" where a criminal's death is not only permanent but permanentized, Heard wrote one other, only slightly less fanciful, short story of Mr. Mycroft, that erudite, irascible purveyor of fact and reason. In "The Enchanted Garden" (1949) a bewitching Eden of lush vegetation, darting hummingbirds, and sparkling waters conceals a far-from-Edenic world where a bizarre and implausible, though certainly possible, murder scheme is enacted once and is only just thwarted the second time. Eden has its magic and its bliss and its enchantment, but how fortunate that Mycroft and humanity ate of the apple of reason and logic and reality.

As eccentric and fanciful as are his two Mr. Mycroft stories, his tale, "The President of the United States, Detective" (1947) is on another plane altogether, for the consequences of its amazing and incredible crime are international and world-shattering. Though the plot is possible (barely), it is unthinkable in its scope and impact, but it does offer a fantastic stage on which careful and perfectly logical detection can show its reach and range. The President's deductions are extraordinary, but no more so than the intended crime; his solution and response are bold and ingenious taking logic and reason to the farthest edges of their domain.

Tony Hillerman

Most of the exploits of the Navajo policemen Jim Chee and Joe Leaphorn are in the several Hillerman novels featuring one or both of them and presenting a world rich with Native American myth and ritual and cultural traditions. That which might seem fantastic or supernatural or at least non-rational to mainstream culture is at the heart of reality for these detectives and their culture. The opening line of the only short story of Jim Chee, "The Witch, Yazzie, and the Nine of Clubs" (1986), lets the mainstream reader know that he's entering a very different world with a vastly different view of rationality, cause-and-effect, and the "natural"—"All summer the witch had been at work on the Rainbow Plateau" (Breen and Gorman, 44). But despite the mythological world of skinwalkers, werewolf tracks, a man turning himself into an owl, a dog transforming to a man, ritual, and the inexplicable disappearance of the loot and the thief, Chee brings logic and deduction into this world, and in the end the witch is dead, but the myth perseveres. The writing is so vivid and "down to earth" that the touch of the fantastic, bordering on the supernatural, seems completely normal, natural, and reasonable—as it is for the traditional Navajo. Fact and fancy blend effortlessly, Navajo tradition and detective tradition are easy bedfellows, and we are left with a "traditional" detective story of unusual richness and intrigue.

Banesh Hoffman

It is not unusual for the fantastic, or at least a touch of it, to show up in spoofs and parodies, for the making fun often borders on the absurd, turning a serious detective tale into a series of incredible incidences, motives, or behaviors on the part of the criminal and/or the detective (for example, see Robert Fish or Arthur Porges in this chapter). "Sherlock, Shakespeare, and the Bomb" (1966) is in some ways in this same vein, but in others fantastically different, for its absurdity—"not only that Shakespeare was a major prophetic genius, but that his knowledge of the future extended to technical details of the most intimate and intricate sort" (Hoffman, 91)—is hauntingly sensible and disturbingly possible. The explication by Holmes of passages from Shakespeare's sonnets and *The Tempest*, though at times far-fetched (as Watson points out), paints a dire picture of nuclear weapons—"...the great globe itself/ Yea, all which it inherit, shall dissolve/And, like this insubstantial pageant faded/Leave not a rack behind" (98)—a future which we all can hope is much more fantastic than real.

P.D. James

James in her "Murder, 1986" (1970) demonstrates how enduring realistic aspects of human behavior and relationships and the detective process can be portrayed and explored powerfully within the context of science fiction elements of place and culture. A personal human tragedy as well as a societal morality play is enacted poignantly within the fantastic parameters of the human race's desperate struggle to survive an epidemic and to maintain its humanity. With tinges of Wells' separation of races in *The Time Machine*, "Murder, 1986" uses the fantastic as fertile ground in which to plant and raise intriguing and important questions about the possibilities and realities of human life.

Clarence Budington Kelland

Ironically, the touch of the fantastic in Kelland's "The Inconspicuous Man" (1951) is the man's utter non-fantastic-ness! The man and the tale are uncommon and fantastic by their utterly unique and inexplicable commonness. Whether he had "schooled himself until he projected the commonplace" or had "been endowed by nature in some freakish mood with that superlative inconspicuousness" (Kelland, 18), the completely unnoticeable man uses that fantastic quality to foster crime and protect criminals. He has somehow defied the "natural law that there shall be individuals, that every created thing shall be itself, distinct, recognizable" (29). Because of this violation of natural law, he is untouchable by human law, but not by detective Alpin Stone, who touches him firmly and painfully with individuality.

Gerald Kersh

"Dr. Ox Will Die at Midnight" (1937) is a remarkable story of an epic psychological battle of wills between a Dr. Pelikan, a psychiatrist, and a violent killer involving mind projection through space and time. The psychiatrist is able to enter into the killer's mind where he finds violence and terror—"The intellect of Dr. Pelikan found itself side by side with the mind of Papke the Ripper. And what I saw horrified me. I watched plan after plan rise to the surface of his amazingly cunning and tortuous mind, like bubbles in a cesspool" (Kersh, 39), but tragically projection of mind and will works both ways. Although the psychological premise in this tale is still in the realm of the fantastic, the battle between good and evil in the minds of men is an enduring reality regardless of how it is conducted.

J.S. Le Fanu

Although the title of Le Fanu's 1872 collection *In a Glass Darkly: The Posthumous Papers of the Occult Detective Dr. Martin Hesselius* refers to Hesselius as an "occult detective," in all but the first story he is more of a framer of the narratives of other people, none of whom is a detective. Even in that first famous story, "Green Tea" (1869), he is more of a consulting physician, though he does investigate the case of the Reverend Jennings from psychological, philosophical, and metaphysical perspectives. Though there isn't much actual "detection," there is considerable speculation with the help of Swedenborg's philosophy about the fantastic aspects of Jennings' obsession and mania—"When man's interior sight is opened, which is that of his spirit, then there appear the things of another life, which cannot possibly be made visible to the bodily sight" (Illes, 36).

The malignant monkey which haunts Jennings may be a hallucination caused by the ingestion of too much green tea, or perhaps the tea operated on the brain fluid, that fluid "being that which we have in common with spirits, a congestion found upon the masses of brain or nerve, connected with the interior sense, forms a surface unduly exposed, on which disembodied spirits may operate" (62). Whether a "surface unduly exposed" or "an inner eye inadvertently opened," Jennings is pursued and haunted by the fantastic beyond anyone else's understanding or imagining and perishes because of it. Hesselius believes he has discovered the cause and solved the mystery, but for Jennings it is too late, and despite the eloquent prose and the intriguing philosophizing, perhaps for detective story readers it is too little.

Arthur Machen

Machen's tales of the fantastic (see also Chapter Seven) are beautifully embedded in the prosaic, everyday reality of the London suburb, which he "dirties up" for the sake of contrast—its "mean limited life ... its utter banality and lack of significance" (Machen, 1922, p. ix). Within this mundane setting lies the fantastic jewel of spiritual and mental adventure—"He who adventures in London has a foretaste of infinity" (xi). Many of his stories are darkly ominous accounts of the remnants of a race of brutal ancients living side-by-side with (but unknown to) modern-day man—"The troglodyte and the lake-dweller, perhaps representative of yet darker races, may very probably be lurking in our midst, rubbing shoulders with frock-coated and finely-draped humanity, ravening like wolves at heart and boiling with the foul passions of the swamp and the black cave" (Machen, 1923, 239). It is clear that for Machen this unrecognized "rubbing of shoulders" with ancient savagery also represents the unacknowledged savage still inside us all, as many of his stories illustrate brutality bursting from beneath its civilized façade. In a series of these tales ("The Shining Pyramid," 1895, "The Red Hand," 1906, and "The Three Imposters," 1926), the frustrated man of literature, Dyson, assumes the role of the detective, following clues and logic to their often gruesome end. In both "The Red Hand" and "The Shining Pyramid," Dyson follows clues that lead him from the modern world of London to the lingering world of "some wreckage of a vanished race, a fragment of another world than ours" (263), which swallows up its victims with no remorse—"So she passed in the Pyramid of Fire, and then passed again to the underworld, to the place beneath the hills" (Parry, 156). Just as the fantastic for Machen lies "beneath the hills," so too it lies beneath the "normalcy" of consciousness and everyday existence.

A.E.W. Mason

"The Affair at the Semiramis Hotel" (1916) reads like a Mid-Summer Night's Eve romance where the everyday is dressed in finery, and reality sparkles in jewels. Before the "play" begins, Ricardo (Inspector Hanaud's "Watson") bemoans the everyday in its working clothes—"Life was altogether a disappointment; Fate, like an actress at a restaurant, had taken the wooden pestle in her hand and stirred all the sparkle out of the champagne" (Mason, 251)—but soon the story unfolds "as fabulous as any out of the Arabian Nights" (255). A dance with a mysterious stranger, a tale of theft intended but supplanted, a murder, a "brilliant bizarrerie" (265) of Mescal-heated dreams; from all this, waking "seemed to be coming out of the real world into a world of shifting illusion" (273)—it all is "a riot in the blood, a recapture of youth, a belief that just around the corner beyond the reach of the eyes, wonder waits for me" (270).

Hard fact—jewel theft and murder and detection—weaves its way among the romance, though even there, "the dream revealing what thought cannot recall" (p. 297) helps Hanaud reason out the crime and catch the criminal. The touch of the fantastic in this tale is like a sprinkling of fairy dust over the traditional detective story, reminding us that indeed the world "is no mere dust heap, but that, on the contrary it is a rendezvous of radiant forces forever engaged in turning dust into dreams, and mind into spirit" (La Gallienne in Higgins, 4). And what stronger justification for the detective tale being touched by the fantastic, and what more telling illustration of the power and beauty of the intersection of the two?

Helen McCloy

While "Through a Glass Darkly" (see above) is a dark, disturbing tale of a brilliant use of Freudian psychology to commit murder, "The Singing Diamonds" (1949) is a strange, fanciful story, which at first appears to be science fiction, but turns out to be about the psychology of "intoxication," the "consistent structuration of the external stimulus world" (McCloy, 52), and the power of suggestion. In a tour de force, McCloy not only provides a rational explanation for an apparently non-rational occurrence (a series of mysterious deaths of witnesses of flying saucers singing at incredible speeds through the sky), but she provides five explanations, all reasonable, but only one true ... and deadly.

Vincent McConnor

"The Man Who Collected Obits" (1967) is an ominous story of a man who makes a fantastic and horrifying discovery—that there is a pattern to each day's obituaries, that each day one last name is the chosen "death name" of the day. He turns detective "on the trail of a mass murderer ... the familiar monstrous hand moved through gray veils of cloud and opened the vast directory of the world. Gigantic fingers turned the vast pages. Each turning page sent a wave of freezing air down from the sky. Then the forefinger would sweep across the page and even from this distance Gerald could see that the printed name had been wiped out" (McConnor, 102 and 105). The fantastic bringer of death hangs heavy over the story and over Gerald and all the chosen, as he frantically tries to investigate and intervene, but in the end the fantastic is only too real for all of us.

Nicholas Olde

Although all of the detective tales in the *Incredible Adventures of Rowland Hern* (1928) are unusual and odd to say the least, some are haunted with a hint of the apparently supernatural or mystical, while others are tinged with a strange mixture of fancy and black humor. "Potter" (1928) is one of the latter, involving the search for an armadillo, an "Ichabod-Crane" zookeeper named Potter, a "grizzly" murder, possible reincarnation, and a vulture haunting. The vulterine appearance of Potter—"a lean, big-boned man with very high shoulders and bony, claw-like hands ... [a neck that was] unnaturally long and thin and red: his head unnaturally small and totally bald" (42) foreshadows the vulture's fantastic revenge and the mercy of the Angel of Death. In all these incredible tales of Olde, touches of the fanciful and the fantastic create very real mystery and peril which only the insight and logic of Hern can unravel and explain.

J.F. Peirce

"The Total Portrait" (1971) is a thought-provoking, psychological story about human personality and the masks we wear, about dualities in life, and about free will and determinism with reference and affinities to Stevenson's *Dr. Jekyll and Mr. Hyde* and Wilde's *The Picture of Dorian Gray*. There are many touches of the fantastic, including a Mephistophelean character who paints portraits that reveal hidden aspects of the self and the subject's inevitable future. As a detective story it has fantastic elements as well, for detective, murderer, and victim are all embodied in the same person!

Hugh Pentecost

Dr. John Smith, the psychiatrist detective, is featured in several novels but in only two short stories—"The Fourth Degree" (1945) and "Volcano in the Mind" (1948) in both of which the motives for the crimes and their explanations exist not in the material but in the psychological: "The motives for murder were to be found, not in bank balances or vaults, not in apparent jealousies or greed, but in the dark and inaccessible corridors of the mind" (Sullivan, 115). Dr. Smith, then, detects accordingly, looking not at physical evidence and natural law, but at the internal "fact" of the fantastic world of the psyche—"You accept the outward physical facts as unassailable, and you make the internal facts fit them. My approach is just the reverse. I believe the internal facts are unassailable" (122). In both stories, the physical facts point in one direction, but the psychological "reality" says otherwise; for Dr. Smith there are "no cigar butts or fingerprints or blunt instruments ... [just] the unconscious testimony of a disturbed mind" (Pentecost, 1945, 20). So even when the killer leaves no trace in physical reality, "he can't erase the clues to murder that are in his mind" (44), which is just where Dr. Smith seeks and finds them.

John Pierce

"Farewell Banquet" (1974) is a perfect example of how a story can stay true to completely logical, reasonable detection while spinning off into the wildest flights of fancy. What do the Alfoors of Poso, the Nufoors of Dutch New Guinea, the killing of Wild Bill Hickok, *La Boheme*, a passage from Epictetus, a "horny" midget, tabus (not taboos), and tubas have to do with an assassination attempt at the farewell banquet for a retiring Inspector? The wacky genius of this story is that the craziness mentioned above is not just peripheral window-dressing, but is actually at the heart of the mystery, at the core of the logical deductions. This story is a prime exhibit in the case that the detective story and the fantastic can not only co-exist but can be co-dependent—the fantastic providing the clues for the logic, and the detection supplying the reason to the fantasy.

Arthur Porges

Porges wrote several "impossible crime" stories, but "The English Village Mystery" (1964) is, though not strictly impossible, so ridiculous as to be as unlikely as any impossibility. Elsie Fyfe was stabbed with a knife; Pickett-Hall was slugged with a cricket ball; Jane Hope was strangled with a rope—murder couldn't possibly get any more absurd (or more poetic!), but Celery Green chose to intervene ... and then "stalked off" (Porges, 1964, 51).

Melville Davisson Post

Best known for his renowned fire-and-brimstone detective Uncle Abner, who has occasional encounters with what seems to be the supernatural, Post was also the creator of several other interesting detectives who were sometimes touched with elements of the fantastic. From the very beginning of "The Great Cipher" (1921) in which the detective M. Jonquelle solves "the finest example of code writing that was ever in the world" (Post, 1923, 27), the reader is bathed in an atmosphere of the fantastic—"It was a night of illusions. The whole world was unreal. There was a sort of fairy vista extending over the gardens. What was the mystery about his death? The current report at the time could not have been the truth. It was too fantastic. Nobody believed it. Nobody could have believed it" (1–2). And as the story of the archeological expedition in search of a lost civilization in the great wilderness of Central Africa and of the resulting death is slowly revealed, the fantastic intensifies, culminating in the appearance of bizarre creatures covered with "frozen and polished flesh, after the skin had been removed" (21), living in underground cites. Although there is reference to the predatory, underground race of H.G. Wells' *The Time Machine*, these creatures turn out to be perfectly natural and the solution to the cipher. Despite the acknowledged brilliance of Post's Uncle Abner stories, some critics have claimed "The Great Cipher" as their very favorite Post detective story—a gripping interweaving of the ominously fantastic with the detective story tradition of the "great cipher."

James Powell

Powell took the fantastic one step further in his many tales of San Sebastiano and its line of detectives, Ganelon I, II, III, and IV. Although his setting was based on Monaco, Powell didn't want to be constrained by that principality's factual history—"Inventing San Sebastiano freed me from the tyranny of facts," (Powell, 2009, 7), so he created an entire fictional history, a wild and crazy history at that. Although none of it violates natural law as we know it, the touch of the fantastic is more like an all-encompassing embrace as the weird becomes the norm and the incredible is commonplace.

A few of his Ganelon stories are or seem for a while to be "seriously" supernatural (see Chapter Seven), but most are fanciful where the traditional detection is surrounded by the almost slapstick. One of the great appeals of these stories is that the fantastic is presented in such a subtle and matter-of-fact way (almost as an afterthought) that it becomes our fact almost without our noticing. "Coins in the Frascati Fountain" (1970), the first San Sebastiano tale of Ganelon IV—the impoverished detective—teems with the quirky if not near-absurdity masked as normalcy: a Baron disillusioned by war dragging his canon all over Europe until he melts it down into "bronzed baby shoes to inspire proud parents with joyful memories" (174); a clock tower which on the stroke of various hours disgorges the Four Horsemen of the Apocalypse, the Seven Deadly Sins, the Nine Muses, the Twelve Apostles, and a "re-enactment of the Battle of the Cornichon when the army of San Sebastiano led by Guido Frascati threw back the Moors under Akbar the Cruel" (177); and the Happy Way, that almost-forgotten art of medieval self-defense based on re-distributing an opponent's body humors—blood, phlegm, choler, and black bile—to produce an instantaneous change in temperament ("with a hip lift and a deft twist of the wrist Ganelon could change a homicidal maniac into a simpering milquetoast or the most civil and obliging of men," 183). Not to be outdone, in "The Flower Diet" (2000) not only is there a man who wants to share the secret of living on the odor of flowers—"I am ready to lead you all through the sinus labyrinth and teach you the secret chemical formula so that you may all slay your Bull of Corpulence" (22)—but there is a unicorn, which has the power to purify a poison cup, a musical spider, an affair with Queen Victoria, and a vow of celibacy which is intended to father a line of "celibate detectives to fight crime as the Teutonic Knights of old battled the gods of the pagan forest" (18). In this elaborate and fabulous history of San Sebastiano, the extravagant and preposterous are the stage, but the action (the detections of the various Ganelons) is relatively straightforward and in line with the detective traditions (Ganelon I is an "armchair" sleuth *a la* The Old Man in the Corner, Ganelon II is Thorndyke-like in his scientific approach, Ganelon III is "hard-boiled," and Ganelon IV is impoverished). In this amazing saga of San Sebastiano and the Ganelons, the fanciful blends so seamlessly with the rational that the reader becomes a fascinated "citizen," following the unfolding of the crimes and the detection without a blink of disbelief, after all "Ganelon's faculty of ratiocination had been named a Treasure of the Principality, First Class" (Powell, 1972, 46).

And even when the setting of Powell's tales is the real world (e.g., San Marino), they are still touched with the fantastic as in "The Stollmeyer Sonnets" (1966) where Acting Sergeant Maynard Bullock of the Canadian Royal Mounted Police, defending himself from a "pistol disguised as a lighter disguised as a pistol" (Powell, 1966, 77) by brandishing a sandwich disguised as a pistol disguised as a sandwich, is called in to prevent an international dispute over stamps from escalating into a "philatelic Armageddon that could destroy them all and stamp collecting as we know it" (69). The "real world" as described in Powell's amazing stories will never be the same "real" again!

J.B. Priestley

Priestley, the renowned English novelist, brought a fanciful imagination and a droll wit to "An Arabian Night in Park Lane" (1947) as the magical unfolding of events at a pomp gala reception "took a queer turn and became an Arabian Nights entertainment" (Priestley, 45) of mad-cap, almost keystone-cop jewelry theft, cheap disguise, the mad hatter, and a walking Christmas tree. The pomposity—Charles William Edmund Alexander Gordon-Fitzstewart, the Most Honorable the Marquis of Gairloch, K.G., P.C., G.C-V.O.—and the insanity verge on the absurd as the fantastic blends with the outrageously real, and the reader has to agree with the detective that "I've had enough o' this high society" (51).

Harold and Jerome Prince

Dubbed "The Princes of Darkness" by Ellery Queen (*EQMM*, September 1950, 31) because of the dark psychology and haunting stream-of-consciousness narration in their first two stories of the detections of Inspector Magruder—"The Man in the Velvet Hat," 1944 (see Chapter Two) and "The Finger Man" (1945)—the Princes wrote only four short detective stories altogether, but these first two are among the finest examples of the integration of fantastic elements of Freudian psychology into the detective tale. Although Magruder is all logic, the telling of the tale drowns the step-by-step reasoning process with the surging ebb and flow of the unconscious expressed in the onrush of unending sentences:

> The room in motion, discords on the piano, Gallegher holding Robinson's head, the doctor elbowing his way through, stethoscope over the heart, eyelids bent back, Jane, saying, hushed, is he dead, the doctor, bending closely over the body, searching for a wound, Jane: is he dead, the doctor, looking up, puzzled, Gallegher, saying, he's not dead—but he must go to a hospital, the doctor, nodding, walking to the phone, Jane, following grabbing him by the arm, saying, then what's wrong with him—what's happened [Prince, 1945, 79].

The tale of the Finger Man is of the unconscious, of complexes, delusions of grandeur, death wishes, and dreams of omnipotence and power to compensate for the materialism and disillusionment of modern life—"The esoteric and the occult have always been the factual concomitants of strange places and alien shores; but the war has brought disenchantment: ancient Gods vanish and the medicine man wears a silk hat when the Marines land with the Coca-Cola and the Saturday Evening Post" (82). This is a gripping, breathless tale where the netherworld of the unconscious is finally brought to light by logic, and the torrent of the unconsciousness finally ends in a period and a harsh and final sentence.

Ellery Queen

Although a vocal critic of the fantastic in detective stories, Queen wasn't beyond using the *appearance* of the supernatural as a foil to a final, carefully reasoned solution (see Chapter Three for "The Lamp of God," praised by many critics as the finest detective novelette or long short story ever written). And although the early Queen stories are known for their "Challenge to the Reader" (overt or implied) followed by brilliant and fastidious, logical solutions, some of the best of these stories brought in a touch of the fanciful as counterpoint to the "severely" logical deductions. "The Mad Tea Party" (1934) is an ingenious and playful tale (as much as murder can be playful) surrounding the logical detection with Alice, the Mad Hatter, "shoes and ships and sealing wax" and "cabbages and kings" where what Alice (and Queen) found *Through the Looking Glass* feeds the logic and solves the crime.

Seabury Quinn

Although many of Quinn's stories of the occult detective Jules de Grandin involve actual supernatural events, quite a few others describe the fantastic experiments of "mad scientists" and bizarre psychological manifestations. De Grandin, "one of the foremost anatomists and physiologists of his generation, and a shining light in the University of Paris faculty, this restless, energetic little scientist had chosen criminology and occult investigation as a recreation from his vocational work" (Quinn, 2017a, 20). And in that first volume of his collected tales, stories with a touch of the fantastic include de Grandin combatting a murderous ape-like thing in evening dress ("The Horror on the Links," 1925), the handiwork of one of those very mad scientists, and a vengeful hypnosis leading to a burial alive ("The Vengeance of India," 1926).

In *The Complete Tales of Jules de Grandin*, Vol. 2, "The Druid's Shadow" (1930) is a powerful tale of racial memories lodged in the unconscious, which in earlier times people called demons and devils—"Long years ago when the scientific patter we mouth so learnedly today had not been thought of, men called such things which troubled them by short and ugly names. She-devils which seduced the souls and bodies of men they called succubi. Today we talk of repressed desires, of unconscious libido, but have we gotten further than to change our terminology?" (Quinn, 2017b, 421–422). Racial memories of druid sacrifice rise up to create havoc and almost murder, but de Grandin, psychologist as well as demon-slayer, uses psychological tools—probing the unconscious and hypnotism—to discover and vanquish the psychological demons. "The Brain Thief" (1930) is a story of East Indian revenge on Westerners through hypnotism—"The brain thief took complete possession of his consciousness and captured his will" (325), making him live an altogether different, and disreputable, life. De Grandin, sometime wielder of fantastic powers in his quest for justice ("He'd corrected maladjusted destinies as though by magic sometimes," 304), in this psychic "adjustment" demonstrates and acknowledges the reality of the fantastic—"It is fantastic, but I damn fear it is *so*, nonetheless" (312).

In *The Complete Tales of Jules de Grandin*, Vol. 3, there are several tales which feature fantastic psychological phenomena. In "The Lost Lady" (1931) Cambodian priests use sympathetic magic to torment victims who believe such magic is possible—"I have seen feet become useless, and seen eyes grow dim and blind. I sought to find some medical explanation and was told there was none. It was simply that some enemy was working sympathetic magic somewhere at a place unknown, and somewhere another poor unfortunate was undergoing excruciating torture that the hated one might also suffer" (Quinn, 2018a, 31). In this agonizing story, a victim is tortured from afar by the torturing of another who resembles the victim.

In "The Dead-Alive Mummy" (1935) in *The Complete Tales of Jules de Grandin*, Vol. 4, a thought of a priestess of Isis persists into the present to haunt a young woman almost into mummy-hood—"Thoughts are things, immortal things. Thought emanations, especially those produced by violent emotions, have a way of permeating physical objects and remaining in them as the odor of the flower lingers in the vase. That was the thought which moved her [the priestess of Isis] when she struck her so abominable bargain with the wizard Ana. And though her body died, the thought lived on" (Quinn, 2018b, 218). De Grandin treats the young woman's Freudian "complex"—"the series of emotionally accented ideas in a repressed state" (219) and allows the thought of the priestess to return to her mummified body and the life of the young woman to return to its own thoughts. In "Frozen Beauty" (1938) a woman is brought back to life after years frozen in a special coffin—"It is the most fantastic thing I ever heard! There's no doubt the freezing process has preserved her wonderfully, but to hope to bring her back to life, that's utterly absurd. When a person dies, he's dead, and I'd stake my reputation that's nothing but a lovely corpse in there" (421). But the fantastic doesn't faze de Grandin—"It was impossible, absurd, and utterly preposterous. Such a thing could not have happened, but there it was" (425). Whether supernatural, preposterous, inexplicable, mythological, or psychologically bizarre, the fantastic for de Grandin is his natural, his everyday reality.

Maurice Richardson

Sometimes a story seems to violate all natural law, not only of the real world but also of the fictional world—a sort of double "scoop" of the fantastic. "The Last Detective Story in the World" (1947), with a touch of the fantastic and a heavy dose of the absurd, pits a team of "good" including such famous fictional detectives as Sherlock Holmes, Father Brown, Lord Peter Wimsey, Hercule Poirot, and Ellery Queen against a gang of "evil" that crosses the fact-fiction line—"The Professor [Moriarty], with characteristic malevolence, is including figures of fact as well as fiction. Nay, more, with cynical disregard of all the rules, he is sweeping into his net the dregs of the supernatural" (Richardson, 63) all in pursuit of an atomic bomb, which "explodes" all realism, and thereby explains the title. With its "touch-of-the-fantastic" absurdity, this apocryphal tale doesn't do much to show that realism and the fantastic can coexist in an effective detective story, but it is great fun to see the real, the fictionally real, and the really ridiculous all "locked" in the same room!

M.P. Shiel

The Prince Zaleski stories (three originals in *Prince Zaleski*, 1895, then an encore sixty years later in *EQMM*, January 1955) are stunning examples of just what bizarre magic can happen in a detective story when meticulous, fastidious logic and deduction meet wild, hyperbolic, rococo setting, plot, and language. Ellery Queen in his introduction to "The S.S." (Queen, 1941, 66) calls these Zaleski stories "remarkable, also fantastic, epic, literary, mystical, scientific, and modern," and he raves about "The S.S."—"As a concept, it will take your breath away. As a fantasy, it can only be described as weirdly delightful. As a detective story, it offers—after almost fifty years!—still the most extraordinary motive for mass murder ever conceived." Although the characters, motives, and crimes in these stories are not outside the possible, they do seem to exist in a different universe where everything is intensified yet diffuse, where you are hyper-sensitive yet languid, where even the simplest object seems much larger than itself, connected to the relics and memories of eons past. The crimes, the conspirators, the setting, the events, even the language ooze fancy and fable and grandiosity beyond the commonplaces of everyday and every place. By whom are these hideous crimes committed—"by man, and for human motives, for the Angel of Death with flashing eye and flaming sword is himself long dead, by men hellish (or heavenly) in cunning, in resource, in strength and unity of purpose; men laughing to scorn the flimsy prophylatics of society, separated by an infinity of self-confidence and spiritual integrity from the ordinary easily-crushed criminal of our days" (Shiel, 1977, 85). And in the midst of this opium-hazed fantasy world, cloistered away in a remote castle, is the brilliant detective mind of Zaleski—"I regarded it as a vast tomb of Mausolus in which lay deep sepulchered how much genius, culture, brilliancy, power!" (4). In "The S.S." Zaleski reads a hieroglyphic code to solve the mystery of the suicide epidemic, and in "The Race of Orven" (1895) his logic diffuses "the sense of the supernatural" to solve a mad plot and a "mechanical" murder.

Shane Stevens

There is a delicious multiple layer of the fantastic in Stevens' "The Final Adventure" (1969), for in this story what "seems to have slight relation to the real world because of its strangeness or extravagance" (see Introduction) is a "blasphemous" and malevolent twist on the "real world" of Doyle's Holmes and Watson. Ellery Queen in his introduction to the story alludes to the "reality" of the Holmes fiction when he anticipates dire consequences for publishing this fantastic blaspheme—"Will we be expelled, ejected, excluded, driven out, dismissed, sent packing, ousted, bounced, ostracized, banished, exiled, excommunicated, and disinvestitured?" (Stevens, 99). Somehow, a murder plot involving the Giant Rat of Sumatra, the Great One and his Watson, and "So much for you and your vaunted powers, Mr. Consulting Detective" (104) is more fantastic (and disturbing) than any violation of natural law or the material world as we know it! But as Queen says, a touch of the fantastic arouses strong emotions and stimulates thoughtful musings, and so "We will bear the whips and scorns so that you may not be deprived of an opportunity to read of an enterprise of great pith and moment" (99).

T.S. Stribling

Ellery Queen's description of Stribling's story "The Mystery of the Chief of Police" (1945) as "one of the most unusual detective stories it has ever been your Editor's privilege to read" (*EQMM,* July 1945, 5) could just have accurately been directed to almost any of Stribling's stories of the psychologist/detective Dr. Henry Poggioli, which are not just unusual but are strange, eccentric, and audacious—fantastic not in the events that occur but in the outrageous criminal connections between them and murder. Whether it's a half-painted house, the eye of a hurricane, forced low prices for a haircut, and typical politicians ("The Mystery of the Half-Painted House," 1952), meteorological and tide charts, a burglar taking notes, sea shells, and an old man's asthma ("Count Jalacki Goes Fishing," 1946), a police department's lack of arrests, a numbers racket, and recovered loot ("The Mystery of the Chief of Police," 1945), or a cock fight, a kilometer marker, Aztec gods of fertility, and a buzzard plunging through a car window ("The Mystery of the 81st Kilometer Stone," 1947), the stories somehow connect ordinary phenomena with fantastic webs of ingenious criminality, which is then brought back to normalcy by Poggioli's insightful detection. It's not that these connections couldn't have happened, but believing they did takes more than a little willingness to believe that the fantastic can touch even the most commonplace of appearances and the most natural of events.

Mark Van Doren

"The Luminous Face" (1963), like a prose-poem glowing in the dark, reveals in the face of a murdered boy the inner world of the soul, even more striking and radiant by its contrast with the prosaic and sordid life of the body and the world that housed it; in the dead face was seen "the pale features on which peace sat as if it were a bird with no intention of flying away. As if were the boy's soul, determined not to leave the body yet ... a rapturous contentment with what the boy had seen, was seeing, when something or somebody killed him" (Van Doren, 86). In this marvelous contrast lies the beauty of the fantastic and the beauty of the rational, which are seen most clearly in juxtaposition with the other. The rational—the detective—in this story is opened by the soul in the dead boy's face to a vision of the universe "as a great curved mirror in which each act, each utterance, each idea is magnified forever ... the mirror a kind of mind, a kind of heart" (89). The boy's face, in death, brings a touch of the fantastic to the body ossified in time, to the mind limited by logic; and yet, it is that very logic and that frozen face that are the vessels of the spirit and of all that defies reason.

Manly Wade Wellman

Best known for his supernatural tales of John the Balladeer and Judge Pursuivant, Wellman also wrote a couple fanciful stories of Doyle's Sherlock Holmes and Professor Challenger working together to help foil the Martian invasion of Wells' *War of the Worlds*. In "The Adventure of the Martian Client" (1967) and "Venus, Mars, and Baker Street" (1972), both narrated by John Watson, Holmes and Watson do deduce that the invaders are not actually Martians but were merely based there, looking for some hospitable home, but other than that they don't contribute much detecting or repelling the invaders as Earth's bacteria adopt that role. However, in the process Holmes thwarts Colonel Moran's son's attempt to kill Watson and to give Earth the secret (from the invaders) of the nuclear bomb. Holmes destroys the information, realizing that humans are not yet ready for such power. It is an interesting twist to merge the fantastic of Prometheus and Wells with the "realistic" of Doyle, though Holmes and detection certainly fade by comparison with Challenger and adventure.

PART 3

The Truly Supernatural

In Part 1 we have seen how incorporating the fantastic or supernatural into a detective story as a straw man or red herring which is eventually debunked by logical detection (or, in the case of a detective, the logical methods beneath the charlatan façade are revealed) can add zest to the story without violating any of the traditional "norms," for the fantastic or supernatural is just a temporary hypothesis that may intrigue without threatening credibility.

In Part 2 it has been shown that a "touch of the fantastic"—detectives with a non-rational sense of evil; mysteries of the unconscious now accepted as "real" by contemporary psychology; archetypal or mythological underpinnings to physical events; or fanciful events that stretch plausibility—can also, if handled by talented authors in a way which respects the detective story tradition, add atmosphere and depth and mystique to the classic detective story. We have cited scores of examples of quality detective stories that have incorporated the fantastic in one or more of these ways—stories whose success relies, at least in part, on the presence of the fantastic.

But what about the "real" supernatural (the world of vampires, werewolves, ghosts, possession, thought-transference, reincarnation), not as a touch or a red herring but as an integral part of the plot and solution? Is this where the skeptics are right in claiming that the detective story and the fantastic are incompatible in assumptions, purposes, and outcomes, that these two "subgenres" are too different, too alien to each other to co-exist?

The detective was the supreme rationalist, grappling with a crime that seemed to violate the very laws of nature. If he failed to find a logical explanation, if only the supernatural would account for a murderer's ability to appear and disappear, or walk across snow without leaving footprints, then we would all be plunged back to a time of ghosts and witchcraft, a new Dark Age far more frightening than Russian spies and secret agents ... only powerful applications of "sittin' and thinkin'" can exorcise the demons and show the clockwork behind the miracles." Carr, 1981, vi.

Part 3—The Truly Supernatural

Can a detective story be successful if the ultimate solution *is* supernatural, if the "clockwork behind the miracles" is shown, itself, to be "miraculous" (i.e., supernatural)? In Part 3 we try to answer this question by examining, in Chapter Seven, detective stories where the sleuth experiences or investigates the "genuine" supernatural, and in Chapter Eight, where s(he) actively combats it. We see in our discussion that in many of these tales, the argument against the detective/supernatural mix has some validity, for so often when the supernatural is "real," the detection isn't—the "detective" does much more experiencing or combatting the supernatural events than actual detection. Often the investigation of the phenomena is in a very simplistic "what happened" sort of way without how's, who's, or why's. In many cases the "what" is so bizarre and frightening that it can easily overwhelm any detective aspects of the story, producing, perhaps, a satisfying supernatural experience but a less satisfying detective story.

Do we, then, discover any support for the claim that the supernatural solution and the detective story can successfully co-exist? Do we find any instances where a talented author has achieved a "fantastic" success by creating an effective and powerful supernatural detective story in which the detective and the supernatural elements enhance each other and create a memorable and satisfying whole?

Seven

The Supernatural
Experienced or Investigated

Before we examine in Chapter Eight by far the most prevalent type of supernatural detective story where the detective must combat a dangerous supernatural adversary, we first look at the occasional story where the detective experiences or investigates a benevolent supernatural entity or phenomenon, where the detective uses his skill to answer questions or to solve problems but not to vanquish a supernatural threat. Since these are not cases, then, where "Mysteries involving the supernatural seek to disarm the reader's [and the detective's] power of logical thought by arousing fear" (Murch, p. 13), the detective's usual arsenal of calm logic and deduction may still be able to function without impairment, so the supernatural and detection have at least a chance to comfortably co-exist.

Exemplars

C.B. Guilford

"Heaven Can Wait," 1953, is a little gem of a story with a profoundly supernatural premise but a meticulously worked out logic that abides by all the "natural" law within that premise. The supernatural is not only benevolent but helpful, so logic can and does function without impediment, and though the central premise is supernatural, the way it plays out conforms to the logic and conventions of the detective story.

Alexander Arlington has been murdered, but doesn't discover that until he meets Archangel Michael at the Pearly Gates. Being a popular author of detective stories, Arlington is adamant about wanting to discover "who dun it": "Here I am, the famous mystery author, who for twenty years asked and answered the question, 'Who did it?' and now—now!—I myself have been murdered and I don't know who did it!" (Herr and Wells, 1961, p. 98). He won't rest until he knows, so he strikes a deal with Michael to be able to return to Earth and re-live his last day, but though Michael can make some minor adjustments in the records, the major events are not subject to change.

The fictional world of his detective novels and the "real" world of his revisit to his life on Earth butt up against each other, for, unlike in his detective stories, now this author has to discover clues before the fact—"You see, in my books—and in real life, too—there are never any clues until *after* the murder. What am I going to do about that?" (p. 108). What he does is use the conventions of the detective story—the final gathering of the suspects—but now, of course, *before* the murder, not after it. Then the fictional world of his detective novels and the "real" world of his reconstructing the crime cleverly intersect again as Arlington plans to use this reconstruction as a plot for his next novel (for he plans to trick Michael and prevent the murder).

Despite all of Arlington's cleverness, however, the "natural law" of Heaven is followed meticulously as the murder occurs again, but in a final clever twist, it is Michael who shows himself to be the detective because in Heaven he has "picked up a few tricks here and there" (118) because of the company he has been keeping—"There's Edgar [Allan Poe] and Sir Arthur [Conan Doyle] and G.K.C. [G.K. Chesterton]. Certainly, Mr. Arlington. Didn't you know that all mystery writers go to Heaven?" (118). And now this mystery writer, Arlington, can rest easy and enjoy the comforts of Heaven, for he has solved his final case. Though the supernatural premise is fantastic, to say the least, we enthusiastically accept it, for the conventions of the detective story are meticulously followed and celebrated.

Margery Lawrence

All the tales of Miles Pennoyer in *Number Seven Queer Street* (1945) *and Masters of Shadows* (1959) are beautifully written explorations of the supernatural overlapping with the natural, of spirits coming into the material world seeking redemption or love or forgiveness, and of the living seeing the joys and beauties of the "world beyond the veil." Lawrence had herself been saved from a mental breakdown by a psychic healer and wrote a celebrated semi-autobiographical study of Spiritualism and the occult, *Ferry over Jordan* (1942), just a couple years before the publication of her first collection of tales of Pennoyer, the psychic investigator or "doctor of the soul." Although the emphasis in these stories is on Pennoyer's "doctoring" of the soul, in some of these tales he does some detecting, ferreting out cause and effect and significance, discovering solutions or at least outcomes with observation, logic, deduction, and compassion. All the stories are poignant and memorable in their delicate and literary portrayal of the intersecting and intertwining of the fantastic and everyday reality, but "The Case of the White Snake" (1945) is probably the most effective supernatural *detective* story, as Pennoyer, to foster the resolution of the spiritual problem and to solve the mystery of the phantom snake—"like a huge fire-hose, hanging from the half-open window to the ground below. It was even in the moonlight still palpable enough to look almost solid. It was alive, vital, palpitant, yet I knew that if I thrust my hand through it, I would feel nothing" (Lawrence, 2003, 114–115)—has to "detect" the psychological and material issues at their core—"for I knew now what it was, and felt awed, amazed, sensing the strength of the subconscious will, the love, and the longing that had sent it forth" (115).

Arthur Machen

"The Inmost Light" (1894) is the most supernatural and probably the most effective of all Machen's Dyson tales as a detective story and as a supernatural one as Dyson follows clues in investigating what he suspects is a murder, but what turns out to be a horrible psychic experiment with the soul and the body, and a "mercy killing" of "the brain of a devil not fit to stay in this world" (Machen, 1922, 269).

As in many of his tales, Machen sets the stage for the fantastic and the supernatural by vividly contrasting the material reality of everyday life ("the maids in slatternly print dresses washing door-steps, the fish-monger and the butcher on their rounds, and the tradesmen standing at the doors of their small shops, drooping for lack of trade and excitement," 264) with the hazy enchantment of the fantastic ("One evening in Autumn, when the deformities of London were veiled in faint blue mist, and its vistas and far-reaching streets seemed splendid," 247). And just as the mystique of romance can venture out from its hiding place within the ordinary, so can the soul emerge in all its glory from the body—"...and within it shone the blue of far skies, and the green of the sea by the shore, and the red of ruby, and deep violet rays, and in the middle of it all it seemed aflame as if a fountain of fire rose up, and fell, and rose up again with sparks like stars for drops" (281). Although this tale of the extraction of the soul is what Joshi in his study of Machen, Dunsany, Blackwood, M.R. James, Bierce, and Lovecraft (*The Weird Tale*) calls an illustration of the transition from "Machen's tales of horror to what might be termed his tales of awe and wonder" (26), it still, as in almost all of Machen's stories of Dyson's detections, contains both—the wonder and the horror of "realities" beyond and beneath the rational.

As with almost all the supernatural detective stories we examine, the awe and wonder and terror of the supernatural stands out in these Machen tales far above any detective story elements; yet, in this Machen story and in a few others described in Part 3 the detection is not completely overwhelmed, for through the fantastic weaves carefully placed clues and logical and reasonable deductions and conclusions that readers can follow and appreciate. For Machen, perhaps partly because of this "grounding in the rational," which helps these stories work as detective stories, his fiction was sometimes criticized for its "tameness"—"His horror, we regret to say, leaves us quite cold … and our flesh obstinately refuses to creep" (Machen, 1922, vii). It's easy to see, then, the challenges inherent in trying to write supernatural detective stories—claims of "hocus-pocus" from detective story traditionalists and moanings of "non-creeping flesh" from supernatural story enthusiasts. However most readers admire Machen for his effective blending of these two genres, though certainly his achievements are far greater in the supernatural realm than in that of the detective story.

Victor Rousseau

Appearing only a year after Blackwood's groundbreaking supernatural detective stories of John Silence in 1908 (see Chapter Eight), Rousseau's tales, much later collected in *The Surgeon of Souls* (2006), recount the "remarkable achievements of Ivan Brodsky, physician, whose investigations into psychic phenomena enabled him to cure spiritual diseases and to exorcise evil spirits from the bodies of their victims" (17). "The Case of the Jailer's Daughter" (1910) and the other tales in that collection combine a bit of "the Blackwood" in their mood and atmosphere and in their philosophical ponderings of the spirit and its incarnations with the additional appeal of the unfolding story of Brodsky and his investigations and experiments in the supernatural. Brodsky is a detective but also a psychologist, physician, and healer, supplementing the traditional detective methods of observation, logic, and deduction with psychological and spiritual methods such as hypnosis, dream analysis, exorcism, and séance.

Other Stories

H.C. Bailey

It is probably a surprise to find Bailey's down-to-earth detective Reggie Fortune involved in a supernatural case, but in "The Rock Garden" (1931) Fortune encounters a benevolent ghost from a generation past, rapping, sighing and crying out to try to save a descendant and his family. The ever-pragmatic Fortune, when asked if it was a ghost, hedges—"I don't know what a ghost is. Somebody, something not in our world, saw another Briggs and his wife getting into trouble in this place, same like they did. And tried to save you" (Bailey, 160). When the skeptical Briggs claims it was all fancy, Fortune gives credence to the fantastic while at the same time avowing his "loyalty" to the rational—"[Fancy?] No. No. I shouldn't say that. I always believe evidence" (160).

Helena Blavatsky

Famous occultist and founder of Theosophy, Blavatsky wrote several occult-themed stories collected in *Nightmare Tales* (1892). Probably her best-known story, "The Cave of Echoes" (1873), presumably based on true events, involves a mysterious and unnamed Hungarian traveler encountering a shaman who uses drums, chants, trances, levitation, and transmutation to reveal and punish a murderer. Although Blavatsky claims the story is based on an eye-witness account and police records, she does concede that the eye-witness, himself, attributes the events partly to "divine interference and partly to the Evil One" (Illes, 66). Whichever, or both, the fantastic is in the eye of the beholder.

Robert Chambers

Although best known for his romantic novels and "yellow" tales of the macabre (e.g., *The King in Yellow*, *The Slayer of Souls*, and *The Maker of Moons*), Chambers did write some sentimental short stories (appearing as chapters in *The Tracer of Lost Persons*, 1907) that involved the supernatural in a romantic role. In "Solomon's Seal" (1906) and "Sameris" (1906) the power of love transcends time and space as the detective—the "Tracer of Lost Persons," Westrel Keen—is able to unite a man with a woman he knows to be dead, who was entombed for thousands of years ("Sameris"), and to help a man find a ghost woman of his visions ("Solomon's Seal")—"Oh, I don't mean one of those fabled sheeted creatures that float about at night; I mean a phantom, a real phantom, in the sunlight standing before my very eyes in broad day!" (86). This "apparition of her own subconscious self" (91) is finally located in the material world with the help of Keen and a cipher involving Solomon's Seal. In these sentimental tales, the supernatural plays a huge role, but the natural triumphs as the most fantastic force of all turns out to be human love.

Agatha Christie

Christie is best known, of course, for her "straight" detective stories of Hercule Poirot and Miss Marple and her parody/pastiches featuring Tommy and Tuppence Beresford, but even in some of those stories she brings in elements of the fantastic. In "The Strange Case of Sir Arthur Carmichael" (1933), featuring none of these detectives, the fantastic ventures into the supernatural, as Dr. Edward Carstairs, serving as narrator and detective, encounters "phenomena that are absolutely unexplainable from the ordinary materialistic standpoint" (Christie, 2003, p. 235), including the meowing of the dead cat and the return of the spirit of the murdered Carmichael to his body. In this case, the supernatural serves justice as the murderer is overwhelmed by the dead cat and the specter of the human victim.

Bruno Fischer

In "The Man Who Lost His Head" (1945) the detective Jim Crane literally loses his head (which is quite shocking to those who see him walking around!) but refuses to stay dead until he solves and avenges his own murder. Though there is more coincidence and fortuitous circumstance than actual detection, the fantastic premise is memorable and brings to mind (to those who still have one) T.S. Stribling's classic story, "Passage to Benares" (see Chapter Nine).

Arabella Kenealy

Some Experiences of Lord Syfret (1896) included in *Supernatural Detectives 3* (2011) is a touching collection of stories about Lord Syfret who, though called a "supernatural detective," is not so much a detective as an observer of the fantastic oddities of life, a man whose curiosity is the only thing that keeps him from the ultimate boredom and suicide. "An Expiation" (1896) is a poignant tale of a tragic murder and its expiation through an innocent infant, an expiation that takes the infant's life and seems to illustrate Syfret's psychic theory—"Death is but a change of identity. Entities in the school of evolution pass through myriad lives in training for eternity, and the ill acts of one existence may not find expiation until a later one" (293).

Margery Lawrence

"The Case of the Haunted Cathedral" (1945) is one of several moving, eloquent tales of Miles Pennoyer, psychic doctor and investigator of the occult, collected in *Number Seven Queer Street* (1945). In some of these stories, Pennoyer actively combats a malignant, haunting presence (see Chapter Eight), but in most of these tales the supernatural is as haunted as haunting—a spirit trying to atone for a crime or to overcome mistreatment in life to find peace. "The Case of the Haunted Cathedral" is a sentimental story of murder, superstition, and guilt, and two ghosts in a cathedral, one seeking forgiveness, the other able to give it. "The Case of Ella McLeod" (1945) is an equally moving tale of a poorly treated Scottish maid flashing back to a past life with the Greek gods when the world was free—"I had caught that look in her eyes that is only shown by those touched by the Finger of the Dark Fool, the Amadan Dhu. She saw back into a past lit with sunshine and freedom and laughter, back into the days when the world was young and happy; the days before the leprosy of cities and civilizations had crept like a spreading sore over the green lands, before love had become twisted so that one could not know it from sin" (Lawrence, 2003, 79). In the end, the call of the past is too strong to resist, and though Pennoyer does little detecting, he is vital to the outcome.

In all these Pennoyer stories, his psychic gift is a blessing and a curse, as the emotions are raw and powerful, and he is intensely aware of both sides of the "curtain"—"One who sees through the ugly, foolish things of every day, the pitiful, shameful side of humanity, through to the further side, where the good, the beautiful, and the true shine forth as an abiding vision" (63). At times he, and we, are almost overwhelmed by the energy and the emotion, as the fantastic intrudes on the "real," and spirits seek to redeem troubled lives. Though the "detection" is limited mostly to observation and some deduction, and the "puzzles" find their own solutions with only a little help from Pennoyer, the stories themselves ask larger questions and pose greater mysteries and ask us to find the place for the fantastic in our lives.

Seabury Quinn

Amidst all the Jules de Grandin stories where he combats dangerous supernatural entities (see Chapter Eight) are a few touching tales where the supernatural is heroic and the tone is romantic and uplifting. In *The Complete Tales of Jules de Grandin, vol. 3* (2018), "The Ghost Helper" (1931) is just such a moving and comforting tale, where de Grandin aids a woman's ghost to get justice and to recover lost love—"Women, children, and dogs know their friends instinctively. So, it would seem, do disembodied spirits. When Madame Marjorie sought one on this earthly plain to help her in her work, whom should she choose but Jules de Grandin. In times gone past he has been known as a ghost-breaker. These last few nights, he has essayed a new role, that of ghost-helper" (52).

Victor Rousseau

Following the introduction of Ivan Brodsky in "The Case of the Jailer's Daughter," in story after story in *The Surgeon of Souls* (2006) Brodsky tries to bring "scientific credibility" to the long-celebrated spiritual knowledge of "the oracle of the Greeks, the Roman Sibyl, the Indian Shahman, or the witch of Endor" (33) as he weaves together the rationality of the detective with the speculation of the philosopher:

> The universe is a palpitating, crowding mass of soul stuff, most of it discarnate, a small part exteriorized in various highly heterogeneous physical forms. Whether this elemental being [a poltergeist] has already gone through the millions of progressive incarnations between the unicellular organism and man, and now is waiting for its first appearance in human shape ... or whether it is simply a leakage from the universal soul stuff, I am not prepared to say.... I should like to make a personal investigation of this matter, for it might put me on the track of a discovery" [72–73].

Whether dealing with a poltergeist ("The Major's Menagerie," 1927), the revivification of an Egyptian mummy ("Homo Homunculus," 1911), the transformation of a wax figure into flesh and blood ("The Fetish of the Waxworks," 1927), or ghosts ("The Woman with the Crooked Nose," 1910), he keeps an open mind, sifts evidence, constantly questions, and tests hypotheses—"if I were in the habit of forming hypotheses without a basis of satisfactory evidence, I should never have learned what little I know about these things" (76). As in even the best of the occult detective stories, Brodsky's detections are more metaphysical than physical, and the mysteries encountered and "solutions" offered are more philosophical than material, so they may, ultimately, be unsatisfactory to the traditional detective story aficionado, though moving and intriguing to readers willing to see "mystery," "crime," and "detection" in a bit broader light.

The saga of Brodsky ends (in "The Ultimate Problem," 1927) with the momentous results of his detections and the ultimate adventure in reason and spirit, though both are perhaps too much for the world as we know it—"Many as were the evils which Brodsky cured during the brief period of our association, the world is better off without this knowledge of his. The risks were too many," (Rousseau, 2006, 169). And yet it appears at the end of the story that this world may get a second chance.

Allan Upward

The several tales of Jack Hargreaves, who tries to clear up "hauntings" so he can make a good profit by selling "haunted" houses he bought cheap, involve him and his "Watson" Alwyne (who is psychic) in encounters with mysteriously dripping blood, spirit tapping, and ghostly presences, but probably the most effective story is "The Haunted Woman" (1905) in which the vision of a corpse, wrapped in linen for the grave, appears in bed beside her stepmother, then rapidly disintegrates. Although there is some "mild" detection on the part of Hargreaves and Alwyne to determine the reasons for the vision, the revealing of the murder is not the result of detection, but of confession, so these Upward stories have very little to offer the fan of detective stories, and, despite some moments of tension and interest, are rather standard and ordinary fare for supernatural tales with a little gentle ribbing thrown in.

Eight

The Supernatural Combatted

Though "the ghost hunter has been an important figure in supernatural fiction for a good many years" (Haining, 9), it may be a stretch to say that "some of the best known of these occult investigators have been bracketed with such illustrious sleuths as the great Sherlock Holmes" (9). We see in this section that, although there are many entertaining, often gripping, stories of "supernatural detectives," in most of them the "detective" doesn't do much detecting other than some research on the history of the place or the people and usually a visit to the "haunting." There are certainly dangers—physical, mental, emotional—but usually more peril to combat than problem to solve, more cameras, pentacles, chants, and holy water than analysis of clues and logical deduction, more dread and mystique than puzzle and mystery. There are many effective tales of the supernatural evoked, engaged, and defeated, but only a few where the classic detective story is successfully commingled with the occult, where reason and the supernatural harmoniously coexist.

Exemplars

Algernon Blackwood

Blackwood's stories in *The Complete John Silence* (1997)—the five stories found in the original *John Silence, Physician Extraordinary* (1908) and "A Victim of Higher Space," first published in *Occult Review*, 1914, then collected in *Day and Night Stories* (1917)—are prime examples of the successful integration of the detective and the supernatural. They are beautifully and evocatively written, the detective uses reason and logic to accompany his psychic talents and sensitivity, and the supernatural energies and entities are more easily comprehended (and more haunting and terrifying) because we're not sure whether they are actually supernatural or are "natural" to the psyche—they seem to exist at least as much in the mind as in the world. John Silence, himself, claims, "I have yet to come across a problem that is not natural, and has not a natural explanation. It's merely a matter of how much one knows—and admits" (Blackwood, 1997, 102). S.T. Joshi, in his Introduction to *The Complete John Silence*, interprets this to mean that "the seemingly supernatural can really be encompassed within the realm of a kind of higher rationality that takes both spiritual and physical phenomena into account. Blackwood is trying to retain the mystery of an awesome universe while at the same time remaining within the domain of human reason" (p. vii). Although Joshi finds this attempt to "live in both worlds" problematic and at times flawed—"The know-it-all Silence obtrudes, usually at the end, with a prosy explanation of the phenomena, introducing a fatal element of rationalism into something that should not be rationalized. Several magnificent tales are nearly ruined by this procedure" (Joshi, 1990, 115)—others find the stories enhanced by this effective blending of the fantastic and the realistic, as we are led to accept the most fantastic improbabilities as natural and to perceive the most natural events as magical. Fire-elementals, werewolves, clairvoyance and possession, reincarnation and transmutation, the lingering traces of emotion on physical objects, drifting through the portals into the "higher space" where all known dimensions are connected—all are handled so delicately and eloquently and with such exquisite attention to their psychological sources and impacts that they do seem to become part of a "higher rationality"—magical, fantastic, haunting, yet somehow reasonable and vividly real. Silence (a perfect name for this physician of the "natural supernatural") is never amazed, just intrigued, for he always has a sensible interpretation and a rational explanation that at least partly normalizes the esoteric and naturalizes the arcane. We accept the premises and follow Silence as he tries to save a soul and unravel the mysteries, using knowledge, research, and logic with very little of the occult detective's usual arsenal of sacred pentacles and holy water.

Although in "Ancient Sorceries" we are left in doubt as to whether the miraculous events actually occurred in fact or just in the protagonist's mind (see Chapter Nine), in several of the other Silence stories, Blackwood balances on the fine line between the fantastic and the rational, seeming to venture into both realms at the same time, so that the fantastic happens but in a strangely rational sort of way.

"A Victim of Higher Space" (1914) is in some ways Blackwood's

145

most fantastic story, but, at the same time it resonates with the fastidious details of believability—as with so many of the other John Silence detective stories, it somehow seems to exist on both planes at once or in rapid succession as a man fades in and out of material existence:

> First he [John Silence] saw a thin perpendicular line tracing itself from just above the height of the clock and continuing downwards till it reached the wooly fire-mat. This line grew wider, broadened, grew solid. It was no shadow; it was something substantial. It defined itself more and more. Then, like someone moving out of deep shadow into light, he saw the figure of a man come sliding sideways into view, a whitish face following the eye, and the perpendicular line he had first observed broadening out and developing into the complete figure of a human being [Illes, 233].

This man, who has come to Silence for help, has become a victim of "Higher Space," which, although defined by Silence as a "spiritual condition" and a "mythical state," is very real for the man, who repeatedly disappears into its endless dimensions when music or color or certain thoughts suddenly throw him into "an intense and terrific inner vibration" (240) where he sees everything in its "weird entirety"—the "essence" behind the physical form. This all seems utterly fantastic, and yet Blackwood, citing various philosophers and metaphysicians, leads us to begin to share Silence's conviction that having "himself advanced sufficiently far among the legitimate paths of spiritual and psychic transformations [he came] to realize the visions of this extraordinary little person had a basis of truth in their origin" (242). The scene where Silence hangs on desperately to the man's leg as he begins to fade into Higher Space challenges the most fundamental assumptions and beliefs of most of us yet is deeply moving in its reality. Again, as in all these John Silence stories, the calm and fastidious detail of event, reaction, and consequence somehow bring plausibility to the bizarre, and Silence's steadfast and matter-or-fact detection and logical deduction bring reason and sense to the incredible and the incredulous.

Lee Killough

Despite its beginning with a murder from the point of view of the victim, "The Existential Man" (1982) seems at first to be a conventional story of a murder investigation by a competent and meticulous cop looking at every clue and following every lead. It slowly becomes something else altogether, however, as the cop and the victim turn out to have a surprising and supernatural relationship. In a dramatic and effective reversal of the stories explored in Part 1, where the apparently fantastic is revealed to be completely natural, in this haunting tale the apparently natural turns out to be anything but—an unconventional and memorable intersection of the supernatural and the harsh realities of crime and detection.

Manly Wade Wellman

Wellman's most enchanting and memorable confronter of the supernatural appeared in the novels and short stories of John the Balladeer, written between 1951 and 1987, the short stories being collected in *John the Balladeer* (1988)—"these stories are chilling and enchanting, magical and down-to-earth, full of wonder and humanity. John is one of the most significant characters in all of fantasy literature" (Wagner Introduction, Wellman, 1988, 7–8). Although John isn't a traditional detective by any means, he wanders through the Southern Appalachians encountering and sometimes actively seeking supernatural evil and using his wits, his music, his knowledge, and his reason to solve fantastic mysteries and dispel evil spells and charms. Balancing the weirdly fantastic—strange beasts like the Bammat, and the Flat, and the Skim, and the Culverin, and the Behinder (in "The Desrick on Yandro," 1952), and witches, ghosts, hoodoo men, familiars, and giants—is the vivid, realistic portrayal of Appalachian backwoods life, its folklore, and its music. As fantastic as are the characters and events, the stories make them seem as real as the valleys and ridges of the mountains and the cabins and daily life of the people. The "John the Balladeer" saga illustrates a powerful and effective blending of the supernatural with the natural, of the fantastic with the rational, if not strictly with the detective, though John is armed with nothing more than intimate knowledge of the terrain (physical and occult), careful observation, courage, logic, a sense for evil, and the power of his music.

Other Stories

Alice and Claude Askew

Although there are some parallels between Aylmer Vance and his assistant and Sherlock Holmes and Watson ("The two investigators

[Vance and Dexter] approach the world of the supernatural in the same fearless and enquiring spirit in which Conan Doyle's heroes [Holmes and Watson] approach the world of crime," Askew, back cover), the blurb goes on to concede that "the parallel is not exact ... [in that] Vance for the most part does not 'solve' mysteries in the way that Holmes does." Although Vance is classified by many anthologists as an "occult detective" (Illes) or a "supernatural detective" (Tyler), the fact that the title of this Askew collection is *Aylmer Vance: Ghost-Seer*, not "Ghost-Detective," is significant, though the term "detective" is used to refer to Vance several times in the text.

These Aylmer stories are illustrative of both the value of integrating the detective and the supernatural and its difficulties and limitations, for though many of the tales are powerful and moving and do involve Vance and Dexter in investigating mysteries and crimes, the investigation is less "detection" than experiencing, and the mysteries and crimes are more psychological, philosophical, and psychic than physical and material—"Do you yearn to discover the secret of the universe—to know more than is good for man to know?" (Askew, 7). Vance and his investigations are given more plausibility and more grounding in traditional detection by the initial caveat, typical of many authors of supernatural detective stories—"I have been the means of detecting several instances of fraud and imposition on the part of so-called 'mediums,' also of proving that natural causes are often responsible for the 'haunting' that is supposed to go on in various houses" (8)—however, the stories in the collection are set apart, for they are cases in which Vance is forced to admit that he has been absolutely baffled, unable to account for what he has seen and heard. Some of these stories are experiences merely observed by Vance (e.g., the demoniacal possession of a young wife by an ancient princess—"The Invader," 1914; the seduction of a young girl by an ancient god—"The Stranger," 1914; a haunting by disembodied fear—"The Fear," 1914), but in several of the tales he actively investigates and solves the mystery, though not always with positive outcomes for the protagonists. "The Fire Unquenchable" (1914) is probably the most intriguing story and the one where Vance's "detection" most nearly approaches the traditional methods of observation and deduction, but even here the main appeal is in the psychic phenomena, though the authors try to "ground" Vance in the detective tradition by connecting the supernatural with the natural—"I hope that we may do good work together, work for the furtherance of human knowledge in the little-known paths of what we now call the super-physical, but which may prove to be the normal and the natural after all" (52). These "fantastic" phenomena may eventually be shown to conform to "natural" law, but for now, they remain "fantastic" and these stories of their "detection," though powerful and appealing, don't entirely succeed as detective stories.

Algernon Blackwood

Blackwood's John Silence stories are wonderful examples of the effective integration of the fantastic and the detective tale, for the fantastic events are often given both supernatural and natural (usually psychological) explanations, which seems to make them more amenable to more traditional detection—"Matters that seemed almost too curious and fantastic for belief he loved to trace to their hidden source" (Blackwood, 1997, 44). For example in "The Camp of the Dog" (1908) the howling "werewolf" is explained as the psychological projection of the man's intense passion—"to bathe in the very heart's blood of the one desired" (213). In "Secret Worship" (1908) a man returns for a visit to the religious school where he spent his youth—a return that results in his "imprisonment," spiritual torment, and almost death (Silence barely rescues him)—but in the end it seems to be a dream, for the school has been abandoned and in ruins for decades:

> But how is it possible? How can it be possible? When I came in here, I saw the building in the moonlight. They opened the door. I saw the figures and heard the voices and touched, yes touched their very hands, and saw their damned black faces [cowled in black], saw them far more plainly than I see you now. Was I so utterly deluded? [168].

Silence explains the man's "delusion" by describing the place as "one of the most haunted—and most terribly haunted—spots of the whole world" (168) where devil-worship closed the school decades earlier. But he goes on to validate the "reality" of the man's dangerous experience by explaining his last-minute rescue—"I saw and heard everything. My plan first was to wait till the end and then to take steps for their destruction, but in the interest of your personal safety, in the interest of the safety of your soul, I made my presence known when I did, and before the conclusion had been reached" (170). The man then realizes, to his horror, that the danger was no dream but was real and the priests were actually alive. But then, the story swings to the supernatural side again as Silence explains that they were just the shells of violent men, "spiritually developed but evil men, seeking after death—the death of the body—to prolong their vile and unnatural existence" (170). The experience and the story seem to occur in an uncertain place where fantastic events have real consequences and reality fades in and out of dream. In "A Psychical Invasion" (1908) the forces of human psychology and the supernatural intertwine effortlessly and again leave us a bit uncertain of their true nature—"At the death of a human being, its forces may still persist and continue to act in a blind, unconscious fashion. As a rule they speedily dissipate themselves, but in the case of a powerful personality they may last a long time. And, in some cases, these forces may coalesce with certain non-human entities who thus continue their life indefinitely and increase their strength to an unbelievable degree. If the original personality was evil, the beings attracted to the left over forces will also be evil" (20).

Despite Blackwood's talents at integrating the fantastic with detective fiction, his Jim Shorthouse stories are nowhere near as successful as his famous stories of John Silence. The supernatural horror—ghostly traces of murder, possession, evil presences, the black arts—is sufficiently malignant and disturbing (especially in "A Case of Eavesdropping," 1900, and "With Intent to Steal," 1906, in which "the shell they left hanging from the rafters in the barn in no way impeded the man's spirit from continuing his dreadful work under new conditions," 1906, 161), but although Shorthouse is referred to as an "occult detective," this is really in name only, as there is much more encountering and combatting than detecting. Blackwood undoubtedly realized this, as there are only four Shorthouse stories (all in *The Empty House and Other Stories*), but it was only two years later that he brought detection and the supernatural together so effectively in *John Silence, Physician Extraordinary*.

Joseph Brennan

Although some of Brennan's stories of the psychic investigator and private detective Lucius Leffing are "straight" detective stories, he frequently combines the detective and supernatural genres, often to great effect. Long, in his forward to the Brennan collection *Chronicles of Lucius Leffing* (1977) is enthusiastic in his praise—"Never to have met Lucius Leffing is to have missed a literary acquaintanceship of rare quality in the realm of both fantasy and mystery fiction" (9). The only two stories (of eight) that have supernatural elements in that collection are "The Dead of Winter Apparition" (1975) and "The Nightmare Face" (1975) both of which involve hideous apparitions of the dead haunting the living—"As we watched on, the swirling shape coalesced until there gradually grew visible the monstrous caricature of something which might once have been human—a ghastly, hunched, spindly-limbed thing with the mockery of a face which expressed such hatred, rage, and suffering as I hope to never witness again" (208).

In the later collection *The Adventures of Lucius Leffing* (1990) a much greater number of the stories combine the supernatural with detection, often involving spirit forms of haunted souls of the long-dead, mistreated in life, or telepathic projections of the living, seeking revenge or manifesting the horror of their tormented lives, or the tortured souls of evil lives perpetuating their wickedness in evil spirits. In "Death on 91" (1990) it is an old man manifesting an image of his long-lost childhood house, which wreaks havoc on the highway; in "The Spruce Valley Monster" (1990) it is the ominous spirit of a mad killer hanged years before; and in "The Haunting at Juniper Hill" (1985) it is the evil ghost of a malicious old woman who beat children to death. In many of the cases, a rational explanation is offered first, but both Leffing and the reader are pleased when it turns out that only the fantastic will suffice—"Your theory may be the correct one, but if so, I might as well admit I will be disappointed. It would all be so—mundane" (150). These Leffing stories don't always work as both detective stories and supernatural ones, but they often do, and even those that don't at least can't be accused of being mundane.

Gelett Burgess

Combining the supernatural with comedy (or farce) is not an easy thing to do and is not accomplished often (see Conan Doyle in Chapter Two for a successful example). Burgess had fun with the charlatan detective, Astro, in *The Master of Mysteries* (see Chapter Four), but he launches an all-out satirical attack on the eagerness of some people to believe in the supernatural and on the Society for Psychical Research in his three stories about Enoch Garrish, who writes ponderous tomes for that Society on such topics as "The Customs and Costumes of Ardent Spirits," "Materialization and Dematerialization of Inanimate Objects," and "Levitation and Semi-Nudity in Dream." In "The Levitant"

(1901)—"How One Gerrish Had an Adventure Quite Nightmare-ish, and Feared That He Would Surely Perish" (Prasil, 57)—he is led on a wild ride in his bed on city streets by a specter; while in "The Spectre House" (1899) his house vanishes and rematerializing around him, and in "The Ghost Extinguisher" (1905) his inventions to trap and extinguish ghosts are not entirely successful as hosts of spirits pursued him with "fatuous fury" (83). These fantastically funny stories are heavy on the spooky satire but light on any real detection.

A.M. Burrage

Many of the stories in *The Occult Files of Francis Chard* (1996) involve that detective of the occult in conflict with dangerous supernatural entities (a spirit compelled to haunt the scene of its crime in "The Pit in the Garden," 1927, an evil spirit accidentally summoned in a séance in "The Affair at Penbillo," 1927, the ghost of a bloody soldier in "The Soldier," 1927, the ghost of a woman murdered by her husband in "The Woman with Three Eyes," 1927), but the aura of the fantastic is tempered somewhat by the skeptical comment of one of the characters that ninety-five percent of what passes for witchcraft and the supernatural is sheer humbug. Of course these cases in the "occult files" are the other five percent.

Burrage also wrote two stories ("The House of Treburyan," 1920, and "The Severed Head," 1920) of the occult detective, Derek Scarpe. In both, Scarpe manages to figure out why ghosts are haunting the living ("When those who have crossed over return to this world, it is generally because some mundane matter is troubling them," Prasil, 261) by doing some research into family history and house architecture and thereby discovering the "mundane matter" and "readjusting things so they can rest in peace" (246). In "The Severed Head," Scarpe discovers that the spirit of a beheaded woman is trying to protect her living husband from attacks—perhaps not exactly a "mundane matter" but one that Scarpe helps her resolve so she can return to the spirit world. These two stories are not particularly memorable, but they are straightforward examples of the "easy" mixture of simple detection and the mildly supernatural.

Lin Carter

Carter's pulp stories of the occult investigator Anton Zarnak were so popular that several authors wrote sequels (e.g., C.J. Henderson, John

French, and Robert Price). Zarnak—"Cultist, perhaps, but charlatan, no" (Carter, 47)—was a brilliant scientist led to pursue occult monsters by the slaying of his wife and baby by a werewolf. In "Dead of Night" (1988) Zarnak uses his extensive knowledge of the occult, incantations, and a "wand of light" to drive away the murderous "underlying emptiness and Silence of Old Night" (115); in "Perchance to Dream" (1988) he destroys an idol from outer space and stops its thought waves from impregnating the living; and in "Curse of the Black Pharaoh" (1989) he manages to counter ancient evil that accompanies the opening of a vile Pharaoh's tomb (18). Zarnak demonstrates a certain amount of detection using his sensitivity to psychic residues, but most of Zarnak is action using both supernatural and physical weapons.

Arthur Conan Doyle

Conan Doyle appears in a surprising number of these chapters, for in addition to the few Sherlock Holmes stories with elements of the fantastic, he wrote several stories which featured the "straight" supernatural. "The Brown Hand" (1899) is a slight but interesting story of a ghost who can't rest until he recovers his missing hand, for "In the case of earth-bound spirits, some one dominant idea obsessing them at the hour of their death is sufficient to hold them in this material world" (Rennison, 115). Only after Dr. Hardacre investigates the ghost and his reasons for ghosting and is able to supply a substitute hand is the spirit able to finally rest.

Dion Fortune

It is difficult to imagine more fantastic detective stories, stories further removed from the rational, than Dion Fortune's tales of the occult investigator/physician Dr. Tavener, whose cases in *The Secrets of Dr. Tavener* (1926) run the supernatural gamut—vampirism, reincarnation, astral bodies, etheric doubles, theft of occult rituals, access of past lives in the Akashic Records through hypnotism and crystal-gazing, gems with consciousness and intention, terror by thought-transference and thought-projection, and shared dreams. Ironically, Fortune (the renowned explorer and author of the occult) introduces these tales by saying that "they may be regarded as fiction, or they may be considered to be what they actually are, studies of little known aspects of psychology," asserting that "they are all founded on fact ... serious studies of the psychology of ultra-consciousness" (vii–viii). They are certainly powerful stories, offering vivid descriptions of the intersection and interplay of the horrors and wonders of what most readers would regard to be supernatural with the material world of everyday reality—"From a cold hell of limitless horror, the flagged space became a normal backyard, the trees ceased to be tentacle menaces, the gloom of the wall was no longer an ambuscade, and I knew that never again would a grey shadow drift out of the darkness upon its horrible hunting" (19).

As fascinating and thought-provoking as these tales are as occult adventures, they work less well as detective stories, for Dr. Tavener is more physician and healer than detective. As he explains in "The Soul That Would Not Be Born" (1926), he investigates the strange phenomena that are brought to him using a repertoire of psychological and psychic techniques—"I use various methods; sometimes I get them by hypnotizing the patients or crystal-gazing, and sometimes I read them from the subconscious mind of nature. Every thought and impulse in the world is recorded in the Akashic Records" (58)—in an attempt to identify the causes and possible cures, and there are clues and deductions of a sort (though usually not accessible to the reader). Nonetheless, these tales are probably too fantastic with too little reason and rationality to appeal to most lovers of the detective fiction genre although Fortune claims they are based on psychological fact and on an actual doctor's experiences. The experiences are presented as physical fact, but not physical fact as most people currently understand it. But despite their implausibility as detective stories, they have appeal as psychic adventures, especially in "A Son of the Night" (1926), the magical and glorious finale for Tavener's "Watson"—"In that enormous stillness of the open heath, remote from all human life and thought, I felt the presence of an unseen existence above me, like walking through invisible water.... Cut off from all human influences, high up on the stark heights of the moors, I met my soul face to face while the unseen life that rose like a sea drew back as if to give me room for my decision" (238–239); and he passed over, like Tavener before him, into the companionship of the "Unseen."

John L. French

One of the many authors to continue the exploits of Lin Carter's supernatural sleuth, Anton Zarnak, French is faithful in tone and plot and "pulpishness" to Carter's flamboyant tales of "monsters and demons, of people getting lost in dreams and of paintings that kill" (Price, 356). In "The Best Solution" (1998), when "logic and reason don't apply, go down to China Alley and see the doctor at Number Thirteen and ask for Anton Zarnak. Tell the Hindu that I sent you, and those two will help you save the world" (356). Several gun battles over drugs, vampires, and a dousing in acid made from holy water later, Zarnak has once again defended the world from supernatural evil and Fu-Manchu-like villainy. Supernatural fun? Yes. Detection? Not really.

Randall Garrett

In his alternate-world England tales (a novel *Too Many Magicians* and two collections of short stories) of Lord Darcy, Chief Investigator for His Royal Highness Richard, Duke of Normandy, Garrett's magician/detective solves a series of cases using classic detective methods but greatly enhanced by supernatural and magical gifts. In "A Matter of Gravity" (1974) a man is killed by "ghosts, demons, black magic, that sort of thing" (Garrett, 6), but Darcy counters with his own unique blend of magical incantations (including the "Preservation Spell" which preserves corpses indefinitely), logic, and deduction, though even his "traditional" detective methods border on the fantastic—"You have the ability to leap from an unjustified assumption to a foregone conclusion without passing through the distance between. Then you back up and fill in" (18). Rarely has traditional detection had such a magical "handmaiden" as in these Lord Darcy tales, but here even the supernatural is governed by "natural" (if not always rational) laws—"There are more things in the universe than the mind of man, and there are laws which govern them" (44).

C.J. Henderson

Henderson wrote several stories extending the saga of Lin Carter's Anton Zarnak, all faithful, as with John French, to the pulpish tone and plots of the originals. In "The Door" (1999) Zarnak teams up with another supernatural sleuth, Teddy London, to protect humanity from the approaching psychic darkness. London had begun as a private investigator of "normal" cases, but he "had become involved in a case which had pulled him beyond the veil of the ordinary into a new understanding of the world that destroyed all his previous perceptions. Since then he had contested with vampires and demons, with changelings and with godlike forms whose mere visages shattered the fragile senses of most who beheld them" (Price, 347). With reference to Seabury Quinn's occult detective, Jules de Grandin, this story evokes quite a tandem of supernatural sleuths, though they don't all survive the fray.

E. and H. Heron

The stories of Flaxman Low were among the earliest tales of a series occult detective. Although they are most noted for their evocation of supernatural threat and terror, Low is a rational detective who uses reason, historical research, and logical deductions in an effort to solve supernatural mysteries and "to make another spot of earth clean and wholesome and safe for men to live on" (*Heron and Heron*, 75). Although he acts upon the premise that "the invisible is real; the material only subserves its manifestation" (67), he is careful to operate on the material level and deal with supernatural problems "on prosaic, rational lines, as we should deal with a purely human mystery" (16). He uses careful observation and measurement, historical research, and calm logic to solve such mysteries as that of a leper ghost ("The Story of the Spaniards, Hammersmith," 1898), an Elemental Earth Spirit with a blind malignity to the human race ("The Story of the Moor Road," 1898), a vampire spirit entering the body of a mummy ("The Story of Baelbrow," 1898), and an earth-bound spirit invading the tendrils of a murderous exotic plant ("The Story of Grey House," 1898). The saga of Flaxman Low ends dramatically with hints of the epic final struggle between Sherlock Holmes and Moriarty in Doyle's "The Final Problem," for Low in "The Story of Mr. Flaxman Low" (1899) engages in a monumental life-and-death struggle, first spiritual then fleshy, with the power-mad Dr. Kalmarkane, who had discovered "not only the secret of etheric energy, but also how to make that energy subservient to the directed will" (183).

Gordon Hillman

Hillman's Cranshawe, "a trained psychic investigator and perhaps one of the best known in America" (Haining, 162), certainly has some ominous encounters with spooky apparitions, ghosts, and avenging spirits, none more fantastic than the ghost ship seeking revenge in "Panic in Wild Harbor" (1986). Despite the innocence of the small fishing village ("The only thing that's ghastly about the town is the smell of fish," 163), the supernatural comes in all its malignancy—"Out of the fog loomed the broken bow of a ship. That ghastly green glow illumined the long, rutted, weed-hung decks, the splintered wheel house, the ribbon of sail stringing from the broken mast ... a sailor, his arms outflung as if to clench some unknown thing, and his face was not the face of a living man" (167). A bell with no rope that tolls at midnight, once for each dead sailor, a fog on a clear and mistless night, a dead ship impaling its nemesis—lots of spooking but no real sleuthing.

W.H. Hodgson

Although the celebrated stories in *Carnacki, the Ghost Finder* (1913) are powerfully written and quite effective at portraying supernatural terrors ("something precious unholy in the air that night," 13), and have led to many enthusiastic sequels by other authors, the detective aspects are usually quite limited, for other than some background research of hauntings (there are usually some murders in the history of the houses), Carnacki spends most of his time setting up pentagrams and candles and sealing doors and windows and using various signs of the Saaamaaa Ritual to ward off the supernatural evil. In "The Gateway of the Monster" (1910), for example, a vast and malignant presence slams doors, throws bedclothes, kills a cat, and threatens Carnacki, and even though "flesh and blood can do nothing against devils" (14), Carnacki and his occult methods manage, barely, to expel it as they do the "squeal of incredible, malevolent anger, piercing through the low honing of the whistle" (57) venting the rage of a man tortured and killed years earlier and threatening body and soul of those now present in "The Whistling Room" (1910). For those who love hauntings and supernatural terrors, the Carnacki stories are some of the finest and best known, but for those looking for a satisfying blend of the supernatural with classic detection, these famous tales may be less satisfying.

Arabella Kenealy

Of the hard-to-classify tales in *Some Experiences of Lord Syfret* (1896) included in *Supernatural Detectives 3* (2011)—stories of the bored observer of life, sometimes referred to as a "supernatural detective"—two have fantastic elements, one of the residue of murder surrounding an infant's soul (see Chapter Seven), the other of a vampirish woman who sucks the life out of those around her. Though neither story involves much detection on Lord Syfret's part other than observation and theorizing, "A Beautiful Vampire" (1896) hovers delicately between the fantastic and the mundane as this beautiful woman, ravenous for life, would "drink blood out of living bodies rather than die" (289), but then "there are a score of such vampires in this very town, vampires in lesser degree. When A talks with me ten minutes, I feel ten years older. He is a rapacious egotist hungrily absorbing the life force of anyone with whom he comes into relation—in other words, a human vampire" (292). Perhaps the myths and legends of supernatural beings are not so far from our reality after all.

Rick Kennett and A.F. Kidd

Kennett and A.F. Kidd separately and in collaboration continued the saga of W.H. Hodgson's *Carnacki, the Ghost Finder* (1913) with several stories collected in *No. 472 Cheyne Walk, Carnacki: The Untold Stories* (1992) and a few other stories published in magazines. As with Doyle in the Sherlock Holmes canon, Hodgson in his original stories makes reference to several other unpublished cases. It was these tantalizing references that inspired Kennett and Kidd to tell the untold tales, very much in the style and mode of Hodgson.

Most of their stories involve "some odd trouble" in haunted houses where eerie presences threaten present inhabitants and endanger the intrepid Carnacki who invariably spends the night armed only with the usual assortment of pentagrams, garlic, candles, and herbs. Although the "Defenses" usually work, in "The Darkness" (1992) Carnacki laments that the only thing that stands between him and being dragged into some foul depths was a Pentacle and a ring of garlic. In Kennett's "The Silent Garden" (1992) the threat is a smothering silence, an intelligence trying to break through into the material world, and again the defense is pentagrams and candles. Though not quite at Hodgson's level of craftsmanship and eloquence, these stories are quite faithful to the original Carnacki tales—effective as narratives of confronting supernatural terrors but less satisfying as stories of detection.

Uel Key

In the stories of Arnold Rhymer, "the young and distinguished savant in psychical phenomena" (Key, 13) there is lots of pulpish, supernatural action (e.g., the revivifying of German corpses as vampires in "The Broken Fang," 1917, experiments in dematerialization in "The Shrouded Dome," 1917), and a bit of rather dubious pseudo-science—when one of the characters says that he "always regarded vampires to be purely mythical" (52), Key responds that "When you become acquainted with the contents of this book [a notebook by German scientists], you'll alter your opinion." A paraphrase of that ultimate rationalist, Sherlock Holmes, brings at least a bit of normalcy to the irrational—"a golden rule which I was taught by a famous detective ... when you have worn out the possible, whatever is left, however impossible, comes mighty near the truth" (25).

Margery Lawrence

Although many of the stories of Miles Pennoyer collected in *The Casebook of Miles Pennoyer* (2003) are more about a psychic doctor, one who deals in the ills that beset the soul rather than the body, than they are about a detective, in some of the tales Pennoyer serves as a classic sleuth who does as much investigation into his clients' psychic ills, their causes, and their effects as "treatment" of these ills. All the tales are powerfully and eloquently written and are extremely effective as tales of the supernatural and a few of them, including "The Case of the Bronze Door" (1945) and "The Case of the White Snake" (1945)—see Chapter Seven for a description of the latter tale—are articulate and moving examples of the blending of the fantastic with the detective. In "The Case of the Bronze Door," Pennoyer battles with the psychic power of an ancient Chinese princess for the heart and soul of a college friend—"I sensed a tiny ripple, a mere thread of vibration, coming stealing through the room towards the sleeping man, and within a few moments that first faint vibration was followed by others and still others until the entire room was quivering and throbbing as though I was in the center of some infernal powerhouse. The sinister Force gathered and whirred about him until I almost heard the hum, like a colossal dynamo, of its vibrations" (26).

Brian Lumley

More in the vein of Lovecraft than in the detective tradition, the Lumley stories of Titus Crowe are powerful and haunting with an atmosphere of occult malignancy and horror. Although Crowe is a psychic sleuth who does do some sleuthing and deducing, most of his time is combatting evil—necromancers, maggots, ancient Black rituals, hypnotism, drugs. "Lord of the Worms" (1983), Lumley's own choice for "the definitive Titus Crow story" (Lumley, 27), is indeed an epic tale of the struggles of Crow to ward off and defeat a 350-year-old magician and coven-leader. This is a gripping and thrilling story where the detection is completely overwhelmed by the horror and decay.

Gordon MacCreagh

Although MacCreagh's Dr. Muncing calls himself a "ghost detective," MacCreagh's term "exorcist" is probably more accurate, for Muncing does little detecting but much encountering and combatting many of those "more horrible things in heaven and earth than are dreamed of in your police records" (Haining, 142). Even Hamlet might have been amazed and appalled by the "palpable, monstrous, deformed thing ... the unleashed malignance of all the ages" (151) that Muncing has to oppose. Iron and an iron will are Muncing's chief weapons (in "Dr. Muncing: Exorcist," 1931, and "The Sinister Shape," 1932) against the "elementals" that are able to penetrate the thin dividing line between the material and the spiritual worlds. Although there is considerable peril to Muncing and his "Watson" in confronting these occult horrors, he might well have said, "Elemental, My Dear Watson."

Fitz-James O'Brien

Harry Escott, O'Brien's occult investigator, first appeared in "The Pot of Tulips" (1855) then again in "What Was It?" (1859), the second (and last) Escott story establishing Escott as the first series occult detective, although he himself denies the supernatural—"I had devoted much time to the investigation of what are popularly called supernatural matters, by those who have not reflected or examined sufficiently to discover that none of these apparent miracles are supernatural, but all, however singular, are directly dependent on certain natural laws"

(Prasil, 14). However, it is not clear just what "natural" laws he is thinking of, for in both stories Escott investigates a ghost—in the former a tortured soul seeking to atone for a living sin, in the latter an aggressive, invisible attacker. Other than a little research into family history in "The Pot of Tulips" there isn't much detection or solving of puzzles—neither Escott nor the reader ever discovers the identity or motives of the invisible assailant. Despite Escott's designation as "the first series occult detective," it wasn't until several decades later that the first successful integration of a "real" detective and the supernatural was achieved with Algernon Blackwood's stories of John Silence.

E. Hoffman Price

Price's Pierre d'Artois, occult detective, combines deep knowledge of the supernatural, skilled swordsmanship, and bravery to combat all sorts of occult enemies including reincarnations of mummies ("The Peacock's Shadow," 1926), the inhabiting of a woman's body by a necromancer's conjured spirit ("The Return of Balkis," 1933), and the hypnotic voice of the dead empowered by occult scientists in the service of the Dark Lord controlling the minds of the living ("The Bride of the Peacock," 1932). A sort of combination of Seabury Quinn's Jules de Grandin and Zorro, d'Artois will follow victims deep into subterranean vaults and to the gates of hell to rescue them from the clutches of supernatural evil. There is some detection in figuring out the horrors behind the crimes, but most of the appeal of these adventure tales lies in the horror itself and in d'Artois' heroic efforts to combat it.

Robert Price

Another of the many authors who continued the "pulp" psychic adventures of Lin Carter's Anton Zarnak, Price brought in Howard's detective Steve Harrison to aid Zarnak to combat black rituals, drug dealers, ancient avatars, and unspeakable cults in "Dope War of the Black Tong" (1996). As in all the Zarnak stories, a world of supernatural evil lurks behind the material world we know, and the detectives exist in both worlds to save ours—"As he walked on through the Oriental Quarter, his huge frame stooped by exhaustion, he felt for the first time, despite the exotic otherworldliness of the place, that on its ancient streets he had re-entered the real world" (Price, 164).

Seabury Quinn

The 93 short stories about Jules de Grandin, investigator of weird psychological (see Chapter Six) and supernatural mysteries and crimes were the most popular stories in *Weird Tales* and are all collected in *The Complete Tales of Jules de Grandin* (2017–2019). Many of these tales are variations on the "Prince Charming-rescuing-the-fair-damsel-in-distress" motif with erotic undertones (or overtones) as they are filled with voluptuous descriptions of slightly-clad damsels in peril (often supernatural peril) for whom de Grandin, the perennial gentleman, is their Knight in Shining Armor. In some of the supernatural tales, de Grandin merely observes and analyzes, but in most of these tales he actively combats dangerous supernatural entities and events, although he himself claims that "There is no such thing as the supernatural. There is undoubtedly the superphysical; there is also that class of natural phenomena of which we do not understand" (Quinn, 2018a, 258). Perhaps at some time we will understand these "superphysical" events as part of the natural order, but for now they counter natural law as we know it, so de Grandin is considered by critics to be an occult or supernatural detective dealing with mostly supernatural incidents and crimes. In Volume 1, stories of combat with the supernatural include battle with a giant serpent—the projection of a dead man's soul—that murders and seduces the innocent ("The Tenants of Broussac," 1925), a disembodied hand under the control of a murderous magician ("The Dead Hand," 1926), a vampire who must replenish his vitality by drinking the blood of a slaughtered virgin ("The Man Who Cast No Shadow," 1927), a werewolf who "recruits" others ("The Blood-Flower," 1927), and a poltergeist who possesses and torments a young woman ("The Poltergeist," 1927). Although at least some of these stories teeter on the edge of pulpish melodrama and wild implausibility, the vivid and realistic description tends to ground even the most fantastic events in the solid and imaginable—"Not human, nor yet wholly bestial it was, but partook grotesquely of both, so that it was at once a foul caricature of each. The cruel lips were drawn sneeringly back from a double row of tusk-like teeth which gleamed horridly in the dim reflection of the open fire, and a pair of round, baleful eyes, green as the luminescence from a rotting carcass in a midnight swamp, glared at us across the windowsill" (Quinn, 2017a, 205)—and the "scientifically" conceivable—"The matter of the universe is little, if anything, more than electrons, flowing about in all directions. For here, now there, the electrons balance and form what we call solids. But may they not coalesce at a different rate of speed, or vibration, to form beings which are real, with ambitions and loves and hates similar to ours, yet for the most part invisible to us, as is the air" (256). The detection, though occasionally involving supernatural "equipment" (e.g., pentagrams, herbs, spells) and the supposition that thoughts are things with form and substance, almost always, even in the most outrageous cases, relies on the standard tools of careful observation, analysis of clues, logic, and deduction.

In all these cases de Grandin ignores incredulity, implausibility, and ridicule ("You're some sort of charlatan from Paris, a dabbler in criminology and spiritualism and that sort of rot," 199) to pursue and defeat the supernatural menace, for "when you have seen such things as I have seen, you will learn to believe many things that fools declare impossible" (96), and "for this sly, clever one, never is the task imposed too great for him" (97). More than once does de Grandin cite the famous phrase from Hamlet that so many authors of the fantastic love to quote, for indeed "There are more things in Heaven and Earth than are dreamt of in your philosophy" (130) and more things in fantastic detective tales than are dreamt of in the more conventional halls of literary academe or Sherlockian scholarship.

In Volume 2 of *The Complete Tales of Jules de Grandin*, 2017, de Grandin battles a murderous skeleton unloosed from a tomb in "The Black Master" (1929)—"When we cast aside the root of mandragoro, we did unseal a tomb which was better left unopened and did release upon the world a spirit capable of working monstrous evil" (Quinn, 2017b, 23). Although de Grandin does historical research and notices subtle clues, his ultimate triumph is with "magical devices"—a silver bullet tipped with a Christian cross—just as in "The Devil-People" (1929) where he rescues a young woman from a race of Malay demon people who can become invisible at will with holy water and lime, in "The Corpse-Master" (1929) where he combats with salt a "spiritless corpse ravished from its grave, endowed with pseudo-life by black magic and made to serve the whim of the magician who animated it" (124), and in "Trespassing Souls" (1929) where he calls on the sacred powers ("Come to my aid, O Powers of Light and Darkness. To me you are bound by the words of Power and Might, nor may ye depart hence till my will be done," 145) to combat a zombie master from the Haitian Cult of Death. In one of the most moving and powerful tales, "Daughter of the Moonlight"

Part 3—The Truly Supernatural

(1930) de Grandin confronts witchcraft, demonic possession, and the rising of the dead from a touch of necromancy and the new moon.

In the gripping tale "Satan's Stepson" (1931) in *The Complete Tales of Jules de Grandin, Volume 3* (2018) de Grandin must combat a horrifying mixture of man and devil who can survive death unless it be a single fatal blow—"Now, together with the werewolf and the vampire, the warlock and the witch, the Russian knows another demon-thing called 'callicantzaros,' who is a being neither wholly man nor devil, but an odd and horrifying mixture of the two. Some call them foster-children of the devil, stepsons of the Devil; some say they are the progeny of evil, sin-soaked women and the incubi who are their paramours" (Quinn, 2018a, 100–101). Two fantastic returns from death later, the callicantzaros meets final death as his victim is reborn into love. In "The Thing in the Fog" (1933) the supernatural adversary is a werewolf, so the fantastic is alive and "well," but de Grandin debunks a bit of the supernatural aura surrounding it as he scoffs at the "traditional" fantastic methods of combatting such a foe:

> What did they know of modern ordnance, those old-time ritualists? Silver bullets were decreed because silver is a harder metal than lead, and the olden guns they used in ancient days were not adapted to shoot iron. The pistols of today shoot slugs encased in cupronickel, far harder than the best of iron, and with a striking force undreamed of in the days when firearms were a new invention. Had the good Saint George possessed a modern military rifle, he could have slain the dragon at his leisure while he stood a mile away [419].

"The Malay Horror" (1933) in *The Complete Tales of Jules de Grandin, Volume 4* (2018) involves de Grandin in confrontation with a "penanggalan," a "sort of nocturnal demon closely analogous to the vampire of Eastern Europe" (Quinn, 2018b, 44) who attacks its victims by hypnotic strangulation. De Grandin, the self-proclaimed "practicing occultist who has spent as much time grappling with the foes of the spirit as with those of the flesh" (39), grapples with both in this case as the penanggalan attempts to kill and convert its victim to one of its own. In "The Mansion of Unholy Magic" (1933) de Grandin must deal with a mummy revivified by a necromancer who needs human blood to persist—"an evil-looking, desiccated thing, skeleton-thin, dark, leather-colored skin stretched tightly as drum parchment on its skull, broken teeth protruding through retracted lips, tiny sparks of greenish light glowing malevolently in its cavernous, hollow eye-sockets" (69). Axe and fire in the hands of de Grandin are the weapons that reduce the fantastic to everyday dust and ash as the millennia catch up to the dead, and life is left to the living. In "Hands of the Dead" (1935) the new hands a woman receives in an operation after a terrible accident are controlled by a malicious magician and hypnotist until de Grandin disposes of the magician and "hands" the woman back her identity and her life. In "A Rival from the Grave" (1936) de Grandin uses x-rays to destroy the ghostly manifestation of a witch trying to possess and destroy a man's body and soul—"Ghostly manifestations, materializations of spirit-forms, are peculiarly creatures of the darkness and the twilight. Bright sunlight seems to kill them as it kills spore-bearing germs. So do certain forms of sound-vibration ... high-frequency electric currents, the emanations of radium salt or the terrific penetrating force of Roentgen rays should have the same effect" (243).

"The Poltergeist of Swan Upping" (1939) in *The Complete Tales of Jules de Grandin, Volume 5* (2019) is a vivid story of a particularly malicious poltergeist whose pranks turn into murder—"But it was no light ethereal vapor, for it plummeted to the floor and hit the oak with a soft slap. For a moment it lay there like a little cone of swirling vapor or, perhaps of fine-ground powder, but suddenly it appeared to take on a semblance of a shape not well defined, but vague and semi-formed, like a mass of colloid substance, or a jelly-fish which had been brought up from the bay. I cannot tell you what it was, but I know that it was very evil. I would not give a centime for the life of anyone whom it attacked" (Quinn, 2019, 88–89). In so many of these de Grandin tales, just as the spirits invade the world of the flesh, so too the fantastic intrudes into the everyday—"The fantastic seems to be the commonplace. Should things keep on going as they are going, only the commonplace will be fantastic, I damn think" (98). In "Stoneman's Memorial" (1942) an aging de Grandin still has what it takes to confront and destroy a stone statue brought back to life by "the secret spell of the magus to bring the dead, cold stone to life" (211) and to do the same to the mad man wielding the spell. In "Death's Bookkeeper" (1944) de Grandin battles a wizard—"just as much a wizard as those dreadful men they hanged and burned in mediaeval days" (216) who has learned "how to turn the hand of death from one man to another" (225). De Grandin's "Watson," Dr. Trowbridge, offers a touch of "reality" amid all the supernatural playing with death, but de Grandin champions the fantastic and disparages its critics, including Trowbridge, in his usual sarcastic manner—"Always you rationalize a thing you do not understand, taking the long route around the barn of Robin Hood in order to arrive at a false conclusion" (220). In "Lords of the Ghostlands" (1945) a mummy of an Egyptian priestess, who was brutally killed for choosing love over devotion to Isis, comes back to take over a young woman's body, and must be chanted by de Grandin back to her eternal sleep, just as he must send a famous, seemingly ageless actress to her long-delayed death after she, for decades, has fed upon the living to keep her youth in "Clair de Lune" (1947). Here, as in Poe's famous "Case of M. Valdemar," we are led to wonder if life itself is the fantastic struggling to be believed as the reality of death claims its due—"The bluish whiteness of her skin turned mottled green, as if already putrefactive micro-organisms were at work there, wrinkles etched themselves across her face like cracks in shattering ice, the luster of her pale-gold hair faded to a muddy yellow, and the hands that plucked at the bed-clothes were like the withered talons of a dead and desiccated bird" (402). In "Vampire Kith and Kin" (1949) we and the detective (de Grandin) are again uncertain where the fantastic and reality lie, for in this case the "vampire" may lay hidden in the psyche or may have emerged from myth into the material world—"In a neurasthenic state of hypochondria she might indeed have wasted away and finally perished. So far a good case for psychopathological illness has been made out; but as yet we lack complete proof. And what disproved it, or at least gave reason for suspecting that some super-physical agent—something you would call the supernatural—intervened? Ghosts and spirits, all kinds of discarnate entities" (418–419). In "The Ring of Bastet" (1951), the very last de Grandin story, Quinn returns to one of his favorite sources for the fantastic—the myths of ancient Egypt—as a ring of the cat-headed goddess wreaks its vengeance on the living, and, as with the entire de Grandin canon, only the detective of reason with a healthy respect for the fantastic and the supernatural can still its influence.

Conrad Richter

In the two stories ("Monster of the Dark Places," 1931–32, and "The Toad Man Specter," 1931) of the supernatural investigator, Matson Bell, sometimes called "The Spook Cop," Richter manages to evoke a sense of malignancy and dread with ghostly presences and inhuman wailing and vivid description of the "Dark Places"—"You couldn't pick a more fitting habitat for the sinister and horrible, the secretive and accursed, the shadowy and unknown than places where the smallest ray of sunshine never penetrates, where it's always midnight, where the tiny lamp of man is swallowed up in the blackness like the flash of a match in cosmic space" (Prasil, 287). The "incredible creatures of nightmare" (280) that populate this tale and "The Toad Man Specter" are a bit spooky and horrifying, but they are easily dispelled by some simple investigating on the part of Bell.

Robert Weinberg

Weinberg's detective Sidney Taine "has earned the nickname 'The New Age Detective' from his use of harmonic frequencies, crystals, and other occult paraphernalia, but he's not a gimmick guy who goes around spouting supernatural mumbo-jumbo" (Weinberg, 16); although he is not adverse to using supernatural assistance (e.g., drinking an elixir which enables him to see the spirits of the dead in "The Midnight El"), he combines these dexterously with the conventional detective techniques.

If his methods are not always fantastic, his cases are, for they involve matching wits with Charon, ferryman of the dead, over a woman not yet dead on the "Phantom Train" whose passengers are those who died that day ("The Midnight El," 1994), seeking the "real" Holy Grail for a king of demons ("Seven Drops of Blood," 1992), battling a werewolf-like creature with the help of the Eternal Society of the Silver Way ("Terror by Night," 1991), and contesting wits with the Beast of the Apocalypse and the prophecies of Nostradamus ("The Apocalypse Quatrain," 1995).

As fantastic as the stories are and as earth-shaking as the peril is, it is the human capacity for reason and imagination that triumphs; Taine illustrates how the very "natural" and human intelligence and wit can bring the supernatural "down to earth."

Manly Wade Wellman

In the stories of John the Balladeer, John's main weapons against the supernatural creatures he encounters (a skeleton come to life in "Can These Bones Live," 1981, a hanged woman trying to suck the life out of him in "Where Did She Wander," 1987, a witch in "The Spring," 1979, the devil himself in "Owls Hoot in the Daytime," 1980) are his steel guitar (steel cuts through the occult) and his music, with a touch of holy water mixed in.

In addition to John the Balladeer, Wellman's other John, the urbane John Thunstone, armed with powerful chants and charms and a silver sword-cane fashioned by Saint Dunston centuries past, seeks out and confronts supernatural perils in *Lonely Vigils* (1981) and in other scattered tales with bravado and compassion for the afflicted. Whether a seductive witch ("The Last Grave of Lill Warren," 1951) or the hideous "familiar" of a witch ("Rouse Him Not," 1982), Thunstone gathers the story from backwoods locals then dispatches the occult with a fantastic flourish but little detection.

An earlier Wellman occult investigator, Judge Keith Hilary Pursuivant, who also has an arsenal of chants and charms, appeared in four stories, the most interesting of which was "The Half-Haunted" (1941) in which Pursuivant is consulted by Seabury Quinn's Jules de Grandin.

Dennis Wheatley

Wheatley's supernatural sleuth Neils Orsen admits that genuine psychical manifestations are very rare, that most apparently supernatural occurrences are either hallucinations or trickery (see Chapter Two), but every now and then he encounters a true supernatural event, as in his stories "The Case of the Long-Dead Lord" (1943) and "The Case of the Red-Headed Women" (1943) where he discovers and defeats earth-bound spirits seeking justice or revenge or relief from earthly guilt. Orsen's detective methods are par for the (supernatural) course— cameras, recording devices, pentacles, historical research—but these stories are appealing for their evocative prose and emotional impact—"A cold whiteness was all about him and with its physical desolation there bore upon his brain another darkness, a sense of evil, too sickening to be borne" (Wheatley, 96).

Henry S. Whitehead

Gerald Canevin, psychic sleuth, was featured in several of Whitehead's stories appearing in *Weird Tales* and other pulp magazines in the 1930s. In "The Shut Room" (1930) Canevin discovers that actually confronting the supernatural (in this case, a ghost of a slain villain seeking his lost holsters and guns) is considerably more challenging and daunting than using the methods of detection to discover the "laws" behind the supernatural—"It is one thing to figure out, beforehand, the science of occult occurrences. It is, distinctly, another to face the direct operation of something motivated by the Powers beyond the keen of ordinary humanity" (Rennison, 283). In these Canevin stories the "distinctly another" plays a much more significant and appealing role than the rather run-of-the-mill "one thing."

PART 4

Supernatural or Natural?

Nine

The Intrigue of
Unanswered Questions

Todorov, in his *The Fantastic: A Structural Approach to a Literary Genre* (1973), makes very fine distinctions between such categories as "the fantastic," the "uncanny," and "the marvelous," defining "the fantastic" very narrowly as occurring only when the reader hesitates between a natural and a supernatural explanation:

> The fantastic lasts only as long as a certain hesitation: a hesitation common to reader and character, who must decide whether or not what they perceive derives from "reality" as it exists in the common opinion. At the story's end, the reader makes a decision even if the character does not; he opts for one solution or the other, and thereby emerges from the fantastic. If he decides that the laws of reality remain intact and permit an explanation of the phenomena described, we say that the work belongs to another genre: the uncanny. If, on the contrary he decides that new laws of nature must be entertained to account for the phenomena, we enter the genre of the marvelous [41].

Although we have decided in this monograph to regard the "fantastic" in a much broader way (as that which seems to have little relationship to the laws of nature as we understand them, and that which includes but is not limited to the supernatural), there are a few (and only a few) detective stories which illustrate this narrower Todorov definition of the "fantastic" (even though Todorov doesn't think a detective story can be fantastic in this sense). It is interesting to note that these Todorovian "fantastic" detective stories, where the hesitation of uncertainty lasts all the way to the end, are among the most daring and memorable of the entire detective genre, probably because they offer no final solutions or explanations—their ambiguity challenges the reader's core beliefs in what is natural and what is real and provokes the reader to contemplate and re-evaluate his beliefs and his life.

173

Exemplars

Algernon Blackwood

The six stories about Blackwood's investigator of the occult, John Silence, are extraordinary, both for their vivid evocation of the fantastic and for how the incredible is made plausible if not believable. He prefers to refer to himself as a "psychic doctor" rather than a "psychic detective," for he investigates strange phenomena but also their even stranger effect on the human mind—"Matters that seemed almost too curious and fantastic for belief he loved to trace to their hidden source. To unravel a tangle in the very soul of things, and to release a suffering human soul in the process, was with him a veritable passion. And the knots he untied were, indeed, after passing strange" (Blackwood, 44).

In most of the stories he probes and combats dangerous supernatural occurrences and forces (see Chapter Eight) whether they exist in the physical world or only in the mind, but in "Ancient Sorceries" (1908) it is not clear whether these occurrences and forces are physical facts operating in the material world or are archetypal memories playing through the psyche. This eerie tale of the man who came upon an ancient town which aroused an ancient, alluring, though terrifying part of himself—"Something utterly remote from his ordinary life, something that had not been waked for years, began faintly to stir in his soul, sending feelers abroad into his brain and heart" (52). "The old, old life within, the life of long ago, the life to which you, too, belonged, and to which you still belong" (68) haunts us as well as the man himself with images of enchantment and seduction, of love and passion, of reincarnation and transmutation, of witches and devil worship. He eventually manages to break the spell and flees back to the everyday world where he seeks out Silence for explanation and solace. As fantastic as his tale seems, it is all told with such subtlety and sensitivity and vivid realism that, though Silence claims "But that the entire affair took place subjectively, in the man's own consciousness, I have no doubt" (81), Blackwood's writing ensures that *we* are not so certain either about Silence or about ourselves. Silence finds evidence that the man was indeed in the town and fled suddenly, but neither he nor we know whether the fantastic resided in the town or just in the man's mind. Silence can "only trust that this gentle soul may soon escape from this obsession of a passionate and tempestuous past," (83), but perhaps we are not even certain if we agree with this, for that past was in many ways his real life.

Ernest Bramah

"The Eastern Mystery" (1923) is another of these cleverly ambiguous stories that blends "traditional" detective methods with eerie, fantastic mood and occurrences. Despite the strangeness, it appears for a while that rationality reigns and there is a "natural" explanation, but there is just enough of the inexplicable and the supernatural to leave doubts and wonder.

A friend of Max Carrados (the detective), who recently returned from the East, brings with him what looks like a rusty, old nail, but which is claimed to be a sacred tooth of the ape-god Hanuman, a talisman given to him in gratitude by a poor man whose son he tried to save. Supposedly it will protect him from harm, but he, a man of reason, is highly skeptical ("Oh, that's all great tom dam foolery. There are a hundred million of them," Queen, 1978, 283), even though his life has been "miraculously" saved on several occasions since it was given to him. When he is saved once again (from an explosion in his bedroom arranged by Indian thugs but which he escapes because he can't remember the address of the building), he, and we, are left to ponder why: "The scientist would perhaps hint at telepathic premonition operating subconsciously through receptive nerve centers. The skeptic would call it a lucky coincidence. The devoutly religious person would claim another miracle" (295). And just which are we, and what do we think? What is this relic—"a monkey's or an ape-god's tooth, an iron-stained belemnite, the fragment of a pagan idol" (297), and what role, if any, is it playing in this man's repeated dodging of death?

We are left in doubt, seeking refuge in our own belief system, as the story has no definite answers, but Carrados (the rational detective) advocates the sacred—"even secular and unfriendly historians have been driven to admit, something out of the order of Nature did shake the heavens" (297), and filters his conclusion through his religious-cultural experience as a child: "To you and me, to everyone who has listened to the story as a little child, it is only conceivable that if miraculous virtues reside in anything inanimate, it must preeminently be in the close accessories of that great world's tragedy" (297). Could this actually "just" be a rusty nail, but a very particular one with particular powers? We will never know, for Carrados and his friend sink it, reverently, in the deepest part of the Atlantic, returning mystery to mystery "safe from any ignoble use" (298).

John Dickson Carr

Carr, the brilliant practitioner of the locked room mystery and the classic clue-puzzle detective story, is also known for his predilection for adding touches of the fantastic and even the supernatural to his classic tales. In most of them, the apparently supernatural is revealed at the end to have a logical, rational explanation, but occasionally the fantastic accompanies the rational all the way to the conclusion (as famously in the novel *The Burning Court*), leaving the reader in a permanent suspended state of uncertainty and "hesitation."

Perhaps the best of his short stories which end in "fantastic ambiguity" is "The Man Who Was Dead" (1935) also titled "New Murders for Old." This haunting tale is heavy with psychology which threatens reason (a nervous breakdown where the protagonist, Tony, has "the conviction, coming in flashes at night, that he was not real any longer, that his body and his inner self had moved apart, the first walking and talking in everyday life like an articulate dummy, while the brain remained in another place" Carr, 1991a, 302). There is a devious murder plot, and there is an ominous, non-rational sense of "active malignancy—of hatred, of danger—surrounding him and pressing on him" (203), which is embodied in a strange figure lurking in the dark, half-concealed in a heavy coat, who reminds Tony of his dead partner. The figure follows Tony as he, Tony, returns from the "dead" to confront his own dead body and his murderer. In the end, Tony gets revenge, but is it fate, karma, or the supernatural who is its agent? Who or what was the figure that followed him, or was it just his own disembodied self? "You tell me" (307).

C.D. King

King's detective, Trevis Tarrant, is the epitome of dogged rationalism, applying and illustrating his premise that "somewhere there is a logically satisfying, causative answer to our puzzle" (King, 96) even to the most bizarre and fabulous mysteries (see Chapter One), but in "The Episode of the Final Bargain" (1935), the final case in *The Curious Mr. Tarrant* (1935) before Tarrant's return several years later at Ellery Queen's request, Tarrant's logic encounters a mystery "to which neat, wrapped up and paid for solutions don't exist" (King, 2003, 143). This "end of adventures and beginning of an Adventure" (143) shakes Tarrant, for it seems to involve evil magic and etheric bodies and a threat of death, which he must sacrifice years of his life to defeat. It is not clear to anyone what really happened—"We were all crazy sitting around listening to that stuff ... all that hocus-pocus" (163), but reason must go in search of a greater knowing as the detective story embraces the fantastic in all its mystery and potency.

Sax Rohmer

Most of the investigations of Rohmer's "occult" detective, Moris Klaw, end up having a logical explanation, though the methods of Klaw are eccentric if not supernatural, based on his special sensitivity to the "vibrations" of thought persisting after death, but one story in particular, "Case of the Veil of Isis" (1913) hovers between the natural and the supernatural, between the psychological and the spiritual. Apparently there were several Klaw investigations that "proved insusceptible of a natural explanation, which fell strictly within the province of the occult," (Rohmer, 142) but Rohmer, cognizant of detective story readers' skepticism of the fantastic in the detective story—"Readers of these pages would be unlikely to appreciate the nature of Klaw's investigations outside the sphere of ordinary natural laws" (142)—failed to record them. In "Case of the Veil of Isis," a case steeped in Egyptian mythology and esoteric practice, Freudian psychology, and hypnosis, the outcome is uncertain—a matter of thought projection ("Thoughts are things—and you gathered together in this house, by that ancient formula, a thought-thing created by generations of worshippers who have worshipped the moon," 158), or is it something more than thought, for the sign of Isis is marked in physical and living flesh. Self-hypnosis? Auto-suggestion? Stigmata? Or is Isis coming down through the centuries?

T.S. Stribling

Stribling's remarkable and disturbing story "Shadowed" (1930) is a masterpiece of uncertainty where the psychological and the supernatural weave in and out, first one then the other seeming to explain the mystery. Here the readers as well as the detective (Professor Poggioli) begin to lose the ability to distinguish between what is "real" and what exists only in the psyche. As one of the characters speculates, "It has sometimes occurred to me that what you might call reality is not the houses and air and men and women which surround us. They are more in the nature of walls cutting off reality, making us for the moment oblivious to reality ... [reality is] our unconditioned selves, our subconscious. When we sleep we are lost in reality" (Stribling, 2004, 75). A newspaper headline about the detective and the case sums up the dynamic tensions that pervade the mystery: "Professor Poggioli pits Western science [including psychology] against Eastern occultism" (55), and the plot unfolds so subtly and with so much left "in the shadows" that we are never quite certain which side we believe all the way to the end. And Poggioli, the detective (and research psychologist), experiences the same quandary, which eventually gets him fired from the University for scientific heresy, as his rational and logical approach to detection and life is profoundly challenged by his encounter in this case with the mysterious depths of the psyche and the supernatural. The story teems with the fantastic— hypnotism, conjuring tricks, numerology, demoniac possession, the 4th dimension, mediumistic exteriorization, unconscious hatred, the survival of the personality after death—but it is never completely clear to anyone how much of the action is propelled by psychological disturbance and how much by supernatural manifestation. The mysteries of this story drive the characters (and probably the reader) to question the very nature of reality and belief:

> ...it suddenly occurred to the psychologist that mankind as a whole must have greatly benefited by this attitude of awe and passive acceptance of the miraculous, or the trait would not be so deeply ingrained in the human race. If that were true, then the awful, the mysterious, the unknowable must, on the whole, have bestowed upon the world of men some great and immeasurable good. And that, of course, was religion [53].

Not only is this story a fascinating, intricate detective story with clues and deductions, but it is a profound meditation on the fantastic and the real, on the intersection of psychic reality with external fact. It is a brilliant illustration of how the "fantastic" can illuminate, deepen, and enrich the classic detective story without weakening its "respectability" or appeal.

Other Stories

Vincent Cornier

"The Throat of Green Jasper" (1934) in Cornier's remarkable collection *The Duel of Shadows* (2011) has some similarities to Christie's

"The Adventure of the Egyptian Tomb," for in both stories the ransacking of an ancient Egyptian tomb appears to have resulted in a fatal curse; however, the Cornier tale is the more effective and memorable, for it ends ambiguously—a contemporary Egyptian beauty brought back from the dead may or may not be possessed by the Egyptian priestess of that ancient tomb, and, fantastically, Barnabas Hildreth, wearing the ceremonial collar of Green Jaspar given him by the Egyptian beauty before she dies again, becomes "something helmeted in pale gold, with poised and glittering royal cobras hung above two glowing eyes I could not meet" (69). However, reason has its say, as Hildreth returns to the rational, reasonable detective in the several following stories.

Jacques Futrelle

Futrelles' famous detective Professor Van Dusen is titled "The Thinking Machine" for good reason—in many ways, he is the prototype rational logician for whom "two plus two makes four, not some of the time, but all of the time" (Futrelle, vol. 1, 2009, 473). In most of his stories, he solves strange problems by pure logic, and so we are reassured that even the most puzzling circumstances are explainable in the end by logic and natural law. But just as we've settled into our secure trust in the world of reason and the rational, The Thinking Machine shakes our confidence—perhaps two plus two doesn't always equal four, perhaps there is something "fantastic" behind all our logic and laws of nature: "Imagination, Mr. Hatch, is the single connecting link between man and the infinite. We can achieve nothing until we imagine it. Just so far as the human brain can imagine it can comprehend. It fails only to comprehend the eternal purpose, the Omnipotent Will, because it cannot imagine it. For imagination has a limit, and beyond that we are not to go—beyond that is 'Divinity' [where] the mind of man merely reels, staggers, collapses" (474). It is unsettling, even shocking, to hear Van Dusen say this, for we have grown comfortable with "2 + 2 = 4" and the conventions of the logical "machine" unshaken by even a glimpse of the fantastic. However, despite these rare philosophical reflections, our confidence is restored by the events in Thinking Machine stories, for they always add up to four as logic and reason prevail and Divinity is only an abstract thought dimly conceived with no power to impact the puzzles and solutions of detection, no power that is until the startling story "The Haunted Bell" (1908).

In this tale Futrelle plays with our expectations and perceptions, presenting a mysterious, seemingly supernatural problem—"It was a thing trivial enough, yet so strangely mystifying in its happening that the mind hesitated to accept it as an actual occurrence despite the indisputable evidence of the sense of hearing" (457)—that slowly resolves itself into a rational explanation, but just as we are breathing a sigh of relief and settling back into the comfort of the "traditional" detective story operating "naturally," we are stunned by the final sentence that peels away the reason and forces us to see the fantastic behind it. It is a tour de force that leaves us uncertain of any assumptions and any realities; it leaves us gasping in doubt, hesitating in unbelief. It is the power of the fantastic to turn our beloved detective story into something transparent but still visible.

Peter Godfrey

Godfrey wrote several impossible crime stories where the psychology plays a large part in the explanation of the crime (see Chapter Six), and he wrote a strange non–le Roux story, "The Lady and the Dragon" (1950) where the psychological workings of the unconscious mind are only part of the explanation; the rest is "Mesozoic," or is it? Is it complex or T-Rex? Is it projection or ingestion? Is it fantastic or is it natural, or is it both?

W.H. Hodgson

With all Hodgson's tales of *Carnacki, the Ghost Finder* (1913) included in *Supernatural Detectives 1* (2011) of serious hauntings and threats from the supernatural (see Chapter Eight), "The Horse of the Invisible" (1910) may be even more haunting because of the uncertainty at the end—much of the horror of the galloping horse was cleverly engineered by a jealous suitor (Parsket), but what of that "last, dreadful thing" (93) when "the look [of shock and horror] on Parsket's face and the thing he called out when he heard the great hoof sounds down the passage seem to show that he had the sudden realization of what before then may have been nothing more than a horrible suspicion?" (93). Could Parsket have created a "kind of induced simulation of his mental conceptions to his desperate thoughts and broodings" (94); are supernatural horrors and hauntings just the projections of mind on the material world? Although Carnacki does use some classic detective techniques (careful observation, logic, and deduction), it is the terror and the uncertainty that leave their mark.

A Story to End All Stories

T.S. Stribling

It is appropriate and satisfying that we end our study of detective stories and the fantastic with another detective story by the Nobel Prize-winning author T.S. Stribling, for "Passage to Benares" (1926) has a shattering, fantastic ending, where a methodically unfolding tale of classic detection by logic and reason is suddenly thrown by the fantastic into a frenzy where the very foundation of logic and natural law is called into question. As in Stribling's earlier tale discussed in this chapter, "Shadowed," we are reassured by reason, as the detective (Professor Poggioli) slowly, logically undertakes the solution to the mystery, but ultimately logic is shown to be but a single, flickering candle bravely but futilely trying to light the blackness of eternity as "space and time had ceased to be" (Stribling, 1929, 316). Even life and death change places as "living things are a result of the struggles of the dead, and not the dead of the living" (319). In the end, or maybe after the end, Poggioli does solve the crime, but it is because of the fantastic that this detective tale is so provocative and shattering and will never be forgotten. Anyone who says that there is no place for the fantastic in the detective story can't have travelled the stunning "Passage to Benares."

Conclusion:
The Detective, the Rational
and the Fantastic

The real and the unreal are seldom compatible in a single short story: straight detection is usually earthbound, grounded by the realistic demands of cold logic and credibility; fantasy, on the other hand, has wings—it may soar into the stratosphere of the weird and even the supernatural [*EQMM*, Sept., 1945, 98].

Queen is certainly not alone in his view that the detective story and the fantastic are, with rare exceptions, incompatible. As was mentioned in the Introduction, Todorov, in *The Fantastic: A Structural Approach to a Literary Genre*, argues that despite some structural similarities between detective fiction and the fantastic, the detective story is fundamentally "the contrary of the fantastic: in fantastic texts we tend to prefer the supernatural explanation; the detective story, once it is over, leaves no doubt as to the absence of supernatural events" (50), for the reader of detective fiction is interested only in the finding of the final solution, which is a logical, analytical, rational process. However, both Queen and Todorov, and other critics, have not precluded authors of "legitimate" detective stories using the fantastic as a "red herring," as an apparent solution only to be debunked by rational detective methods. Notice that Todorov says, "the detective story, *once it is over* [emphasis added], leaves no doubt as to the absence of supernatural events." This certainly leaves room for the *apparently* supernatural or fantastic to enter into a detective story, as long as it is later explained away by logic and deduction. Although Queen seems to say that the "earthbound" and the "soaring" are incompatible, he has great admiration for the classic locked-room mystery and other impossible crime stories, the solutions to which initially appear to be explainable only by fantastic or supernatural means. So, it seems fair to conclude that neither Todorov

183

Conclusion

nor Queen, nor other critics, would claim that detective fiction and the *apparently* fantastic are incompatible.

In Part 1 of this work, we have listed and described over two hundred detective stories, many among the most respected and popular in the genre, which have used the apparently fantastic or the supernatural in this "red herring" way. The list of authors is impressive, including many of the biggest names, both classic and more contemporary, in the detective short story field—Allingham, Bramah, Brand, Carr, Chesterton, Christie, Freeman, Futrelle, Gardner, Godfrey, Halter, Hoch, Innes, Kemelman, C.D. King, P. MacDonald, Palmer, Poe, Porges, Post, Powell, Pronzini, Sayers, Simenon, Wallace, and even that bastion of reason, Conan Doyle, and even Ellery Queen himself. And so, it is clear that when the "real" triumphs in the end, when the apparently fantastic explanation to an impossible crime is supplanted in the end by a logical, rational solution, the real and the unreal—the "demands of cold logic and credibility" and the "wings" of the "weird and even the supernatural"—can not only co-exist, but can enhance each other to create an effective, legitimate, and popular detective story.

In Part 2, we have described over one hundred detective short stories where the fantastic (but not the supernatural) is used as a "genuine" part of the detection or the solution—detectives using non-rational methods (special sensitivity or intuition) or detectives using traditional methods to reveal non-rational explanations and solutions, usually those involving psychological or mythological elements. Authors of these types of stories include such luminaries as Boucher, Chesterton, Christie, Conan Doyle, Derleth, Eberhart, Futrelle, Heard, Hillerman, P.D. James, Jesse, Le Fanu, Machen, Mason, Pentecost, Post, Powell, Priestley, Queen, and Stribling. Clearly, what is considered "fantastic"—contrary to natural law or having slight relation to the real world as we understand it—changes over time, as many non-rational aspects of the psyche, which are considered "real" today were considered fantastic or even supernatural before Freud and Jung and modern psychology. We have seen that there are numerous effective, renowned, and "legitimate" detective stories whose plot and solution depend on non-rational but currently acknowledged "realities" of the unconscious. When it comes to detectives with non-rational detecting abilities, the situation is a bit more problematic, but with skilled authors (e.g., Eberhart and Jesse) whose detectives follow up on their intuition with classic, rational methods, the stories can avoid the accusation of "mumbo-jumbo" and can be effective and popular.

So, we have argued that the detective story can effectively incorporate the apparently fantastic (to eventually be debunked by reason) and touches of the fantastic (non-rational elements of psychology and mythology) that become central parts of the solution. But what about the fantastic that is still believed by most to be completely fantastic—the supernatural, especially the supernatural that threatens and terrifies? Some critics have been adamant in claiming the supernatural and horror have no legitimate place in the detective story—"The combination of the horror tale and the detective tale is about as grotesque an idea as can be imagined" (Joshi, 115), for "Mysteries involving the supernatural seek to disarm the reader's power of logical thought [and the detective's] by arousing fear" (Murch, 13), and, so the argument goes, without logical thought, how can you have a detective story? In Part 3, we have seen that this argument has some validity, for although there is a long history of supernatural or occult "detective" stories, many of these are far more effective as supernatural tales of horror than as detective tales. However, we have also seen that such an integration is possible, for in the hands of a supremely skilled writer grounded in the conventions of the detective story the horror of the supernatural does not preclude the puzzles, clues, and rational detection of the classic detective tale. In Chapters Seven and Eight we have described quite a number of supernatural detective stories where the detective experiences or combats supernatural forces, which have varying degrees of success integrating the "real" and the supernatural. Clearly, this is the most difficult and rarely achieved type of integration, for the assumptions, parameters, and conventions of the detective story are in many ways inimical to the supernatural, especially the supernatural of terror. However, it has occasionally, been done effectively and powerfully.

Finally, in Part 4, we have seen that even when the "fantastic" is defined in the strictest possible way as the period of uncertainty about whether something is "real" or not, there are a few detective stories that have incorporated (and gloried in) the fantastic. A case could be made that these few stories, by such master writers as Blackwood, Bramah, Carr, Futrelle, and Stribling, are among the very finest of the detective genre.

And so despite many risks, pitfalls, and challenges in trying to integrate the fantastic with the detective story, it seems that some of the very best detective tales can be truly fantastic!

Bibliography

Works Discussed

Adams, Samuel Hopkins. 1903. "The Flying Death." *Ellery Queen Mystery Magazine (EQMM)*, January 1944.

Agis, Alexander. "The Science of Anticipation." *EQMM*, February 1974.

Allingham, Margery. 1937. "The Border-Line Case." In *The Black Lizard Big Book of Locked-Room Mysteries.* Edited by Otto Penzler. New York: Vintage Books, 2014.

Anderson, Poul. "The Martian Crown Jewels." *EQMM*, February 1958.

Arden, William. "The Bizarre Case Expert." *EQMM*, June 1970.

Arthur, Robert. 1951. "The 51st Sealed Room." In *Tantalizing Locked Room Mysteries.* Edited by Isaac Asimov, Charles Waugh, and Martin Greenberg. New York: Walker and Company, 1982.

Asimov, Isaac. 1968. *Asimov's Mysteries.* Garden City, NY: Doubleday and Company.

Askew, Alice, and Claude Askew. 2006. *Aylmer Vance: Ghost-Seer.* Hertfortshire, England: Wordsworth.

Bailey, H.C. 1931. *Mr. Fortune Explains.* London: Ward, Lock and Company.

Barr, Robert. 1985. *The Triumphs of Eugene Valmont.* New York: Dover.

Barr, Stephen. 1965. "The Locked Room to End Locked Rooms." In *The Black Lizard Big Book of Locked-Room Mysteries.* Edited by Otto Penzler. New York: Vintage Books, 2014.

Baxt, George. 1982. "Clap Hands, There Goes Charlie." In *Fifty Years of the Best from Ellery Queen's Mystery Magazine.* Edited by Eleanor Sullivan. New York: Carroll and Graf, 1982.

Begbie, Harold. 2002. *The Amazing Dreams of Andrew Lattner.* Ashcroft, Canada: Ash Tree Press.

Biggle, Lloyd. "Department of Future Crime." *EQMM*, September 1966.

Blackwood, Algernon. 1906. *The Empty House and Other Stories.* London: Nash.

_____. 1914. "A Victim of Higher Space." In *The Weiser Book of Occult Detectives.* Edited by Judika Illes. Newburyport, MA: Weiser Books, 2017.

_____. 1997. *The Complete John Silence.* Mineola, New York: Dover Publications.

Blavatsky, Helena. 1873. "The Cave of Echoes." In *The Weiser Book of Occult Detectives.* Edited by Judika Illes. Newburyport, MA: Weiser Books, 2017.

Block, Lawrence, and Lynn Wood Block. 1997. "The Burglar Who Smelled Smoke." In *The Black Lizard Big Book of Locked-Room Mysteries.* Edited by Otto Penzler. New York: Vintage Books, 2014.

Bodkin, M. McDonnell. 1898. "Murder by Proxy." In *Death Locked In.* Edited by Douglas Greene and Robert Adey. New York: International Polygonics, 1987.

Boucher, Anthony. 1955. *Far and Away.* New York: Ballantine Books.

_____. 1969. *The Compleat Werewolf.* New York: Ace Books.

Bramah, Ernest. 1923. "The Eastern Mystery." In *Masterpieces of Mystery: the Old Masters.* Edited by Ellery Queen. New York: Davis Publications, 1978.

Bibliography

_____. 1923. *The Eyes of Max Carrados.* London: Richards.

Brand, Christianna. 1983. *Buffet for Unwelcome Guests.* Carbondale: Southern Illinois. University Press.

Braun, Lilian Jackson. "SuSu and the 8:30 Ghost." *EQMM,* April 1964.

Breen, Jon. 1982. *Hair of the Sleuthhound.* Metuchen, NJ: The Scarecrow Press.

Brennan, Joseph. 1977. *Chronicles of Lucius Leffing.* West Kingston, RI: Donald Grant.

_____. 1990. *The Adventures of Lucius Leffing.* Hampton Falls, NH: Donald Grant.

Brittain, William. 1974. "The Impossible Footprint." In *The Mammoth Book of Perfect Crimes and Impossible Mysteries.* Edited by Mike Ashley. New York: Carroll and Graf, 2007.

_____. 2018. *The Man Who Read Mysteries.* Cincinnati, OH: Crippen and Landru.

_____. "Mr. Strang Finds an Angle." *EQMM,* June 1971.

_____. 1976. "Mr. Strang Accepts a Challenge." In *The Mammoth Book of Locked-Room Mysteries and Impossible Crimes.* Edited by Mike Ashley. New York: Carrol and Graf, 2000.

Brown, Fredric. 1943. "The Spherical Ghoul." In *Locked In.* Edited by Douglas Greene and Robert Adey. New York: International Polygonics, 1987.

_____. "The Dijinn Murder." *EQMM,* January 1944.

Burgess, Gelett. 1899. "The Spectre House." In *Giving Up the Ghosts,* Edited by Tim Prasil. Greenville, OH: Coachwhip Publications. 2015.

_____. 1901. "The Levitant." In *Giving Up the Ghosts,* Edited by Tim Prasil. Greenville, OH: Coachwhip Publications. 2015.

_____. 1905. "The Ghost Extinguisher." In *Giving Up the Ghosts.* Edited by Tim Prasil. Greenville, OH: Coachwhip Publications. 2015.

_____. 2008. *The Master of Mysteries.* Surinam Turtle Press.

Burke, Thomas. 1929. "The Bloomsbury Wonder." In *Fifty Years of the Best from Ellery Queen's Mystery Magazine.* Edited by Eleanor Sullivan. New York: Carroll and Graf. 1991.

Burrage, A.M. 1920. "The House of Treburyan." In *Giving up the Ghosts.* Edited by Tim Prasil. Greenville, OH: Coachwhip Publications, 2015.

_____. 1920. "The Severed Head." In *Giving up the Ghosts.* Edited by Tim Prasil. Greenville, OH: Coachwhip Publications, 2015.

_____. 1996. *The Occult Files of Francis Chard.* Ash Tree Press.

Carr, John Dickson. 1981. *The Department of Queer Complaints.* Boston: Greg Press.

_____. 1991a. *The Door to Doom.* New York: International Polygonics.

_____. 1991b. *Fell and Foulplay.* New York: International Polygonics.

_____. "The House in Goblin Woods." *EQMM,* November 1947.

Carter, Lin. 2002. *Lin Carter's Anton Zarnak.* Marietta, GA: Marietta Publishing.

Chambers, Robert. 1906. *The Tracer of Lost Persons.* New York: D. Appleton.

Charteris, Leslie. 1943. "The Man Who Liked Toys." In *The Black Lizard Big Book of Locked-Room Mysteries.* Edited by Otto Penzler. New York: Vintage Books, 2014.

Chesterton, G.K. 1905. *The Club of Queer Trades.* New York: Harper and Brothers Publishers.

_____. 1911. *The Innocence of Father Brown.* London: Casell.

_____. 1922. *The Man Who Knew Too Much.* London: Casell.

_____. 1926. *The Incredulity of Father Brown.* London: Casell.

_____. 1929. *The Poet and the Lunatics.* New York: Sheed and Ward.

_____. 1934. *The Scandal of Father Brown.* London: Casell.

_____. 1951. *The Father Brown Omnibus.* New York: Dodd, Mead, and Company.

Child, Charles B. 1950. "The Long, Thin Man." *EQMM,* July 1954.

_____. 2002. *The Sleuth of Baghdad.* Norfolk, VA: Crippen and Landru.

_____. "The Man Who Wasn't There." *EQMM,* April 1969.

Christie, Agatha. 1939. *The Regatta Mystery.* New York: Dodd Mead.

_____. 1984. *Partners in Crime.* New York: Berkley Books.

Bibliography

_____. 1986. *The Mysterious Mr. Quin*. New York: Bantam Books.

_____. 1991. *Problem at Pollensa Bay*. London: HarperCollins.

_____. 2003. *The Hound of Death*. London: Harper.

_____. 2011. *Miss Marple: The Complete Short Stories*. Boston: William Morris.

_____. 2013. *Hercule Poirot: The Complete Short Stories*. Boston: William Morrow.

Cole, G.D.H., and M. Cole. 1928. *Superintendent Wilson's Holiday*. London: W. Collins Sons and Company.

Coles, Manning. "Handcuffs Don't Hold Ghosts." *EQMM*, May 1946.

Collins, Michael. 1963. "No Way Out." In *The Mammoth Book of Locked-Room Mysteries and Impossible Crimes*. New York: Carroll and Graf. 2000.

Commings. Joseph. 2004. *Banner Deadlines*. Norfolk, VA: Crippen and Landru.

Conan Doyle, Arthur. 1883. "Selecting a Ghost." In *The First Lenaur Book of Supernatural Detectives*. Edited by Morgan Tyler. Leonaur. 2015.

_____. 1898. "The Lost Special." In *Vintage Mystery and Detective Stories*. Edited by David Stuart Davies. London: Wordsworth.

_____. 1899. "The Brown Hand." In *The Supernatural Sherlocks*. Edited by Nick Rennison. Herts, England: No Exit Press, 2017.

_____. 1902. "The Leather Funnel." In *The Weiser Book of Occult Detectives*. Edited by Judika Illes. Newburyport, MA: Weiser Books, 2017.

_____. 2005. *The New Annotated Sherlock Holmes*. New York: W.W. Norton.

Copper, Basil. 2017. *The Secret Files of Solar Pons*. London: DIP.

Cornier, Vincent. 1929. "The Flying Hat." In *The Black Lizard Big Book of Locked-Room Mysteries*. Edited by Otto Penzler. New York: Vintage Books, 2014.

_____. 1937. "The Courtyard of the Fly." In *Murder Impossible*. Edited by Jack Adrian and Robert Adey. New York: Carroll and Graf, 1990.

_____. 2011. *The Duel of Shadows*, Norfolk, VA: Crippen and Landru.

Crispin, Edmund. 1951. "Beware of the Trains." In *The Black Lizard Big Book of Locked-Room Mysteries*. Edited by Otto Penzler. New York: Vintage Books, 2014.

_____. "The Name on the Window." *EQMM*, February 1953.

Crofts, Freeman Wills. 2001. *The Mystery of the Sleeping Car Express and other Stories*. London: House of Stratus.

Crowley, Aleister. 2012. *The Simon Iff Stories and Other Works*. Hertfordshire, England: Wordsworth.

Cummings, Ray. 1925. "The Confession of Rosa Vitelli." In *The Black Lizard Big Book of Locked-Room Mysteries*. Edited by Otto Penzler. New York: Vintage Books, 2014.

Daniels, Harold. "The Haunted Woodshed." *EQMM*, August 1961.

Davies, David Stuart. 1999. "The Curzon Street Conundrum." In *Vintage Mystery and Detective Stories*. Edited by David Stuart Davies. London: Wordsworth, 2006.

_____ . 2000. "The Curse of the Griswold Phantom." In *Vintage Mystery and Detective Stories*. Edited by David Stuart Davies. London: Wordsworth. 2006.

de Crespigny, Rose Champion. 1999. *Norton Vyse: Psychic*. Ash Tree Press.

de la Torre, Lillian. "Murder Lock'd In." *EQMM*, December 1980.

_____. "The Triple-Lock'd Room." *EQMM*, January 1952.

Derleth, August. 1982. *The Solar Pons Omnibus*. Sauk City, WI: Arkham House.

Doyle, Adrian, and John Dickson Carr. 1992. *The Exploits of Sherlock Holmes*. New York: Barnes and Noble.

Dunsany, Lord. 1952. *The Little Tales of Smethers*. London: Jarrolds.

Eberhart, Mignon. 1934. *The Cases of Susan Dare*. Garden City, New York: Doubleday, Doran.

_____. "Postiche." *EQMM*, November 1944.

_____. "The Flowering Face." *EQMM*, November 1948.

Ellin, Stanley. 1967. "The Twelfth Statue." In *The Black Lizard Big Book of Locked-Room Mysteries*. Edited by Otto Penzler. New York: Vintage Books, 2014.

189

Bibliography

Ellis, Kate. 2000. "The Odor of Sanctity." In *The Black Lizard Big Book of Locked-Room Mysteries*. Edited by Otto Penzler. New York: Vintage Books, 2014.

Fairman, Paul. 1959. "Recollection of the Future." *EQMM*, July 1964.

Fischer, Bruno. 1945. "The Man Who Lost His Head." In *Best Detective Stories of the Year*. Edited by David Cooke. New York: E.P. Dutton, 1946.

Fish, Robert. 1990. *Schlock Homes: The Complete Bagel Street Saga*. Bloomington, IN: Gaslight.

Fortune, Dion. 1926. *The Secrets of Dr. Tavener*. Columbus, Ohio: Ariel Press.

Freeman, R. Austin. 1909. "The Aluminum Dagger." In *The Black Lizard Big Book of Locked-Room Mysteries*. Edited by Otto Penzler. New York: Vintage Books, 2014.

French, John. 1998. "The Best Solution." In *Lin Carter's Anton Zarnak*, Edited by Robert Price. Marietta, GA: Marietta Pub., 2002.

Futrelle, Jacques. *Mystery and Detection with the Thinking Machine, vol. 1*. Landisville, PA: Coachwhip Publications, 2009.

_____. *Mystery and Detection with the Thinking Machine vol. 2*. Landisville, PA: Coachwhip Publications, 2009.

_____. "The Statement of the Accused." *EQMM*, May 1945.

Gardner, Erle Stanley. "The Clue of the Runaway Blonde." *EQMM*, March 1971.

Garrett, Randall. 2013. *Lord Darcy Investigates*. N.p.: Jabberwocky Literary Agency, e-book.

Giesy, J.U., and Junius B. Smith. 2013. *Semi Dual: the Occult Detector, vol. 1*. Boston: Altus.

Godfrey, Peter. 1979. "Out of this World." In *Death Locked In*. Edited by Douglas Greene and Robert Adey. New York: Polygonics, 1987.

_____. 2002. *The Newtonian Egg*. Norfolk, VA: Crippen and Landru.

_____. "A Dagger of the Mind." *EQMM*, March 1951.

_____. "The Lady and the Dragon." *EQMM*, September 1950.

Guilford, C.B. 1953. "Heaven Can Wait." In *Bodies and Souls*. Edited by Dan Herr and Joel Wells. Garden City, NY: Doubleday and Company, 1961.

Halter, Paul. 2004. *The Night of the Wolf*. Rockville, MD: Wildside Press.

Harrison, Micheal. 1968. *The Exploits of the Chevalier Dupin*. Sauk City, WI: Mycroft and Moran.

Heard, H.F. "The Adventure of Mr. Montalba, Obsequist." *EQMM*, September 1945.

_____. "The Enchanted Garden." *EQMM*, March 1949.

_____. "The President of the United States, Detective." *EQMM*, March 1947.

Henderson, C.J. 1999. "The Door." In *Lin Carter's Anton Zarnak*. Edited by Robert Price. Marietta, GA: Marrieta Pub., 2002.

Heron, E., and H. Heron. 2011. "The Experiences of Flaxman Low." In *Supernatural Detectives 3*. Landisville, PA: Coachwhip Publications.

Hillerman, Tony. 1986. "The Witch, Yazzie, and the Nine of Clubs." In *Sleuths of the Century*. Edited by Jon Breen and Ed Gorman. New York: Carroll and Graf, 2000.

Hillman, Gordon. 1986. "Panic at Wild Harbor." In *Supernatural Sleuths*. Edited by Peter Haining, London: William Kimber.

Hoch, Edward D. 2017. *All But Impossible: The Impossible Files of Dr. Sam Hawthorne*. Norfolk, VA: Crippen and Landru.

_____. "The Case of the Musical Bullet." *EQMM*, March 1974.

_____. 2018. *Challenge the Impossible: the Final Problems of Dr. Sam Hawthorne*. Norfolk, VA: Crippen and Landru.

_____. 1971. *City of Brass*. North Hollywood, CA: Leisure Books.

_____. 2000. *Diagnosis Impossible: The Problems of Dr. Sam Hawthorne*. Norfolk, VA: Crippen and Landru.

_____. "The Impossible Impossible Crime." *EQMM*, April 1968.

_____. 1985. *Leopold's Way*. Carbondale, ILL: Southern Illinois University Press.

_____. "The Man Who Shot the Werewolf." *EQMM*, February 1979.

_____. 2006. *More Things Impossible: the Second Casebook of Dr. Sam Hawthorne*. Norfolk, VA: Crippen and Landru.

_____. 2014. *Nothing is Impossible: Further Problems of Dr. Sam Hawthorne*. Norfolk, VA: Crippen and Landru.

_____. 1984. *The Quests of Simon Ark*. New York: The Mysterious Press.

_____. 1997. "A Shower of Daggers." In *The Mammoth Book of Perfect Crimes and Impossible Crimes*. Edited by Mike Ashley. New York: Carroll and Graf. 2007.

_____. "The Theft of the Venetian Window." *EQMM*, November 1975.

_____. "The Treasure of Jack the Ripper." *EQMM*, October 1978.

Hodgson, W.H. "Carnacki: Ghost Finder." In *Supernatural Detectives 1*. Landisville, PA: Coachwhip Publications, 2011.

Hoffman, Banesh. "Sherlock, Shakespeare, and the Bomb." *EQMM*, February 1966.

Hunsberger, H. Edward. 1985. "Eternally Yours." In *The Mammoth Book of Perfect Crimes and Impossible Mysteries*. Edited by Mike Ashley. New York: Carrol and Graf, 2007.

Innes, Michael. 1975. *The Appleby File*. North Yorkshire, England: Stratus.

_____. 2001a. *Appleby Talking*. North Yorkshire, England: Stratus.

_____. 2001b. *Appleby Talks Again*. North Yorkshire, England: Stratus.

_____. "The Magic Painting." *EQMM*, January 1957.

James, P.D. "Murder, 1986." *EQMM*, October 1970.

Jesse, F. Tennyson. 1931. *Solange Stories*. New York: Macmillan and Co.

Keating, H.R.F. 1972. "Inspector Ghote and the Miracle Baby." In *The World's Greatest Detective Stories*. Edited by Herbert van Thal. London: Magpie Books, 2005.

_____. 2000. "The Legs that Walked." In *The Mammoth Book of Locked-Room Mysteries and Impossible Crimes*. Edited by Mike Ashley. New York: Carroll and Graf, 2000.

Kelland, Clarence Budington. "The Inconspicuous Man." *EQMM*, January 1951.

Kemelman, Harry. 1967. *The Nine Mile Walk*. New York: G.P. Putnam's Sons.

Kenealy, Arabella. 1896. "Some Experiences of Lord Syfret." In *Supernatural Detectives 3*. Landisville, PA: Coachwhip Publications. 2011.

Kennett, Rick. 1972. *No. 472 Cheyne Walk, Carnacki: the Untold Stories*. The Ghost Story Society.

Kersh, Gerald. "Dr. Ox Will Die at Midnight." *EQMM*, October 1970.

_____. "Open Verdict." *EQMM*, October 1959.

Key, Uel. 2015. *The Broken Fang and other Experiences of a Specialist in Spooks*. Ramble House.

Kidd, A.F. 1972. *No. 472 Cheyne Walk, Carnacki: the Untold Stories*. N.p.: The Ghost Story Society.

Killough, Lee. 1982. "The Existential Man." In *Supernatural Sleuths*. Edited by Charles Waugh and Martin Greenberg. New York: Penguin, 1996.

King, C.D. 2003. *The Complete Curious Mr. Tarrant*. Norfolk, VA: Crippen and Landru.

King, Rufus. 1925. "The Man Who Didn't Exist." *EQMM*, August 1947.

King, Stephen. 1987. "The Doctor's Case." In *The Black Lizard Big Book of Locked-Room Mysteries*. Edited by Otto Penzler. New York: Vintage Books, 2014.

Krohn, William. 1965. "The Impossible Murder of Dr. Satanus." In *The Mammoth Book of Perfect Crimes and Impossible Mysteries*. Edited by Mike Ashley. New York: Carroll and Graf, 2007.

Lawrence, Margery. 2003. *The Casebook of Miles Pennoyer*. Ashcroft, British Columbia: Ashtree Press.

Le Fanu, J.S. 1869. "Green Tea." In *The Weiser Book of Occult Detectives*. Edited by Judika Illes. Newburyport, MA: Weiser Books. 2017.

Le Queux, William. 1917. "The Colour-Criminologist." In *Supernatural Detectives 5*. Landisville, PA: Coachwhip Publications. 2012.

Lipman, Clayre, and Michel Lipman. "The Walking Corpse." *EQMM*, September 1950.

Bibliography

Lonstar, Conway. "The Weapon from Nowhere." *EQMM*, November 1970.

Lumley, Brian. 1987. *The Compleat Crow*. Buffalo, NY: W. Paul Ganley.

Lupoff, Richard. 2000. "The Second Drug." In *The Mammoth Book of Locked-Room Mysteries and Impossible Crimes*. Edited by Mike Ashley. New York: Carroll and Graf, 2000.

MacCreagh, Gordon. 1932. "The Sinister Shape." In *Supernatural Sleuths*. Edited by Peter Haining. London: William Kimber, 1986.

_____. 2011. *Dr. Munsing, Exorcist*. Worcestershire, England: Read Books, Ltd.

MacDonald, Philip. 1952. *Something to Hide*. New York: Doubleday and Company.

_____. "The Green-and-Gold String." *EQMM*, October 1948.

Machen, Arthur. 1922. *House of Souls*. New York: Alfred Knopf.

_____. 1895. "The Shining Pyramid." In *The Supernatural Solution*. Edited by Michel Parry. New York: Taplinger Publishing Company, 1976.

_____. 1923. *The Three Imposters*. New York: Alfred Knopf.

Marsh, Ngaio. 1946. "I Can Find My Way Out." In *Death Locked In*. Edited by Douglas Greene and Robert Adey. New York: International Polygonics, 1987.

Martin, A.E. "The Flying Corpse." *EQMM*, September 1947.

Mason, A.E.W. 1917. *The Four Corners of the World*. London: Hodder and Stoughton.

Mathiesen, Theodore. "Leonardo da Vinci, Detective." *EQMM*, January 1959.

McBain, Ed. "Nightshade." *EQMM*, August 1970.

McCloy, Helen. 2003. *The Pleasant Assassin*. Norfolk, VA: Crippen and Landru.

McConnor, Vincent. "The Man Who Collected Obits." *EQMM*, February 1967.

Meade, L.T., and Robert Eustace. 1898. "John Bell: Ghost Explorer." In *Supernatural Detectives 1*. Landisville, PA: Coachwhip Publications, 2011.

Meade, L.T., and Robert Eustace. 1902. "The Dead Hand." In *Giving Up the Ghosts*. Edited by Tim Prasil. Greenville, OH: Coachwhip Publications, 2015.

Muir, Augustus. 1935. "The Kestar Diamond Case." In *The Black Lizard Big Book of Locked-Room Mysteries*. Edited by Otto Penzler. New York: Vintage Books, 2014.

Nevins, Francis. "The Ironclad Alibi." *EQMM*, November 1974.

Newton, Douglas. 1936. "Contrary to Evidence." In *The Mammoth Book of Perfect Crimes and Impossible Mysteries*. Edited by Mike Ashley. New York: Carroll and Graf, 2007.

O'Brien, Fitz-James. 1855. "A Pot of Tulips." In *Giving up the Ghosts*. Edited by Tim Prasil. Greenville, OH: Coachwhip Publications, 2015.

_____. 1859. "What Was It?" In *Giving up the Ghosts*. Edited by Tim Prasil. Greenville, OH: Coachwhip Publications, 2015.

Olde, Nicholas. 1928. *The Incredible Adventures of Rowland Hern*. Ramble House.

Palmer, Stuart. "Monkey Murder." *EQMM*, January 1947.

_____. "The Riddle of the Tired Bullet." *EQMM*, March 1948.

Peirce, J.F. "The Total Portrait." *EQMM*, April 1971.

Pentecost, Hugh. 1945. "Volcano in the Mind." *EQMM*, January 1967.

_____. 1948. "The Fourth Degree." In *Fifty Years of the Best from Ellery Queen's Mystery Magazine*. Edited by Eleanor Sullivan. New York: Carroll and Graf, 1991.

Pierce, John. "Farewell Banquet." *EQMM*, March 1974.

Poe, Edgar Allan. 1927. *Collected Works of Edgar Allan Poe*. New York: Walter J. Black.

Porges, Arthur. 1960. "No Killer Has Wings." In *The Mammoth Book of Perfect Crimes and Impossible Mysteries*. Edited by Mike Ashley. New York: Carroll and Graf, 2007.

_____. 2009. *The Curious Cases of Cyriack Skinner Grey*. Surrey, England: Richard Simms.

_____. "Her Last Bow: an Adventure of Stately Homes." *EQMM*, February 1957.

_____. "Murder of a Priest." *EQMM*, September 1967.

_____. "The English Village Mystery." *EQMM*, December 1964.

Post, Melville Davisson. 1923. *Monsieur Jonquelle*. London: D. Appleton and Company.

_____. 1929. *The Bradmoor Murder*. New York: J.H. Sears.

_____. 1977. *The Complete Uncle Abner*. Del Mar, CA: University of San Diego.

_____. 2006. *The Sleuth of St. James Square.* Los Angeles: Aegypan Press.

Powell, James. 2009. *A Pocketful of Noses.* Norfolk, VA: Crippen and Landru.

_____. "The Stollmeyer Sonnets." *EQMM,* October 1966.

Price, E. Hoffman. 2017. *E. Hoffman Price's Pierre d'Artois: Occult Detective.* Wildside Press.

Price, John Basye. 1954. "Death and the Rope Trick." In *The Mammoth Book of Perfect Crimes and Impossible Mysteries.* Edited by Mike Ashley. New York: Carroll and Graf, 2007.

Price, Robert. 1996. "Dope War of the Black Tong." In *Lin Carter's Anton Zarnak.* Edited by Robert Price. Marietta, GA: Marietta Publishing, 2002.

Priestley, J.B. "An Arabian Night in Park Lane." *EQMM,* March 1947.

Prince, Jerome, and Harold Prince. "The Finger Man." *EQMM,* January 1945.

_____. "The Man in the Velvet Hat." *EQMM,* May 1944.

Pronzini, Bill. 1973. "Proof of Guilt." In *The Mammoth Book of Perfect Crimes and Impossible Mysteries.* Edited by Mike Ashley. New York: Carroll and Graf, 2005.

_____. 1978. "The Pulp Connection." In *The Mammoth Book of Locked-Room Mysteries and Impossible Crimes.* Edited by Mike Ashley. New York: Carroll and Graf, 2000.

_____. 2011. *Case File: A Collection of Stories Featuring the Nameless Detective.* New York: John Curley and Associates.

_____, and Jeffrey Wallman. "The Half-Invisible Man." *EQMM,* May 1974.

Pronzini, Bill, and Michael Kurland. 1975. "Thin Air." In *Tantalizing Locked Room Mysteries.* Edited by Isaac Asimov, Charles Waugh, and Martin Greenberg. New York: Walter and Co., 1982.

Queen, Ellery. 1967. *The Ellery Queen Omnibus.* New York: Dorset Press.

Quinn, Seabury. 2017a. *The Complete Tales of Jules de Grandin, Vol. 1.* New York: Night Shade Books.

_____. 2017b. *The Complete Tales of Jules de Grandin, Vol 2.* New York: Night Shade Books.

_____. 2018a. *The Complete Tales of Jules de Grandin, Vol. 3.* New York: Night Shade Books.

_____. 2018b. *The Complete Tales of Jules de Grandin, Vol. 4.* New York: Night Shade Books.

_____. 2019. *The Complete Tales of Jules de Grandin, Vol. 5.* New York: Night Shade Books.

Rawson, Clayton. 1940. "Death out of Thin Air." In *The Black Lizard Big Book of Locked-Room Mysteries.* Edited by Otto Penzler. New York: Vintage Books, 2014.

_____. 1979. *The Great Merlini.* Boston: Gregg Press.

_____. 2004. *The Magical Mysteries of Don Diavolo.* Ontario, Canada: Battered Silicon.

Reed, Mary, and Eric Mayer. 2000. "Locked In Death." In *The Mammoth Book of Perfect Crimes and Impossible Mysteries.* Edited by Mike Ashley. New York: Carrol and Graf, 2007.

Rees, Arthur. 1911. "The Invisible Ray." In *Vintage Mystery and Detective Stories.* Edited by David Stuart Davies. London: Wordsworth, 2006.

_____. 1926. "The Finger of Death." In *The World's Best 100 Detective Stories.* Edited by Eugene Thwing. New York: Funk and Wagnalls, 1929.

Richardson, Maurice. "The Last Detective Story." *EQMM,* February 1947.

Richter, Conrad. 1931a. "The Toad Man Specter." In *Giving up the Ghosts.* Edited by Tim Prasil. Greenville, OH: Coachwhip Publications, 2015.

_____. 1931b. "Monster of the Dark Places." In *Giving up the Ghosts.* Edited by Tim Prasil. Greenville, OH: Coachwhip Publications, 2015.

Rittenberg, Max. 1913a. "The Mystery of the Sevenoaks Tunnel." In *The Mammoth Book of Perfect Crimes and Impossible Mysteries.* Edited by Mike Ashley. New York: Carroll and Graf, 2007.

_____. 1913b. "Dr. Xavier Wycherley, the Mind-Reader." In *Detective 2.* Landisville, PA: Coachwhip Publications. 2011.

Rogers, Joel Townsley. 2006. *Night of Horror.* N.p.: Ramble House.

Rohmer, Sax. 1977. *The Dream-Detective.* New York: Dover.

Bibliography

Rosaire, Forrest. 1939. "The Poisoned Bowl." In *The Mammoth Book of Perfect Crimes and Impossible Mysteries*. Edited by Mike Ashley. New York: Carroll and Graf, 2005.

Rousseau, Victor. 2006. *The Surgeon of Souls*. N.p.: The Spectre Library.

Sayers, Dorothy. 1972. *Lord Peter*. New York: Harper and Row.

Scrymsour, Ella. 2012. "*Sheila Crerar*." In *Supernatural Detectives 4*. Landisville, PA: Coachwhip Publications. 2012.

Shiel, M.P. 1977. *Prince Zaleski and Cummings King Monk*. Sauk City, WI: Mycroft and Moran.

Simenon, George. 1947. "The Little House at Croix-Rousse." In *The Black Lizard Big Book of Locked-Room Mysteries*. Edited by Otto Penzler. New York: Vintage Books, 2014.

Skvorecky, Joseph. 1988. *The Mournful Demeanor of Lieutenant Buruvka*. Toronto: Lester and Orpen Dennys, Publisher.

Somerlott, Robert. "The Hair of the Widow." *EQMM*, January 1965.

Stevens, Shane. "The Final Adventure." *EQMM*, February 1969.

Stribling, T.S. 1929. *Clues of the Caribbees*. Garden City, NY: Doubleday, Doran.

_____. 1975. *Best Poggioli Detective Stories*. New York: Dover.

_____. 2003. *Dr. Poggioli: Criminologist*. Norfolk, VA: Crippen and Landru.

Symons, Julian. "As If By Magic." *EQMM* (British), January 1964.

_____. 2006. *The Detections of Francis Quarles*. Norfolk, VA: Crippen and Landru.

Talbut, Hake. 1944. "The Other Side." In *Murder Impossible*. Edited by Jack Adrian and Robert Adey. New York: Carroll and Graf Publishers.

Upward, Allan. 1905. "The Haunted Woman." In *The Black Veil and Other Tales of Supernatural Sleuths*. Edited by Mark Valentine. London: Wordsworth.

Van Doren, Mark. "The Luminous Face." *EQMM*, August 1963.

Vivian, E. Charles. 1926. "Locked In." In *The Mammoth Book of Vintage Whodunits*. Edited by Maxim Jakubowski. New York: Carroll and Graf, 2006.

Wallace, Edgar. "The Ghost of John Holling." *EQMM*, April 1963.

Weinberg, Robert. 2005. *The Occult Detective*. Chicago: Twilight Tales.

Wellman, Manly Wade. 1947. "A Knife Between Brothers." In *The Black Lizard Big Book of Locked-Room Mysteries*. Edited by Otto Penzler. New York: Vintage Books, 2014.

_____. 1981. *Lonely Vigils*. N.p.: Carcosa.

_____. 1988. *John the Balladeer*. New York: Baen Books.

_____. "The Adventure of the Martian Client." *Magazine of Fantasy and Science Fiction*, December 1967.

_____. "The Half-Haunted." *Weird Tales*, September 1941.

_____. "Venus, Mars, and Baker Street." *Magazine of Fantasy and Science Fiction*, March 1972.

Wheatley, Dennis. 1943. "Gunmen, Gallants, and Ghosts." London: Hutchinson and Company.

Whitehead, Henry S. 1930. "The Shut Room." In *Supernatural Sherlocks*. Edited by Nick Rennison. Harpenden, Hertsfordshire: No Exit Press.

Yaffe, James. 2016. *My Mother, the Detective*. Norfolk, VA: Crippen and Landru.

_____. "The Department of Impossible Crimes." *EQMM*, July 1943.

_____. "The Emperor's Mushrooms." *EQMM*, September 1945.

_____. "The Seventh Drink." *EQMM*, September 1944.

Other References

Adrian, Jack, and Robert Adey, eds. 1990. *Murder Impossible: an Extravaganza of Miraculous Murders, Fantastic Felonies, and Incredible Criminals*. New York: Carroll and Graf.

Ashley, Mike, ed. 2000. *The Mammoth Book of Locked-Room Mysteries and Impossible Crimes.* New York: Carroll and Graf.

Ashley, Mike, ed. 2007. *The Mammoth Book of Perfect Crimes and Impossible Mysteries.* New York: Carroll and Graf.

Asimov, Isaac, Charles Waugh, and Martin Greenberg, eds. 1982. *Tantalizing Locked Room Mysteries.* New York: Walker and Company.

Blackwell, Laird. 2018. *The Metaphysical Mysteries of G.K. Chesterton.* Jefferson, N.C: McFarland.

Breen, Jon, and Ed Gorman, eds. 2000. *Sleuths of the Century.* New York: Carroll and Graf.

Contendo, William, and Martin Greenberg. 1991. *Index to Crime and Mystery Anthologies.* Boston: G.K. Hall and Company.

Davies, David, ed. 2006. *Vintage Mystery and Detective Stories.* London: Wordsworth.

Detection Club. 1946. "The Detection Club Oath." In *The Art of the Mystery Story.* Edited by Howard Haycraft. New York: Simon & Schuster.

Fodorov, Tzvetan. 1973. *The Fantastic: A Structural Approach to a Literary Genre.* Ithaca, New York: Cornel University Press.

Greene, Douglas, and Robert Adey, eds. 1987. *Death Locked In: An Anthology of Locked Room Stories.* New York: International Polygonics.

Haining, Peter, ed. 1986. *Supernatural Sleuths: Stories of Occult Investigators.* London: William Kimber.

Herbert, Rosemary, ed. 1999. *The Oxford Companion to Crime and Mystery Writing.* Oxford, England: Oxford University Press.

Herr, Dan, and Joel Wells, eds. 1961. *Bodies and Souls.* Garden City, NY: Doubleday and Company.

Higgins, James. 1970. *Beyond Words: Mystical Fancy in Children's Literature.* New York: Teacher's College Press.

Hoch, Edward, ed. 1981. *All But Impossible: an Anthology of Locked Room and Impossible Crime Stories by Members of the Mystery Writers of America.* New York: Ticknor and Fields.

Hubin, Allen. 1994. *Crime Fiction II: a Comprehensive Bibliography, 1749–1990.* New York: Garland.

Illes, Judith, ed. 2017. *The Weiser Book of Occult Detectives.* Newsburyport, MA: Weiser Books.

Jakubowski, Maxim, ed. 2006. *The Mammoth Book of Vintage Whodunnits.* New York: Carroll and Graf.

Jones, Stephen, ed. 1999. *Dark Detectives: Adventures of the Supernatural Sleuths.* Minneapolis, MN: F and B Mystery.

Joshi, S.T. 1990. *The Weird Tale.* Austin: University of Texas Press.

Knox, Ronald. 1929. "A Detective Story Decalogue." In *The Art of the Mystery Story.* Edited by Howard Haycraft. New York: Simon & Schuster, 1946.

Levison, Richard, and William Link. 1981. "Introduction." In *The Department of Queer Complaints,* by Carter Dickson. Boston: Gregg Press.

Melville, Herman. 2002. *Moby Dick.* Hertfordshire, England: Wordsworth Classics.

Murch, A.E. 1958. *The Development of the Detective Novel.* London: Peter Owen Limited.

Nieminski, John. 1974. *An Author/Title Index to Ellery Queen's Mystery Magazine, Fall 1941–January 1973.* White Bear Lake, MN: The Armchair Detective Press.

Parry, Michel, ed. 1976. *The Supernatural Solution.* New York: Taplinger Publishing Co.

Penzler, Otto, ed. 2014. *The Black Lizard Big Book of Locked-Room Mysteries.* New York: Vintage Books.

Prasil, Tim, ed. 2015. *Giving Up the Ghosts.* Greenville, OH: Coachwhip Publications.

Price, Robert, ed. 2002. *Lin Carter's Anton Zarnak, Supernatural Sleuth.* Marietta, GA: Marietta Pub.

Bibliography

Queen, Ellery. 1941. *101 Years' Entertainment.* New York: Modern Library.

_____, ed. 1946. *The Queen's Awards, 1946.* Boston: Little, Brown, and Company.

_____. Introduction. *The Exploits of Chevalier Dupin* by Michael Harrison. Sauk City, WI: Mycroft and Moran.

Rabkin, Eric. 1976. *The Fantastic in Literature.* Princeton, NJ: Princeton University Press.

Rennison, Nick, ed. 2017. *Supernatural Sherlocks.* Herts, England: No Exit Press.

Santesson, Hans, ed. 1968. *The Locked Room Reader: Stories of Impossible Crimes and Escapes.* New York: Random House.

Stephensen-Payne, Phil. 2008. *Crime, Mystery, and Gangster Fiction Magazine Index.* www.philsp.com.

Sullivan, Eleanor, ed. 1991. *Fifty Years of the Best from Ellery Queen Mystery Magazine.* New York: Carroll and Graf Publishers.

Swinfen, Ann. 1984. *In Defense of Fantasy.* London: Routledge and Kegan Paul.

Thwing, Eugene. 1929. *The World's Best 100 Detective Stories.* New York: Funk and Wagnalls.

Todorov, Tzvetan. 1975. *The Fantastic: a Structural Approach to a Literary Genre.* Ithaca, New York: Cornell University Press.

Tyler, Morgan, ed. 2015. *The First Leonaur Book of Supernatural Detectives.* Leonaur.

Tymn, Marshall, Kenneth Zahorski, and Robert Boyer. 1979. *Fantasy Literature: a Core Collection and Reference Guide.* New York: R.R. Bowker Company.

Valentine, Mark. 2015. *Haunted by Books.* North Yorkshire, England: Tartarus Press.

_____, ed. 2008. *The Black Veil and other Tales of Supernatural Sleuths.* Hertfordshire, England: Wordsworth.

van der Beek, Suzanne. "Agatha Christie and the Fantastic Detective Story." *Clues,* 34 (1) 2016.

Van Dine, S.S. 1928. "Twenty Rules for Writing Detective Stories." In *The Art of the Mystery Story.* Edited by Howard Haycraft. New York: Simon & Schuster, 1946.

van Thal, Herbert, ed. 2005. *The World's Greatest Detective Stories.* London: Magpie Books.

Wagner, Karl. 1988. "Introduction." In *John the Balladeer* by Manley Wade Wellman. New York: Baen Books.

Waugh, Charlie, and Martin Greenberg, eds. 1996. *Supernatural Sleuths.* New York: Penguin Books.

Index

Index

Index

Index

Index

Index

Index

Index

Index

Index

PARACHUTE MINDS:

Light Switch

To Mike!

Mid

by

Jeremiah Sanchez

DORRANCE
PUBLISHING CO
EST. 1920
PITTSBURGH, PENNSYLVANIA 15238

Dorrance Publishing Co
585 Alpha Drive
Pittsburgh, PA 15238
Visit our website at www.dorrancebookstore.com

ISBN: 978-1-6386-7270-8
eISBN: 978-1-6386-7621-8